Starless Rivers

Underground Adventures
by

Des Marshall

First publication: 2019

ISBN: 978-1-84524-288-6

Cover photo: Paul Deakin
Cover design: Eleri Owen

Published by Gwasg Carreg Gwalch,
12 Iard yr Orsaf, Llanrwst, Wales LL26 0EH
tel: 01492 642031
email: books@carreg-gwalch.cymru
website: www.carreg-gwalch.cymru

Printed and published in Wales

STARLESS RIVERS

The first river gallery in Nare
(credit: Untamed River Expedition)

Biography

Born and bred in the Lake District Des has always had an interest in outdoor adventure especially as a rock climber and mountaineer. In the late 70's he became a caver but still maintained his love of mountains. Instead of adventuring above ground he adventured below! Not content with being a 'weekend climber' he became an instructor firstly as a climber and then caving and became a trainer and assessor of cave leaders. He then went on to become an adviser in caving activities. As well as organising caving expeditions to Europe he also ran his own adventure holidays to the Himalayas and Africa. Having lived in Mid Wales for many years, where he started to write walking guides he moved to the USA climbing many of the snowy peaks of Oregon and Utah as well as exploring some remarkable lava tubes. Now retired Des still climbs and walks as often as possible and now lives on the Llŷn Peninsula close to Snowdonia. He continues to write books about Snowdonia.

Contents

The big shaft of Gradisnica, Slovenia

Acknowledgements

I would like to thank all my caving friends over the years for the many great adventures I was privileged to undertake with them. Initially I would like to thank members of the Eldon Pothole Club but especially Bob Dearman and Alan Gamble who started it all off again for me. I would like to thank the late Dave Edwards for inspiration and much support and my first really big caving trip – the Gouffre Berger – when just the two of us rigged the whole cave. He was most instrumental and influential in my becoming a caving instructor. Thanks to Dave Gill for inviting me on the Untamed River Expedition in 1984, without him the expedition would not have taken place.

I would like to thank Steve Reay for all the years of many really memorable days out in the Dales, Ireland and the Vercors; Donald Rust, for going first into narrow holes checking out whether I would fit through or not and for some amazing through trips together both at home and abroad; John Cliffe for Irish and European trips; Pete McDonald for trips at home and the Vercors including a second trip down the Berger.

I would also like to thank the many trusting clients I took on the frequent European caving adventures I organised twice or three times a year. They took everything in their stride and I appreciate their patience and support.

I would like to thank too, members of the rejuvenated Kendal Caving Club, especially Richard Mercer, Bill Hogarth, Andrew Kirk (Kirky) and Ken Wood and the Kendal 'Lads' for great Yorkshire days out and much fun.

As a cave instructor I would like to thank all the outdoor centres and organisations who asked me for advice, training, assessments or just instruction, for all the wonderful years of being involved with them at whatever level. I thank especially Lyn Noble the Head of Centre at Whitehall Centre for Open Country Pursuits near Buxton in the Peak District who trusted me and appreciated my caving competence at an early stage thus heralding for me a great working life in caving; Mike Davies from the Hampshire Mountain Centre near Brecon and Bob Burson from Longtown Outdoor Education Centre. Also I would like to thank Bill and Wendy Mountford at Buxton Activity Centre who helped in setting up my first guiding trip to the Vercors. I would also like to thank John Barnatt who is administering the late Paul Deakin's photographs for continued use of photographs given to me by Paul after the Gouffre Berger photographic trip in August 1985. Thanks also to Dave Gill for unfettered use of the photographs from the Untamed River Expedition October to December 1984.

Finally this book would not have been written without the support and drive from my ex-wife, Sandie, who wanted me to put down in writing the many stories I had related to her over a long period of time.

Thank you, one and all. If I have left anyone out my sincere apologies, but please accept my heartfelt thanks for all the fun and adventure we had together.

Introduction

Rain had fallen all week, the rivers were a frothy brown and I was going caving for the first time. I was excited and looking forward to a memorable day. It was. Not for the caving but having to be rescued from a rapidly filling passage by the turbulent stream. Fortunately rescue was, fortuitously, at hand. An on surface member from another caving club raised the alarm when he realised that no-one could get out. Once we had all been safely brought out I reflected on the day to the extent that it was, at that time, the worst experience I had ever endured. I was wet, very cold and just wanted to get home into a warm bath. I vowed that I would never venture underground again but have my adventures above ground. How wrong that turned out to be and how time clouds the mind. When I did weaken and venture once more into the realm of darkness many years later I realised that it could be fun. Much of the thrill was because I perceived it as real adventure. It allowed me, at times, to explore places where only a few of us in the whole world of 6.5 billion people had ever been. As the title of a CD performed by the cave diver Steve Thomas states, 'More People have been to the Moon.'

'La Riviere sans Etolies', The Starless River, is found 400 metres down in the Gouffre Berger. It inspired the title for this book. For, yes, these rivers and streams are starless once their underground journey begins but they dance, twinkle and shimmer when lit by a caver's light.

Caves are damp, dark and mysterious filling mortals with dread. Maligned and much hated by the early scholars, they were the haunts of the devil, dragons and demons. Even today many people have just as much dread. Many, many people say they are claustrophobic. Some in fact are, but very few. It is just their fear of the unknown and their own supposition of what it is like. This is because caving gets a very poor press whenever there is an accident. Caving, often referred to as potholing, is perceived as forcing a way through tight miserable little holes in the ground that are full of mud and water. Frank Booth, a friend of mine for many years and a very good climber, but a non-caver, once said to me at the top of Lancaster Hole 'It's like going into a grave'. 'Yes, but you are alive and there are some wondrous sights to see', I replied. There are magnificent galleries that buses can pass down as well as viewing fantastic cloud like formations of dangling straw stalactites hanging effortlessly from the ceilings of cave passages. That is the thing about caving. You have to make an effort to see what is there. Mountains on the other hand can be driven to and you needn't leave your car, if you do not want, to admire them.

In caving there are questions. Where does the water go? Where does it come out? Or even, where does it come from?

Although many show caves exist around the world, the true feeling of being underground comes only when you have your own personal light for the journey. This is the excitement, the adventure. It may at times be wet, muddy and cold but when approaching the exit, the thrill of smelling the outside air is quite exquisite. Darkness reigns supreme down there, for without light it is impossible to see anything, never ever, no matter how long you stayed down. It is impossible to see your hand thus giving the feeling of losing two senses, sight and hearing. In caves where no water flows silence is absolute, except for the thumping of your heart and the occasional drip of water.

Caves are natural phenomena with most of them found in limestone. In Britain limestone was formed in a warm shallow sea between 275 and 350 million years ago when the country was somewhat nearer the equator. Caves form when weak carbonic acid in the water dissolves the rock imperceptibly slowly along the horizontal bedding planes, the feature between beds of limestone; or joints, vertical cracks. Rainfall picks up carbon dioxide from the atmosphere before flowing along the ground to collect more carbon dioxide. Combining with the water it forms a weak solution of carbonic acid. Over many millions of years caves develop, firstly by a process of solution or corrosion and forming water filled tubes and then as the water table drops the void becomes incised by corrosion or the down cutting of the acidic water and the tumbling of stones. Continued wearing away at floor level forms deep meandering passages, or canyons that wander snake like through the cave as the water table drops or the land rises, sometimes forming keyhole shaped passages. In the later stages of cave development collapse often plays a major role in enlarging passages, as thinly jointed walls or thin beds in the roof collapse.

Out of the prying eyes of the world, almost in secret, it is one of only three activities where 'original' exploration can be undertaken. The other two are space travel, very expensive and only open to a very few lucky individuals and deep sea diving. Where is the deepest cave in the world? Nobody knows, but at present (2018) it is found in Georgia not far from the Black Sea. Known as the Krubera/Voronja system it is an astonishing 2,140 metres deep. That could change today, tomorrow, who knows when. The deepest known cave in the world has seen many changes over the years. It is possible that only 10% of the caves in the world have yet been explored.

On May 24th 1953 the entrance to a cave that was to become the first 1,000 metres deep cave was discovered in the Vercors region of France close to Grenoble. It became known as the Gouffre Berger, named after the discoverer Joe Berger, a shepherd. Explorations commenced that year and in August 1956 the first time anyone had gone below 1,000 metres was achieved after the descent of a shaft that is aptly named Hurricane. Explorations still continue to find THE deepest cave in the world. Everest has been known for a long time as the highest mountain because you can see it and survey it. Caves, being unseen, have to be found, explored and surveyed before their depth and length can be ascertained.

I am often asked 'what is the difference between a cave and a pothole'. Caving is the generic term used for all underground trips. To be more descriptive though, caving is going horizontally or basically so, whilst potholing is going vertically down.

I have tried within this book to focus on the fun and friendship one gains from exploring caves, the epics, sporting trips, expeditions, instructed and guided caving as well as mining experiences of later years.

Having lived in Wales since 1994 on and off apart from a spell in the States I have explored many slate mines in North Wales. Although 'constructed' by human endeavor they provide exciting experiences with some being quite exceptional because, for instance, some have streamways, akin to many caves, flowing through them. Visiting some of these mines though is definitely not for the faint hearted!

Having 'graduated' from caves into mining, mines are a perfect venue for bodies behaving like iron bars as age increases. Generally they are spacious and, on occasion, contain fine calcite formations. Exploring a slate mine I am always gobsmacked by the amount of effort that went into extracting slate and the huge voids the miners left behind. Roofs in massive chambers, supported by huge pillars of often good slate, are sometimes unseen except by the brightest of lights. So as my body became more aged and progressively more knackered, mining enabled me to continue exploring underground whilst at the same time appreciating the highly dangerous job of slate mining in those years long ago.

Chapter 1

Rescue

Born and bred in Kendal, conveniently placed between the Yorkshire Dales and the Lake District, I discovered a love for the mountains and crags of the Lake District at an early age. It just seemed logical to become involved with them for youthful adventures. I was walking in the mountains from the age of seven with my father and when I was fourteen secretly going off climbing. It was only when I was eighteen that I had my first real caving adventure.

I always remembered my father saying to me whilst on a walk around the Langdale Pikes when I was nine or ten that I must never go rock climbing as it was far too dangerous. That statement was like a red rag to a bull. We were descending from Loft Crag, an outlying summit close to the famed Langdale Pikes, late in the day when Gimmer Crag loomed ahead, its black forbidding profile silhouetted by the setting sun. I set my heart on wanting to climb it, but how and when was this going to be achieved? I wanted to climb rocks! Almost as soon as I went to Kendal Grammar School at 11 years old, in September 1955, I joined the school mountaineering club. Here I learnt the rudiments of rock and ice climbing, eventually venturing out, secretly, on my own.

The master in charge of the club, Arthur Morton, was

our chemistry teacher. My first chemistry lesson was entertaining to say the least. I went in to find that Arthur was boiling some wax over a Bunsen burner when all of sudden it overflowed and set on fire. However, Arthur was prepared for this. He had his home made fire extinguisher to hand. Aiming the thing at the burning mess he fired it. The force of the jet knocked him backwards. Arthur was totally unprepared for this. He was catapulted back into the acid cabinet breaking bottles which spilled acid all over the place, but at least the fire was extinguished. Now, because of the ever growing pond of mixing acids the class had to evacuate the room.

I was useless at chemistry but Arthur, or 'Morty' his nickname, engendered a huge enthusiasm in me for mountaineering and rock climbing. My first real rock climbs were on Gill Crag in Dovedale in 1958. We had a winter expedition to Scotland in March 1961, long before the journey became quick with modern day motorways. In fact as we drove up the A74 the construction of the dual carriageway had just commenced. We camped initially for the first few days in Glencoe where we traversed the Aonach Eagach ridge in ideal winter conditions and ascended easy snow gullies on Stob Coire nan Lochan before moving on to Ben Nevis, the highest mountain in Britain at 1342 metres. Here we camped at Lochan Meall an-t-Suidhe about half way up the mountain. This is where the tourist path continues up to the summit whilst a path from our camp took us around to the famed north face. In the team was Arthur, Margaret his wife, Mike Lee and I along with Rikki and Tavy, two Siamese cats. Margaret acted as cat minder whilst the 'boys' went climbing.

Although the weather was not good we managed to swim up Number Three Gully and on to the summit of Ben Nevis in near white out conditions. After I left school in

May 1961 I was a frequent guest at Arthur and Margaret's house in Kentmere some 9 miles from Kendal. They were both very keen and interested to hear about my latest adventures and showed them slides of these. It was quite ironic that when Arthur died and Margaret moved away another climbing friend, Max Biden, bought their house.

When I was sixteen whilst rock climbing I fell 80 metres down the side of Middlefell Buttress in the Langdale Valley. I was carried down on a stretcher to the Old Dungeon Ghyll Hotel sporting a hole in my head and lots of 'rock-burn'. Here I was told there were no bones broken but with lots of red stuff leaking from the hole in my head! I had my flattened ego to attend to as well. A visit to Doctor Lancaster in Ambleside was made to stitch the hole before going home to face the music. I was duly told off, but, surprise, surprise, I was given a birthday present a couple of weeks later by my father that totally amazed me. It was a weekend rock climbing tuition with a mountain guide, Jim Cameron. This was a gigantic step forward in the right direction as they realised they were unable to quell my desire and they thought that Jim would give me a good grounding in the techniques of the day. I could at last go rock climbing with parental blessing and the ensuing climbing adventures are another story.

However, more to the point, I was told that caving was an even more risky and idiotic pastime and on no account was I ever to consider going underground. They said it was wet, with tight miserable holes to crawl through and extremely muddy with every chance of being stuck for all time down there! At that time in 1962 it had only been three years since Neil Moss had become stuck irretrievably in Peak Cavern. The story was still very fresh in everyone's mind as, unfortunately, the rescue team were unable to free him from the rocky jaws.

I had been to White Scar show cave near Ingleton in the Yorkshire Dales as a tot and had been fascinated by all the formations and rock architecture. Although the cave was for public consumption the seed had been sown for a real underground adventure. The Yorkshire Dales is the finest area in Britain for potholing. Wild, windswept moorlands, lots of rain and a thick skin of jointed limestone host some magnificent shafts.

Paradoxically South Wales has the deepest cave in Britain, Ogof Ffynnon Ddu, at 308 metres, where the caves generally follow the bedding down slope, whereas Yorkshire having predominantly vertical systems, has the longest in the Three Counties, Lancaster/Easgill system with some 44 miles of passages.

In the early 1960's Kendal had a well respected caving club and a close group of climbers. We drank in the same pub from time to time, so after a long session one night each bragging about the respective merits of each 'sport', it was agreed that the cavers would take the climbers caving and us climbers would take the cavers climbing. I was a rock climber first and foremost in those days. But would the cavers offer to take us caving first or would we take them climbing? By mutual agreement we, the climbers took the cavers first. We went up to Gill Crag, Dovedale on a beautiful sunny day in early August. It was a hot, non-serious, day with lots of banter and easy climbing.

On the 26th August 1962 it was our underground day. Rain had fallen most of the week and on the Sunday it was still raining. We were to visit Alum Pot to explore 'The Churns'. These are Lower Long Churn and Upper Long Churn. Alum Pot Beck was brown and frothy and my instincts told me that we should perhaps adjourn to the pub and talk caves. But no, we were assured that all would be OK. We went firstly up into Upper Long Churn to 'test' the strength of the water. I remember it being quite strong and managed to get completely soaked by the time we reached the highlight of the cave. This is a 10m high chute of water that plummets into 'Dr Bannister's Hand-basin.' The amount of water made it totally impossible to climb. Turning around we were almost immediately swept off our feet. Back on the surface I breathed a sigh of relief. We could all now, perhaps, go to the pub.

Alas, not yet. It was decided that we should, perhaps, have a look at Lower Long Churn. So we set off into the cave fighting some very fast flowing and foaming water. A short way down the entrance stream-way, the passage steps up into a higher one. This fortunately was dry apart from some pools of water and wet walls. Slowly we made our way to 'Double Shuffle Pool' and then on to 'Plank Pool'. These often provide a wetting for the careless or not very confident as they involve traversing around their walls. On this occasion it did not matter as we splashed our way across, we were all wet anyway! Ominous, very audible booming sounds, I was told were coming from the adjacent Diccan Pot, became louder as we progressed. Lindsay Greenbank one of our leaders reckoned that we should perhaps make our way out after all. There was another team in the cave that day, a group from Bradford.

Everyone started to exit the cave. The clothing I was wearing very similar to the others was by now sodden and very heavy from various wettings. My woollen pullover had stretched so much it was hanging down by my knees and the jeans were so restricting I could hardly move. My walking boots were soft and squishy and I felt thoroughly miserable. What a dreadful sport. I would be glad to get out. Exiting was not going to be easy I thought to myself. In fact it turned out to be impossible without assistance because the stream had risen so much that our retreat was far too dangerous to attempt. Certainly we would have been swept off our feet and washed down to goodness knows where.

Fortunately a member of the Bradford team had stayed on the surface. Whilst his team was underground he recognised that there was a serious problem and had gone to raise the alarm. The rescue team duly arrived and sorted the problem quickly and easily. They floated what appeared to be a ships mooring rope down the rapidly rising water to the 12 of us trying to keep out of the water in various nooks and crannies. The guy next to me, from Bradford, asked if I could tie a bowline as he could not. He was very relieved when I said yes I could. Some had a lifeline whilst others dispensed with it. We were all intensely relieved when we were back arrived at the surface on 'dry' land. OK then very squelchy land. It did not matter as I was out in the open again. Little were we to know then that years later we would be immortalised as incident number 66 in the excellent book about the Cave Rescue Organisation. Titled 'Race Against Time' it lists some 1054 incidents from the formation of the C.R.O. in 1935 through to 1988.

There and then I resolved never ever to go caving again. What a daft sport. Wet, cold and miserable, although the rock features were truly fascinating. Squelching and shivering I walked down the track back to the cars. This time I thought my parents were right after all. They did not like the idea of me groveling around in the bowels of the earth anyway.

Alum Pot is a fine, wide open shaft 75 metres deep ringed with trees with a variety of ways to reach the sump at the bottom. First descended by Boyd Dawkins in 1870 the hole now has two magnificent descents. For the proficient in Single Rope Techniques (S.R.T.) the best of these is the northern end, where, after a short descent against the wall the rope is re-belayed on the lip of an overhang which allows for an interrupted free hanging descent into the bottom of the shaft. Less proficient cavers, however, have another option to reach here, the descent of the much easier Lower Long Churn. This is a classic beginner's trip. Nowadays many novice groups from outdoor centres come to the cave but stop before the cave becomes technical before the descent of the aptly named 'Dolly Tubs' pitch. When the cave is not crowded with groups it is a very fine trip.

Dolly tubs were used in the old days when people did not have electric washing machines. We even had a dolly tub at home complete with a separate handled mangle! The tub was a circular, galvanised barrel and clothes were washed in this using a wooden 'posher'. The spindles on the base of the 'posher' twiddled the clothes around just like modern washing machines.

The Dolly Tubs are two circular holes part way down the 14 metres pitch which is usually abseiled. The pitch lands in a short length of passage which leads out to daylight part way down the main shaft of Alum Pot for perhaps, the most famous and classic view in a Yorkshire pothole. A stream at the far side of the shaft tumbles freely down for 60 metres in a huge, spectacular arc. Now at the half way point down the shaft the remaining descent is mostly daylight. This makes the place feel much bigger. After descending the 'Greasy Slab' a traverse along the west wall follows an exposed ledge to a huge block, 'The Bridge', spanning the shaft. There were several deaths from here in the old days, when protection was seen to be 'wimpy', because the potential fall is over 15 metres. From the bottom of 'The Bridge' the descent continues somewhat damply down some climbable cascades to an 8 metres pitch which is descended to enter a high passage. Darkness is regained and after a dry oxbow the huge waterfall of the final pitch of Diccan Pot is encountered thundering down from the roof above close to the sump pool of Alum Pot, an awesome place in wet weather.

Diccan Pot, one of the finest sporting trips in the Dales, had the dubious distinction many years ago, before the advent of S.R.T. of having the wettest pitch in the Dales. The descent down the 45metres final pitch on ladders was in the full force of the water. Nowadays there is none of this nonsense. S.R.T. allows for a dry descent of this fine and very spectacular pitch to be made in low to moderate water conditions, ending at the sump pool as for Alum Pot.

The above two 'rescue' incidents are the only ones where I have had the services of a rescue team to help me out. Falling off the climb was one of stupidity and too big an ego and the caving one due to complete and utter ignorance of what water can do in the underground drainage channels of an active cave. I have seen flood water in caves since but at a safe distance or been able to keep out of it if caught in a sudden pulse. I have fallen off climbs since then especially when the move turned out to be more strenuous or awkward than I thought, but with the security of a rope and protection on these infrequent occasions.

Clothing in those early caving days was not conducive to keeping warm let alone dry. Leather boots, wool socks, jeans, 'T' shirt, woollen pullover and a waterproof or cotton overall was all that was typically worn. Helmets were made from papier-mâché and the helmet mounted light was an ancient, heavy lead acid miner's type. Nowadays it is possible to keep perfectly dry in all but the wettest caves because equipment has developed to such an extent that it is lightweight, comfortable and keeps you warm even when wet. Fleece under-suits worn by most cavers today underneath a nylon or PVC over-suit are such items. Lighting too has advanced to such an extent that many days of illumination can be had by using a helmet mounted and lightweight LED unit.

Being a glutton for punishment my next foray was to a totally different type of venue. This time it was a mine. In fact it was the Seathwaite Graphite Mine at the head of Borrowdale in the Lake District. We were staying for the weekend at the 'K' hut at the edge of the hamlet, ostensibly being there for a climbing weekend. That was entirely kicked into touch due to the monsoon rain that fell for most of it. So we all decided that a mining trip would help pass the time of day before the pub on Saturday evening.

The 'K' hut belongs to the 'K' Fellfarers, a group of people who enjoyed being in the mountains walking, climbing or even just being there. They all worked at, the once well known, 'K' Shoes factory based in Kendal. As I worked there myself at that time along with many of the climbers and cavers we were able to use the hut more or less at any time we wished.

The short walk from the hut across the valley floor was sodden with the river rising very quickly. After struggling up the hill between the spoil heaps and poking our heads into various openings we decided that enough was enough and returned to the warmth of the hut and subsequent trip to the Scafell Hotel Riverside bar.

Sunday was no better and by the time we were all packed to go home the valley was somewhat full of water and driving home was out of the question. What were we to do? No beer and little food. An idea was formulated that we should send a beer collection team to the pub. As such a team of two was duly dispatched in the afternoon with the order to bring a crate of Double Century bottled beer back to the hut. Bill Duff and I, suitably dressed in borrowed wet suits swam down much of the road to the pub some three miles away.

No longer was it the Riverside Bar when we arrived at the Scafell Hotel, it was the River Bar!! Water was swirling almost waist deep inside and Bill the very friendly barman was amazed to see us, his first customers of the day. This was hardly surprising, really. No-one in the valley could drive anywhere. So we bantered for a while, had a beer or two then set off back to the hut with our crate. It took a great amount of effort to drag our burden against the flow of water. We arrived back at the hut after what seemed a long time, cold and very shivery but to the huge delight of the inmates who had long ago given up all hope of ever having any beer at all that day, let alone seeing us again. Well that was that.

I had no intentions of ever caving or mining again. Both experiences had left me wet, cold and not very happy. However, I continued to be intrigued by dark mysterious holes, even venturing into the twilight zone of many. But, the question remained. Why did people go underground? Why did they want to get muddy, wet and cold with the constant fear of flooding or getting stuck? I was to find out many years hence.

Chapter 2

I get hooked

A new girl friend heralded a move to Buxton in May 1978. I was so into climbing that this was an absolute joy for me. Superb gritstone edges with literally thousands of climbs all over the place. I was like a little boy in a chocolate factory! This lovely rough and solid rock is, without doubt, my favourite for climbing. There was limestone too, but I was much more into rough grit than the polished shiny limestone cliffs, even though I did manage to lead several of the harder limestone classics.

After I had been living there for 6 months or so I met with various members of the Eldon Pothole Club some of whom I climbed with on subsequent occasions. One of these characters was Bob Dearman. He was great fun and so full of enthusiasm that it was hard not to get swept along with it. In no time at all he was taking me caving. A pioneer of many difficult free and aid climbs in the 60's and 70's, Bob was a really good caver as well. Even to this day he maintains this interest. So in March 1980 he picked me up from home and after changing into a borrowed wet suit we set off to Giants Hole. Here he pronounced that we would do the Round Trip. On reflection this, as an introduction, was some trip. Not only did it have ladder climbs but there were also several 'tighter' bits too.

Climbing down the 6 metres long ladder at 'Garlands Pot' was intimidating but I was not letting Bob know that. Soloing short ladder pitches in those days seemed quite normal!! I was then confronted with a high but narrow slit in the wall ahead of me. This was the start of the 'Crab Walk', half a mile of twisting and very sinuous passage. Here I had to emulate a crab by walking sideways as I gradually descended the narrow rift through countless tight hairpins until I reached the tight bit at the end, 'The Vice'. This I dealt with by laying down in the water and pushing forward, although for 'thinnies' it was possible to climb up higher up and avoid getting wet. I have always had to lie down in the water and push myself through although on one occasion and feeling 'thin' I tried it higher up in an effort to keep drier longer but.... Yes, I got stuck for the first time of several. I managed to solve the position I was in by doing a kind of forward roll and crashing head first into the stream-way at the far side of the snug bit.

We descended the aptly named 'Razor Edge Cascade' before climbing down the 3 metres section of iron ladder at 'Comic Act Cascade' into 'Great Relief Passage'. This took us to the 'Eating House'. A passage leads off to 'Geology Pot', a 13 metres deep circular hole. The descent of this and the ensuing section of cave reaches the end of the cave after several sections of wet and sporty caving. From the 'Eating House' we turned to our right into 'Maggin's Rift' and continued to a junction. Left would take us to 'Poached Egg Passage' and the infamous and extremely miserable section of cave simply called 'The Connection'. This links Giants with the Oxlow/Maskill system. Many rescues have occurred in this innocuous sounding passage. It is wet, very low and tortuous for all of its 300 meters length.

Once Bob had filled me with dread about 'The

Connection' we fortunately turned right through 'Letterbox Passage' to enter 'Ghost Rift'. At the far end of this a low entrance took us into the 'Giants Windpipe'. Not a particularly fine place to be on a first caving trip as it is mostly filled with water. Sometimes this passage is sumped. When this happens a return has to be made to the 'Eating House' and back up the 'Crab Walk". Fortunately today we crawled through spluttering and cursing until we were able to get out 20 metres further. Very shortly we were in the roof of the 'Crab Walk'. Abseiling, from a single bolted in hanger, we dropped into the 'Crab Walk' very close to the ladder dangling down 'Garlands Pot'. Scampering up the ladder, again without a safety line, we were then quickly on the surface.

I had really enjoyed the experience. Bob had made it fun for me with much banter. Less than a week later we were in the depths of Oxlow, a deep, abandoned lead mine, but with some natural passages as in 'Pilgrim's Way'. Six pitches took us to the bottom beyond 'West Chamber'. The long iron ladder leading up into 'Pilgrim's Way' from 'West Chamber' is now long gone, being replaced by a pull back rope system. An amusing rescue incident happened here one very snowy night. As I was a member of the Derbyshire Cave Rescue Organisation (D.C.R.O.) there was a call out to rescue some cavers who had tried 'The Connection' that appallingly miserable stretch of cave briefly mentioned above between Giants and Oxlow, but had bottled out of it. The reason they had to be rescued was they had pulled their ropes down from all the pitches in Oxlow on their way in as they were confident in getting through. This cut off all hope of their retreat in case anything had gone wrong. Thinking they could use the iron ladder propped against the wall they attempted to get out. Unfortunately for them the ladder was much too short, so when they became overdue we were called out to rescue them.

Having gone to the final wet chamber as well as going up into and along Pilgrim's Way, we set off out. I think Bob might have had a sneaky desire to do 'The Connection' but perhaps realised in time that I may not have been ready for it, or indeed would I fit! Once out of Oxlow Bob whisked me down the road a couple of miles to P8 so that we could 'wash off'. This cave is sometimes called Jackpot. It was called this because when it was entered in 1964 people thought it would lead to the Master Cave. (A Master Cave is where all the water is collected from inlets in an active system to form an underground river). All the local Buxton cavers believe such a cave exists. The 11 caves and pots, or swallet holes, including Giants are situated below Rushup Edge. They each have separate streams that flow eastwards determined by the east west mineral veins. Most of this swallet water flows via the Speedwell Stream-way whilst the Peak Cavern stream-way carries the percolation water from the limestone area to the south. The water emerging in the back garden of a house in Castleton 3 miles distant in a straight line has had a 3 day journey having flowed through what is likely to be quite a complex maze of flooded passages.

After an uneventful trip to the sump and back Bob asked if I wanted to join the Eldon Pothole Club (E.P.C.). This was an accolade indeed. The E.P.C. were a bunch of very hard cavers who not only found, pushed and forced miserable little holes in the ground to their end, but had also been very forceful in expedition caving in Europe especially the Gouffre Berger, the Pierre San Martin, Gouffre de Fromagere, the Antro del Corchia and the Spluga della Preta. They had their headquarters in Buxton behind the Barbecue, a hostelry long since gone after the improvements to the Spring Gardens shopping area.

This hostel was home to many. It was rough but very comfortable. I was fortunate to stay there whilst hitch hiking from the Lakes to climb on the grit in 1965, before moving to Buxton 13 years later. After I had moved there I was sad to hear that the Barbeque HQ was no more and long gone. I always wondered what happened to the many 'trophies' the Eldon had on display in the hostel.

I was then invited to Peak Cavern by Bob who wanted to explore 'Wind Tunnel' in the depths of the cave. I'd heard stories about this wretched tight crawl and was very glad that I met up with Clive Westlake another Eldon member who was undertaking a much less arduous trip into Ink Sump. I went with him! Bob had a willing crawler to go with him, so all was well. Clive, a very experienced cave diver, was not diving on this trip. Having booked in at the Technological Speleological Group (T.S.G.) headquarters in Castleton, as part of the access procedure, we walked the short distance to the cave. Changing in the entrance and leaving spare dry clothes there we set off along the show cave section. Leaving this an initial damp and low section through the 'Mucky Ducks' took us to where the cave became large and impressive. At Surprise View the large stream-way is met. We descended into the magnificent and circular tunnel. Firstly we went downstream following a lively river to a sump. Returning, we continued upstream passing Surprise View and continued up to Ink Sump. Clive was interested in diving this at a later date. The wonderful clear blue water of this was incredible. We ducked under an arch where I gurgled and spluttered until we could go no further. Back at the cave entrance we dropped down from the entrance terrace to the rope making paraphernalia, an attraction for the tourists. Below this was located Swine Hole. This is a heavily scalloped but perfect example of a phreatic tube and I thought it was well worth the visit to view this short section of cave. Peak Cavern is a spectacular cave and although an easy day I had thoroughly enjoyed it.

Later, after visits to Water Icicle Close, Eldon Hole where I learnt the intricacies of S.R.T. and Knotlow Cavern, I was invited on an Eldon meet to South Wales. There were not many of us in the team, Alan Walker, Jim Dale and Ray King plus me. The weather was cold and frosty as it had been for several days. It was forecast to remain so for the weekend so we were quite happy that the water was not going to rise as we were going to be underground for several hours on a long trip into Dan yr Ogof on the Saturday. As it starts off life as a show cave, like Peak Cavern, we needed permission from the owners. This had been obtained several weeks in advance of our visit. Being winter we had to use the lower cavers' entrance at river level being unable to walk through the closed show cave. Descending to the river by the locked front doors we followed the river a short distance before climbing up into the show cave and through another locked gate for which we had the key.

At the end of the show cave the wetness begins and things become much more serious. The first of three lakes loomed in front of us. Being tall I was able to bottom walk and was just able to keep my nose clear of the water. The smaller members of the team had to swim. Once clear of the lakes we carried on until we came to the 'Long Crawl'. Well it wasn't that long, about 5 minutes I seem to recall, but it certainly had my heart racing as it was the first really snug crawl I had done. Having long legs the difficult bit for me was the actual start to get around the right angled bend. I asked Alan to go first. He was about the same height as me but thinner, also with long legs.

Once out of that we quickly arrived in 'Gerard Platten

Hall'. Here we made a detour to see the marvelous straw formations in 'Flabbergasm Chasm' taking care as we traversed around the 'Crystal Pool'. Continuing, we passed through the aptly named and superbly decorated 'Cloud Chamber' having many long straw stalactites hanging from the ceiling. I was now really enjoying the trip. It was exciting, long and had lots of pretty formations. However, we stopped at the beginning of a fearsome looking stretch of water. This was the 'Green Canal'. Green it wasn't, black it was. I was really glad I was wearing a wet suit although there were several flotation devices bobbing up and down. I could see now why wet suits were obligatory for this trip as well as being part of the access agreement at that time. On a trip some years later I saw a flotation device that creased me up no end, a blow-up Indian war canoe.

We slid into the black looking liquid and immediately I was out of my depth in the freezing cold water. Part swimming and part traversing the walls with my hands the floor gradually rose to meet my feet. What a relief. I also realised that we were going back the same freezing way. On another trip I went the lower route both in and out to avoid the cold swim along the 'Green Canal'. This way started from 'Gerard Platten Hall' and continued through the wonderful 'Bakerloo Street' but it involved a very slippery climb up 'The Abyss' to reach the far end of the 'Green Canal' not to mention the awkward climb over the 'Camels Hump' before this. It was possible to go through a slot, tight and not for me, or over which was very slippery. Take your pick. The climb down 'The Abyss' on the return journey is no easier. Having been both ways I prefer the 'Green Canal' and all my subsequent trips were done that way.

Continuing, the way ahead was much more pleasant. We reached 'The Rising' where the flow of water rises up from a sump. Here a conveniently placed ladder allowed us to climb up above it. When the ladder ended the climb continued higher on slippery rock and reached a window. Entering this was a serious step and roll over. This was followed by a difficult climb down into a fairly tight rift that lead to the head of the pitch descending into the 'Great North Road'. After a snug start against the wall the 15 metres long ladder swayed gently as it hung freely down into the water at the bottom, the same water as 'The Rising'. Various obstacles were passed as we continued upstream. When we reached the 'Far North Choke' we could go no further. Turning around we now looked forward to the way out! What an amazing six hour adventure. It had been great fun with lots of banter and lots of encouragement for each other. I was beginning to like this clambering around and exploring in the dark.

Sunday was again cold and frosty and the choice of cave was Little Neath River Cave. Although reasonably short the cave starts off snug and very wet. The entrance is on the side of the River Neath, well, in the river bed would be more precise. Our wet suits were frozen solid, we had been camping, and it was quite a struggle both physically and mentally to get these on. Once we had bent and twisted them to reduce their armour like feeling we struggled to get them on after which we shivered violently. We all creaked as we walked the short distance to the entrance from the car park. When we saw what was entailed the idea of doing this cave faded instantly. However, we each had a go. Facing flat down in the freezing water, I poked my head inside and scuttled out like a rabbit, as did everyone else in turn. No-one was prepared to push it. I know that if one of us had gone in the rest of us, like sheep, would have followed!

Instead, we opted for the much easier Bridge Cave.

Situated just a few steps away from the car park, a short, dry, easy entrance crawl took us to a short boulder choke. Threading our way through this we reached the short but lively stream. Following this the passage suddenly became huge and the stream spilled across the boulder floor. We walked easily down this until the cave narrowed. Looking up we saw the bridge above our heads. This is a remarkable feature that gives the cave its name. The passage became smaller but still of walking size and also quite pretty until a short, but low crawl took us to the sump leading into Little Neath River Cave. The weekend was, for me, a really fine introduction to longer caves and caving.

When I finally did Little Neath River Cave many years later with Don Rust, I found it a very fine trip after I had negotiated the 60 metres long awkward entrance crawl. It was a lovely summer's day. The flowing trickle of water was not quite your bathwater at home temperature, but almost. What a difference to that first attempt. It was pure joy. All my subsequent trips have all been in summer with warm water conditions!

By now I was beginning to think that caving would be my main activity but climbing won 51% to 49% but I was keen to do more caving. After another trip into P8 and having met Dave Edwards I was invited to go and do Penyghent Pot, a 160 metres deep pothole. This is regarded as a truly great trip being, perhaps, the finest stream cave in the country and was graded 5, the hardest cave category. Dave was an instructor at Whitehall Outdoor Education Centre and one of the best cavers around. What he did not know about caving was not worth knowing. He was a master of invention. His caving gear seemed to consist of tyre inner tubes! But it all worked. I was very fortunate indeed to have met Dave early on in my caving days and we did many memorable trips together of which more later on.

It was with some trepidation that I set off from Dale Head to walk to the cave. I had heard stories about the long wet canal at the start, the 11 pitches and how quickly the water can rise if rain starts to fall. The day was sunny and warm and the forecast was great. That was a relief to me straight away. Would I have the bottle to do such a trip so early on in my caving career? We arrived at the cave and having kitted ourselves we climbed down the short entrance shaft. My heart was racing. The canal was quickly reached and the start of the descent started for real. Although low the 330 metres long canal posed no difficulty and I was greatly relieved.

The vertical element, with sections of passage between, now started with two short pitches to reach the main 40 metres pitch, 'Big Pitch'. This was, fortunately, dry otherwise we would have had to retreat. The pitch was descended in two sections. From the base of this pitch the cave continued refreshingly down short pitches and cascades, a couple of which we free climbed, 'Flake Pitch' and 'Niagara'. The final short or eleventh pitch took us down to a high rift chamber. At the far end of this a drop down took us into the Lower Main Stream Passage. Easy walking and stooping lead us to a small cascade that dropped into a foreboding looking sump. All that remained was the hard bit getting out. On a subsequent trip into Penyghent I noticed that there were some fish in the entrance canal. Now where did they come from! Please send your nswers on a postcard please.

Taking only 4 hours it was for me a very satisfying experience. It was wonderfully exciting and I enjoyed every single second of the cave. I believed that caving now was something I could get totally engrossed in, but it took another year for that to be confirmed!

Caves are graded as to their seriousness as follows:

Grade I: Easy caves. No pitches or other difficulties.
Grade II: Moderate caves and small potholes.
Grade III: Caves and potholes without any particularly hazardous, difficult or dangerous sections.
Grade IV: Cave sand potholes which present some hazard or difficulty such as a long underground pitch or a long wet crawl.
Grade V: Caves and potholes which include very strenuous sections, wet underground pitches or tight, long wet crawls.

I have been in some grade I caves and found them incredibly tight, for me, whilst in some of the grade V's I found them great fun and enjoyable. I suppose being a bit on the large side I very much enjoyed the technical rigging side of the sport and not the wriggly snake holes!

The first trip of 1982 was with Carol, my wife of 3 months. She had an interest in caves as her previous boyfriend, Ron Hammond, was a caver. She had never been into P8 though, so one evening in January after work on a bitterly cold, freezing night we visited the cave under an incredibly starry sky. I had taken the precaution of taking an ice axe with me as I thought we may have to chop our way in. I was correct. The entrance was covered over by a sheet of ice. Breaking this there was a grille of beautiful icicles dangling down barring entry. After chopping these away we were able to reach the warmth of the cave. Yes, warmth by comparison. Caves in the UK have a constant temperature of 8 to 10 degrees C summer and winter. In winter therefore caves feel warmer than the outside air and in summer refreshingly cool! I took the precaution of leaving the axe inside the cave just beyond the bottom of the entrance climb, just in case. It was so much warmer inside. In fact it felt very hot! We had a great trip to the sump but I had to clear more icicles before we could exit.

The final confirmation that I wanted to explore more caves came after I went on another Eldon trip some months later. This one was to Birks Fell Cave. Whilst I found the trip quite arduous it was a great experience. We went underground on one of those lovely warm, cloudless autumn days. I would normally have been climbing but this was a cave difficult to get permission for so I thought it would be a good idea to do it. After reaching the bottom we started the return journey and I came out some time ahead of the others, who seemed to be taking it slowly, in the early evening to a warm and balmy atmosphere. The golden sun made all the hillsides look as though they were glowing. The Eldon seldom started early in the day, so it was lunch time by the time we entered the cave. Sitting on a tussock of grass with my wet suit steaming I began reflecting. I had already had many astonishing experiences with some really great people. I had enjoyed their support, friendship and confidence in me. Yes, I wanted and was definitely going to do much more caving.

Chapter 3

Eldon Exploits

I now wanted to go from the deepest part of Britain to the highest in under 24 hours. Being on the fringe of becoming a member of the Eldon Pothole Club, members were always keen for any mad escapade or stunt, I asked around who wanted to do this. George Cooper, a good climber and caver, was interested along with Bill Chiswell and Alan Gamble (AG). It was decided that we would, instead of going through Ogof Ffynnon Ddu, we would descend Penyghent Pot. Although not THE lowest to highest trip, Penyghent Pot was going to be a challenge although it was known to all of us. At one time it was a 2 day expedition with many ladders and ropes having to be hauled in and out by a somewhat larger team than the mere four of us.

Going from the entrance to the bottom and back out once again in 4 hours we found the next bit the hardest. This was the drive north. We were using my car, a 2 litres Ford Cortina Estate, so that we could carry both caving and climbing gear. We had an enforced stop at Hamilton when the exhaust developed a rather loud sound as one part had decided enough was enough and blew a large hole. George being practical managed to procure some exhaust repair tape and duly sealed the hole in the pipe.

With no further problems the rest of the journey to Fort William was uneventful.

The 2 hours walk up the Allt a Mhuillin to the foot of Tower Ridge was tiring due in part to it being it's usual boggy self, but also from the cave and drive. We were relieved to be able to dump our kit at the Scottish Mountaineering Club hut, the Charles Inglis Clark memorial mountain hut. Being a member of the club I had booked us into the hut. It is situated close to the foot of the climb we were going to do, Tower Ridge. Before setting off though we made ourselves a brew.

We raced up the ridge in no time at all and continued to the summit of the Ben. Tower Ridge, at 700 metres, the longest ridge on the mountain is one of the easiest and is, perhaps, the grandest of them all. It makes a very fine and enjoyable way to the summit of the mountain. Clothed in winter conditions it is also a grand and classic ascent, although considerably much more difficult. The cloud free summit of Ben Nevis had been reached 19 hours after entering Penyghent Pot. Back in the hut after stumbling down Coire Leis we had a great evening of celebration and story telling, sinking a couple of bottles of whisky in the process.

When underground and far from the surface it is necessary to trust your friends. Trusting the people you are with is an integral part of the experience. Equipment needs to be in perfect working order and to have trustworthy ropes and hardware to descend a vertical shaft, or committing yourself to enter a small hole or squeeze. These are quite apart from trusting your mates to rig ropes correctly when it is their turn to rig and having due regard to the prevailing weather. The difficult part for me, was, and still is the entry into a small hole. Being quite big I often had no idea where they ended or even whether it was possible to get out at the far end. Fortunately most people that caved with me have been smaller than me and I've sent them down tight looking holes first to check them out lighting their dimensions as they pushed forwards and reporting on their size. I have often persuaded a 'boy to go in first'. That said I was having a great amount of fun and not too phased by snug spots. I became a fully paid up member of the Eldon in the autumn 1982, membership being a formality rather than a process.

Soon after arriving in Buxton I started climbing with George Cooper who was a gregarious person, a wry sense of humour but great fun. Our first caving trip together was to Eldon Hole. In the 16th century it was reputed that a local peasant had been lowered 60 metres down the entrance shaft into the dank depths, only to be brought back to the surface a gibbering and frightened idiot. Another story told of a goose flying into the cave and, so the story is related, emerged 3 days later, singed and burned, out of Peak Cavern. However, the first recorded descent was around 1770 by John Lloyd, a scientist. During my first few visits to Eldon in the early 80's there was always a 10 metres high pinnacle of ice at the bottom of the shaft. This remained for at least 2 years before it disappeared.

'Damocles Rift' in Eldon Hole had been found in 1964 by Jim Kinsman. He had climbed up the 25 metres high calcite wall from 'Miller's Chamber' into a large and pretty roof passage from which a further climb up lead into the rift. A pull back line had been left in place to facilitate the ascent from 'Miller's Chamber' for other people. Unfortunately, this had long since disappeared denying access to all, so George and I decided it was time to replace the line with something much more substantial. We both had several attempts over 2 weekends to reach the top of the chamber, each of us getting a little further each time. George solved the climb by the cunning use of some aid by threading a thin piece of nylon line threaded through a small hole in the calcite flowstone.

Having secured himself he brought me up to the top. The continuation passage started with an almost pristine, steep upward slope of twinkling calcite. It must have been many years since anyone had trod this slope as there were no signs of footprints. At the top of the slope there was an obvious place to start a 13 metres climb leading up into a narrowing rift. I lead this, but at the top of the climb I ended up having to contort myself through a small window to where I was below some very fine and remarkable formations. Although not quite as hard as the climb below, it had its moments. We felt that a fixed line was, perhaps, not necessary here feeling that we should leave it for others to climb if they wanted to see the fine formations. Having abseiled back to the twinkling calcite slope we pulled our ropes down.

The rusting hangers in place at the top of the climb up from 'Miller's Chamber' did not inspire an abseil. Managing to find a thread we linked a rope from this into the decaying hangers before descending to the boulder strewn floor of the chamber, leaving our rope rigged for our next trip. Before the next trip George had found a rather over the top fixing plate for a pull back line so four days later we were back at the pitch head drilling holes, by hand, for the bolts that would anchor the plate to the wall. You could have anchored a battleship to the large ring welded to it, never mind cavers. Having discussed the pros and cons about fixing a pull back line for the climb up into 'Damocles Rift' we decided, after all, that it would be helpful to people, so we left one in place. Once we were back on the floor of 'Miller's Chamber' we joined an end of the pull back line to an end of our abseil rope and pulled it down and then knotted the two ends of the pull back line together and secured it to the wall.

Christmas was looming large and less than a fortnight away and I wanted a stunt. The idea of having a pre Christmas Dinner in a cave was quite appealing so I set about organising this. People had their own ideas regarding the venue but most had been discarded as either too mundane or easy to get to. I mooted the idea of the 'Eating House' in Giants as the precursor to the annual dinner and stomp in the New Year. It also meant everyone managed a caving trip before the meal as the venue is almost a mile from the entrance so would be hungry on arrival! Preparations began. Invitations, although verbal were responded to and eventually catering for 22 people had to be arranged. The Sunday before Christmas was chosen as the most appropriate as it allowed married or partnered cavers to avoid, at least in part, the hectic last-minute shopping and seething crowds.

Being the main perpetrator I discussed with people what would be a suitable meal, bearing in mind that it had to be easily transported through the cave. Three courses: with soup, chilli con carne and rice, fruit salad and cream for dessert followed by coffee, liqueurs along with after dinner mints seemed the order of the day. It was decided to pre-cook the chilli before transporting it in sealed, airtight containers. Dr. Hugh Kidd was co-opted as chief medical officer (he was the Cave Rescue Doctor anyway). His wife, Mary also a Doctor, was co-opted as chief chef, a master (mistress!) of all things hot and spicy. Her curries were renowned throughout Buxton. Large pans for re-warming the food were obtained from the local outdoor centre, Whitehall, on the strict condition that they were returned dent free! Umm, that might be a problem as they had to negotiate the 'Crab Walk', but I did promise they would be returned in a fit state still able to be used!

We were almost there. The planning regarding food and quantities was by complete courtesy of Mary. Having extorted the necessary fee from the 'guests', food was bought as well as streamers, party hats and party poppers. (It was decided that if people wanted liqueurs they would have to bring their own). All the chilli ingredients were handed over to our chief chef, who in turn nominated several under chefs because many hands make light work. All and sundry set to and concocted the delicacies to the chefs precise specifications. Little soup and chilli kitchens burst in to life all over Buxton, preparing for the big day. All we had to do now was to arrange how to carry everything down the cave.

The Thursday evening before the dinner was the dress rehearsal. Lots of grubby little hands mustered all the decorations, cutlery, plates, cups, bowls, stoves, pots and pans. Our oversize aluminium containers were pushed, bent and noisily scrunched down the 'Crab Walk'. What a racket they made! It was going to need someone of an excellent engineering mind to take out all the dents in the pans if I was to return them dent free. 'The Vice' was a problem and the pans became flatter. Soon, however the muscle of the Eldon had everything in place. Anything that could become damaged in the wet atmosphere was left in sealed containers. What would happen if the cave flooded on the day? We dared not think the unthinkable, after all, it was an Eldon enterprise and we could conquer all or it would be just 'another Eldon Epic'.

The day of the Dinner dawned bright and cold, not a flood in sight. Along with the other menu makers I set off earlier than the guests to reheat the food which we carried in sealed, watertight containers. Once we had arrived at the 'Eating House' the food was decanted into the not too circular pans and the site prepared, making it comfortable for the party goers as they arrived from their meeting place a short distance away, the Wanted Inn. We had no sooner finished the decorations when much merriment was heard in the passage below and the first decorated revelers arrived clutching small but precious bottles of liqueurs for a relaxed drink after the meal plus some extra decorations for adorning the wet grey walls of the 'Eating House'. Never did the cave look so pretty!

Hugh, our medical officer soon had his first case. One of his friends had become, reportedly irretrievably, stuck in 'The Vice'. This unfortunate was cursing his bad luck, believing that the party would start before he arrived and there would be no food left for him, not to mention those marooned behind also having to go hungry.

We delayed the start. Very quickly the cave telegraph system announced that the 'stuck man' had been freed and everyone could 'come on down'. Apparently, it had been a supreme effort of all those involved to free him. Place settings were pretty arbitrary; sit where you could, pick up a bowl of soup, a serviette and get on with it! What did we eat with? Like all proper dinners we did have cutlery, not silver service mind, just good old stainless steel.

The rather hot chilli quickly warmed everyone through and every last bit was consumed. Fruit salad and cream followed, not, as you might expect in the same bowl, but served in a separate clean one. The decorations certainly improved the ambience partially hiding the bare, damp scenery. Streamers hung from the ceiling struck an odd, almost farcical air to the proceedings. People wearing wetsuits were adorned with party popper streamers, party hats replaced caving helmets. Once all the food had been devoured people started relaxing, legs intermingling with other legs. The purr of conversation was akin to being in a sumptuous lounge in a posh hotel as people reclined, replete, burping, farting and making all the other noises of total contentment.

As the mess was slowly tidied away and stowed ready for the 'long carry' out of the cave, little glasses appeared out of peoples' emergency bag, having been carefully packaged to avoid breakage. Liqueurs were duly poured and supped slowly along with coffee and after dinner mint creams. If only we had thought about bringing a piano!

Eventually the fun had to stop. Some, especially those who had eaten the most and the one who had become stuck on the way in, went out the long way thus completing the 'Round Trip'. The rest of us who perhaps had not eaten quite as much opted for the short way back via 'The Vice'. Whichever way people went they were given something to carry even though they had paid hard cash for the experience. Further bending and bashing soon had the pans at the surface and the cave once more returned to a place of peace and quiet.

No-one was poisoned and no-one the worse for wear, surprisingly, although some party goers had become hungry and thirsty after their exertions on the return journey. They returned to the local hostelry for further sustenance. However, most of us went home to commiserate with wives, husbands, partners or whatever and to pack Christmas presents or sleep on the sofa. The pans again resumed their normal service back at the centre. I never found out, though, how all the dents disappeared. That escapade ended the club celebrations for the year.

I was by now doing much more caving than climbing even to the extent of digging. However, that activity only related to Maskill Mine to ensure that it remained open.

Some temporary shoring in the entrance shaft was looking very dodgy indeed so John Middlemist (Mouse) and I spent several evenings making things safe. One night we exited much later than we had anticipated after a particularly great nights work. We were very surprised to see loads of flashing blue lights on the road below us. Were we about to be rescued? Were we that late? Perhaps we were. Fortunately for us, but unfortunately for another team of cavers, the Cave Rescue team, of which we were both a part of, had been called out to P8. That rescue over they decided to see if we were OK. How thoughtful, but worrying in case Carol or Mouse's girl friend at the time, Sally, had called them out.

Mouse and I went to the Yorkshire Dales for an Eldon meet. Others went to a different cave but Mouse was intent on doing Washfold Pot. I'd heard many stories about this and I had remembered some from 1962. I'd heard that it was a serious wet hole with a tight section before the main pitch. It was a glorious day seemingly set fine. Mouse and I quickly reached the tight bit and after a bit of thrutching and emulating a neatly pressed shirt I was through to the head of the 45 metres pitch. We rigged the shaft carefully as there was a little bit of water flowing. A deviation on the far wall kept us clear from most of it. From the base of the pitch we followed a flat out crawl. Lying in the stream we pushed through to an easier passage. Following this we reached some awkward climbs down that took us to the short final three pitches to reach the sump.

From there we started our return journey. We both looked at each other as we had noticed a significant change in the rate of flow of the stream. It had risen somewhat and by the time we had reached the top of the awkward climbs the stream was in full flow, brown and frothy. We arrived to where the low crawl leading to the big pitch should have been but could not find it. The reason being, it was sumped.

Now, being prudent cavers and listening to what you should take underground with you we had our foil blankets and chocolate bars. Foil blankets were believed to be THE thing for survival situations all those years ago. Finding a comfortable ledge above the water we wrapped ourselves in these like turkeys and ate our chocolate. But instead of cooking we froze. They were useless.

Fortunately, after 3¾ hours of shivering misery the water had dropped sufficiently for us to start out once more. With six inches of air space we forced the low passage to reach the base of the pitch where we found the rope twitching like a tormented snake in the spray. Fortunately with the deviation in place the rope was out of the main flow of water. The ascent was still wet but amenable. Ironing myself once more to become a pressed shirt we glided through the tight bit and back to the surface where the sun was shining! What was going on? Apparently there had been a localised thunderstorm. When we met up with the others and spoke to them they had had nothing at all and they were only 5 miles down the road in Meregill.

Mouse and I finished our shoring job in Maskill. This made the entrance much safer with the mine becoming a superb S.R.T. trip as well as an even better exchange trip with Oxlow. We were pleased with the result. After I had done a through trip from Top Sink to Lancaster Hole, Dave Gill and I went down to South Wales. We were going into Otter Hole. Sid Perou had been filming there and needed his equipment taking out. Dave, who knew Sid, and I duly obliged. We knew that it was a superbly decorated cave but a little bit of effort is needed as well as a bit of planning to see the formations.

My 'Nare Cake' made by Carol

Me exiting the Scialet Michellier into the ploughed field, Vercors, France

On the way to the Jean Bernard near Samoens, France

*Dave Edwards and me arriving back at camp on the Sornin
Plateau after bottoming the Gouffre Berger, Vercors, France*

On the way to Pot Deux, Vercors, France

Steve Reay at the entrance to the Trou de l'Aygue, Vercors, France

Andy Kirk (Kirky), on the surface with Bill Hogarth entering the Trou qui Souffle, Vercors, France

The Guiers Mort entrance into the Dent de Crolles,
Trou de Glaz system

Pete McDonald descending the Pot
de Loup, Vercors, France

Looking out of the entrance to the
Grotte de Bournillon, Vercors,
France

Donald Rust at rest after the Pierre St Martin through trip, Pyrenees, France

Dave Edwards digging out the entrance to the Grotte de l'Ermoy, near to Flaine, France

Curtains in Shatter cave, Mendip

Me at the Antro del Corchia, Tuscany, Italy

Nick Eve in the Antro del Corchia, Tuscany, Italy

Climbing back out of the Scialet de Malaterre, Vercors, France

My farewell dinner at the Scafell Hotel in Borrowdale before the Nare Expedition. L to R Me, Bill Hogarth and Carol

Looking up at the 'direct'. The black speck on the right is actually Tim descending (credit: Untamed River Expedition)

Grotte de Gournier, traversing in the main river passage

Slogging along on all fours in the Trou qui Souffle

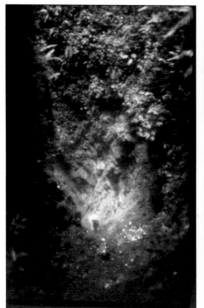

The entrance to Kille Cave
(credit: Untamed River Expedition)

Me after coming out of Otter Hole
in the Wye Valley

Dave Gill on 'The Dirty English Sneaky Bit'
(credit: Untamed River Expedition)

The Canals –
Gouffre Berger
(credit: Paul
Deakin)

Hall of the
Thirteen –
Gouffre Berger
(credit: Paul
Deakin)

Nare from the air
(credit: Untamed River Expedition)

*Me contemplating going down the
Tanne de bel Espoir, Parmelan
Plateau above Annecy*

*Roger Silver on left and me at Ole's Cave near to Cougar,
Washington, USA*

The Pillars of Fire, Lava Tube, near Trout Lake, Washington, USA

*Pillars of Hercules in the lava tube of the same name, near
Cougar, Washington, USA*

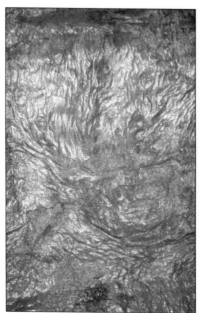

Lava flow marks on the passage wall of Pillars of Fire lave tube, Trout Lake, Washington, USA

Sandie at Arnold Ice Cave near Bend, Oregon, USA

Hidden Forest Cave, near Bend, Oregon, USA

Sandie exiting Ape Cave, near Cougar, Washington, USA

Josh Hydeman and Kim Lauper at Christmas Canyon, near to Cougar, Washington, USA

Kim Lauper in the tight squeeze near the entrance to Deadhorse Cave, Trout Lake, Washington, USA

Sandie in Sawyer's Cave near Bend, Oregon, USA

Matt Skeels abseiling into Little Belknap Cave, near Bend, Oregon, USA

Patale Chhango, Pokhara, Nepal Deka at entrance 2

The river at the far side of Armageddon – Apocalypse Now (credit: Untamed River Expedition)

Sandie in Labyrinth Cave, Lava Beds, California, USA

Entrance depression to Dynamited Cave, near Cougar, Washington, USA

*Josh Hydeman in
Dry Creek Cave,
near Cougar,
Washington, USA*

*Pete and Me –
Hall of Thirteen,
Gouffre Berger*
(credit: Paul Deakin)

*Me and
Formations – Salle
Bourgin, Gouffre
Berger*
(credit: Paul Deakin)

The cave is, I believe, unique in Britain. Although the entrance is dry it quickly becomes full of sticky, brown sea and river mud. Situated on the bank of the River Wye close to Chepstow in South Wales the cave runs underneath the racecourse. The formations are guarded by a sump. This rises and falls with the tide because the Wye at this point is tidal. Flat out crawling through passages following a pipe as it guided us through the horrendous aqueous mud to an area where the mud was even more glutinous. This was the infamous sump. Wallowing through the arch we climbed up to where we were able to drop down to a small stream where we washed off some of the clinging mess. The passage climbed up away from the stream, through some more crawls to where it suddenly opens out to the 'Hall of Thirteen' at the start of all the wondrous formations.

We explored the remainder of the cave totally amazed by all the fantastic formations returning through the sump to fresh air again after 13 hours. I have found that doing an over tide trip gives plenty of time to see everything without any rush. Whilst we explored the cave the arch by the sump disappears under water and exit is denied for about 6 hours. Timing our exit correctly when we arrived back at the sump we were able to go straight out. Leaving the cave everyone looks like a melted chocolate bar. Everything was smeared with sticky glutinous mud.

On another trip I did in Otter, on a lovely sunny day in June '84, we set up camp on the racecourse before going underground. After sorting out the tidal situation we entered the cave around 16.00. The team was comprised of Tim Allen, Steve Reay, Hugh Kidd, his son Alasdair and myself. We had picked Tim up in Worcester whom I had recently met as a member of the Untamed River Expedition. After an uneventful trip exploring the cave we arrived back at the sump a little too early. We waited for 30 minutes. All of a sudden fierce gurgling noises were heard ahead. These were quite startling but amazing to listen to. It sounded as though the cave was going to erupt. Suddenly, there was a huge rush of air as the eyehole cleared and ripples could be seen on the water beyond indicating that the way ahead had begun to be opened. Being impatient we forced our way through the eyehole, swam across the pool to enter the small passages beyond and out. We arrived back at the car park to an early sunrise after a cursory wash in an abandoned bath. Somebody had been thoughtful and enterprising to lug that down there. Hugh, resourceful as ever produced an interesting mix of goodies from the depth of his car boot. Sardines, he loved them, chocolate he couldn't get enough of, oranges and of course a 24 pack of lager to wash it all down. After gorging ourselves on all this we drove back to the campsite ready for a good mornings sleep.

No sooner, or so it appeared, we were asleep that 'Hugh, I don't want to sleep, Kidd' was asking what Sunday papers we wanted and what would we like for breakfast. We'd had about 2 hours in the flat, unconscious zone. Hugh was an amazing, very genuine and kind person, as was is wife Mary. He was always inviting us for happy hours. In fact happy hours often turned into happy nights with cars being abandoned outside his house to be picked up the following morning!

Bob now increased the tightness stakes. Winnats Head Cave was renowned for having a very unpleasant tight crawl through the many loose boulders adorning the entrance series. He wanted to lay a telephone line through into 'Fox Chamber' and install a telephone there, just in case the boulders decided to rearrange themselves. I managed the first few feet but then I was stopped in my tracks. I had no idea how to get through the hole that confronted me. Bob shot through but waited for me. No way was I going to fit through, I didn't really want to fit, so out we came. Very unhappy with myself I went back with him a few weeks later and I wondered why I had backed off the first time. Although tight it was not too bad. We reached 'Fox Chamber' with our roll of wire. The phone line was in place. This is a serious cave even for lovers of loose boulders.

I was always attracted to the name of Black Shiver Pot. It has an 90 metres deep pitch almost at the end of the trip and the description of the tight entrance crawl was very off putting but I had been through Pippikin, a very, very snug cave for me of which more later! I found the entrance crawl to be much larger than expected. The first time I did this we all almost fell in to it as we blundered around the area looking for the short entrance drop. As it was in the depth of a Yorkshire winter it was completely covered over by snow. It was a great trip to the bottom. The 90 metres deep big pitch, 'Black Rift' is magnificent and fortunately had very little water flowing down it. To reach the head of the huge void a short crawl lead to the 'Eagles Nest' from where the first 23 metres drop is rigged and descended to two massive boulders bridging the shaft. Although the pitch can be split here in complete isolation I decided after a 'black shiver' to continue down the remainder of the shaft. My light barely lit the walls and the rest of the team above looked a long, long way away. The final short pitch was much wetter than expected. At the awkward 'Black Dub', the third pitch, we used a ladder to facilitate getting out of the fairly snug rift to descend the pitch but more importantly getting back into the rift again on the way out. This approach did make life much easier and thoroughly recommended. On exit Ingleborough was framed very dramatically and loomed large above me.

The deep Meregill Hole, Juniper Gulf, Long Kin West, Diccan Pot and Alum Pot, where the waterfall was almost frozen making a most memorable and magnificent sight, followed over the ensuing weeks. Long Kin East, Nick Pot and Rift Pot, all these again with deep shafts combined with many other trips locally in Derbyshire continued until I found myself in South Wales with Alan Gamble, Mouse and Paul Deakin. They wanted to do the 'Grand Circle' in Agen Allwedd. I had been in the cave before but only up the 'Turkey Stream-way' and around the 'Summertime Series'. The D.C.R.O. had been on standby as had all the other cave rescue teams in Britain a few weeks before. A caver had slipped at the far end of the mile long 'Southern Stream Passage' a very long way into the cave and broken his leg. It took some 58 hours to get the victim to the surface. Inside the cave the medics used a new type of cast made from fiberglass to stabilise his leg during the rescue.

We had a really good fun trip with AG his usual, dry humoured, self. I was having a hard time with 'Biza Passage', yes, it was tight, and AG wanted to be in front of me so that he did not have to go back, complaining about 'chunkies' or more like 'fat bastards' getting in his way. This was all good banter and it was a really great trip. I was really doing some fine trips with the Eldon and having a good time underground.

After the trip we visited the Chelsea Caving Club hut at Whitewalls at the start of the tram-road walk to the cave. Inside, behind the front door was the Daren Cilau rescue kit. For many years Daren was a particularly awkward cave being just a snug and miserable crawl of 517 metres. The entrance is situated in the escarpment behind the Chelsea hut. At the end of 1984 whilst we were in Papua New Guinea a caver removed a boulder at the end of the nastiness to enter a passage that eventually lead into the remainder of the cave. Rescue from beyond the entrance crawl would be difficult in the extreme if not impossible. Some wag had therefore placed a derringer pistol behind the hut door, labeling it 'Daren Cilau Rescue Kit'!

Being a victim here was not high on my list of priorities. It was brought home to me very forcefully, when, with Steve Meyers in April 1986, I did a trip into Daren. It went through magical sounding places such as 'The Big Chamber Nowhere Near The Entrance' and 'The Time Machine', still the largest passage yet found in Britain, to the 'Terminal Sump' via the 'Bonsai Stream-way'. The 517 metres long entrance crawl commences with a tight wet squeeze before you have even left daylight. Some say this is the tightest bit, but I found the second calcite squeeze almost at the end of the tortuous passage most difficult, taking two attempts to pass through. I found, after experimenting, that by putting my left shoulder in the tiny floor slot I could push through. Acting on some good advice from AG for this trip before doing it I took some goodies in with me and stashed them at various points so that I had something good to look forward to on the way out. Taking two tins of peaches and various chocolate bars I placed them at regular intervals for our outward journey.

It was a memorable trip and wish that I had visited other parts of the cave, especially 'Antler Passage', where the aptly named antlers, helictites, grow out sideways from the wall. That will, unfortunately, be in my next life! However, I was well pleased with having reached the Terminal Sump and I was glad that I had stashed goodies for the way out at various intervals. They were a huge moral booster.

In the early 70's a climbing mate Eric 'Spider' Penman, who had also done some caving in South Wales, had been waxing lyrically about the crawl into Daren that did not go anywhere. He rated it as one of the most miserable places he had been and also quite arduous. Explorations still continue to find the link with Agen Allwedd. Spider also talked fondly about Ogof Ffynnon Ddu, in which I was to spend many happy hours exploring this very complex cave a few years later.

I had first met Spider around 1962 whilst climbing in Llanberis. He had a reputation as a hard climber and I next met him after he had moved to Tilberthwaite near Coniston in the Lake District in the early 1970's to become a Lake District National Park Warden. Unfortunately Spider disappeared to South Africa around 1975. However, whilst not exactly keeping in touch over the years, we made contact again when I visited Durban in 2006 and we were able meet a couple of times further whilst I was there. He still worked in the outdoors as a climbing instructor.

I was fortunate to visit Christmas Swallet three times towards the end of 1986. Situated close to Giants Hole the water was tested and found to arrive in Castleton from the same resurgence as all the other water from caves in the area. Dave Arveschoug, an Eldon member, was very friendly with the then owners of Peakshill Farm, Tom and Betty Watson and their son also called Dave. They had allowed Dave A and invited friends to start the exploration of this particular cave. It is very wet and quite tight in parts, but very sporting. I reached the sump on the 3rd trip having placed anchors for the 4 pitches on the way. High water on the other 2 trips stopped us from going down further than the 2nd pitch. Unfortunately very few people outside the Eldon managed to get down this one! It was a 'who you know trip'.

Chapter 4

Yorkshire Tales

At a Buxton Speleological Society dinner in December 1982, Hugh Kidd introduced me to Steve Reay who was to become my main caving partner for the next 8 years. Hugh was thinking about retiring as the Cave Rescue doctor and wanted to train someone much younger for this role. Many pints later I had arranged to take Steve on a trip shortly after New Year. We went down a very wet P8. Steve seemed to enjoy this, so along with various members of the Eldon I trained him in S.R.T. (Single Rope Techniques). To be the D.C.R.O. doctor he had to be able to descend ropes quickly and climb back up them. I was often his 'bag carrier'. He learned quickly and was very keen and enthusiastic to do more, not only in Derbyshire but elsewhere too.

Steve's wife Viv was also interested in caving. Although she worked and had three children I was able to introduce her to the dark delights of caves. On one occasion I took her to P8. I had done this cave many times and towards the bottom of the cave a short traverse is required above a section of shallow stream-way. A local enthusiastic digger, the late Keith Bentham (Ben) had been exploring a roof passage excavating tons of material in the process, dumping mud and stones from the high level passage into the stream below. This had, unfortunately, made a very effective dam, which in turn lead to the water becoming much deeper! I had not realised this, having not been in the cave for several weeks. At the start of the traverse I was surprised how close the level of the water was to the actual traverse line. My memory dimmed as I recollected the water not to be as close to the traverse line and only to be welly top deep. How wrong this memory lapse turned out to be! Viv asked me if the water was deep. My reply indicated that, no it wasn't, it was only welly deep!

At one point there is an awkward, slippery step. Viv slipped. Sploosh she went, totally disappearing. I was stunned. All I could see was a dirty brown helmet several inches down under the water. Fortunately I pulled her up spluttering and cursing my misinformation on the way! We had a good laugh about it later.

Although the safe number for venturing underground is 4, one to stay with a victim and two to go out, I found that caving with Steve was quick, speedy and allowed the pair of us more flexibility. We decided that we would visit Yorkshire on a regular basis. Taking it in turns to drive on each trip north we would leave Buxton around 06.00 and drive until we saw a convenient breakfast stop. After a 'vegetarian' full fat bacon and sausage breakfast we set off to the chosen cave. Steve's wife Viv was a vegetarian so I told her that her husband had been a good boy. After the caving trip we would have a meal in a pub close to where we had caved. Steve was always starving hungry after a trip and consumed huge amounts of fuel to the extent of often having two puddings, especially if Black Forest Gateau was on the menu. Food and a beer or two, when I wasn't driving, always had the same effect on me afterwards as I would react like a nodding dog in the passenger seat for the journey home. Similarly the reverse would happen to Steve when I drove.

Yorkshire Tales

Our first major trip together was to Meregill Hole, 165 metres deep, one of the finest trips in the Dales. We had a very early start for this. Having done this cave previously I knew that it could take a while. Entering via the short but snug and awkward 'Aven Entrance' we soon reached the bottom of all the fine pitches. 'Aven Entrance' avoids the 'mere', a large semi underground lake near the normal entrance, but rigging the first pitch is awkward. The long passage at the bottom of all the pitches continues via a couple of short drops each of which had a pool at their base. Now Steve, not being a climber, was not clever at staying on the rock so peeled off several times. This resulted in him becoming somewhat wet, well, soaked might be more precise. Laughing about it we continued along a fine, walking passage for 500 metres. The next 250 metres looked too miserable to contemplate so we turned around and headed out.

It did not take long to surface. Steve was more than happy to de-rig the ropes. I was very pleased for him to do so as he was a young, strong lad. It was still early afternoon so I persuaded him that another trip was in order. He was up for it. We drove over to Kingsdale and geared up before walking up the hill to the magnificent 105 metres deep Rowten Pot. I had been in here a while back with John Gillett but, due to very high water conditions, had not progressed very far. It was good to be attempting this again. We again made rapid progress to the sump and back out again. Poor Steve, again volunteering to de-rig, had his heart in his mouth as he swung out form he floorless rift into the main shaft. What a day. This showed me that a fast competent team can do a lot of caving in one day and keep warm in the process as there is much less waiting around.

Steve used much energy, emotionally and physically. Because of this I could always tell when he was close to the

73

surface. Cloud-like vapour would rise from the depths as though a smouldering volcano was about to erupt. Even inside caves when pitches were long, Steve was always enveloped by his personal 'cloud'. I could also tell when Steve had a problem or was upset about something. He would always whistle, not any kind of recognizable tune, just whistling. When the whistling stopped, which was very seldom, look out. He would be angry.

Some years later I was doing Meregill on a gorgeous summer day with some mates from Kendal, Richard Mercer, Bill Hogarth and Andrew Kirk (Kirky). It was so dry that we decided to enter via the 'mere'. This saved us the snug crawl and awkward rigging manoeuvre in the 'Aven Entrance'. We had made rapid progress to the head of the fine fifth pitch when I noticed that the water had changed colour.

"Right", I said "we are off out now".

"Why, what's up with you" they replied in unison.

"Because the cave is going to flood" I retorted.

"Don't be daft it's a fine day outside".

"No, seriously, the water has changed colour and to get out fast we need to tandem prussik".

They drew lots as to who was going to prussik with me, the chunky, and Bill lost. So we all set off out, Richard and Kirky followed by Bill and me.

As we approached the bottom of pitch 2 we heard a roar, just like an express train. A huge jet of water suddenly plummeted out of the roof. Fortunately, I had rigged the ropes out of harms way. We reached the entrance arch with water up to our waists. The Mere had risen dramatically due to a freak thunderstorm that had not been forecasted. At least we were all out of the cave with only the short 'mere' pitch to regain the surface of the moor above. Bill set off first and had only gone up a couple of metres when he fell out of his harness. He landed with a thump but was unscathed. His central maillon had somehow come undone. Or, as this was unlikely, had he neglected to screw up the maillon before going underground? This was a very sobering thought, one that left me checking everyone's central maillon before committing to rope on future trips.

An invitation to instruct on a specialist caving week in the Yorkshire Dales for Whitehall, an Outdoor Centre close to Buxton came in August 1983. I was thrilled and happy to accept. On an evening off from instructing, fellow instructors Dave Edwards and Al Hindle, convinced me that I would fit down Pippikin Pot. I knew this was a particularly tight hole as I had seen pictures of thin people just fitting the various tight slots, especially 'Stemple Squeeze'. Excited and encouraged with their enthusiasm, but worried too, I set off. We rigged Link Pot for our exit before continuing up the hill to the entrance. My heart was racing as we descended the first pitch and I felt very uneasy about what was to follow. Once the rope had been pulled down I had to go all the way through or wait for the others to do the trip and then come for me. This would have entailed a very long cold wait.

The cave at once became tight and almost immediately I found the tightest part of the trip. There was no way I was going to fit through the hole in front of me. I really did think that Dave and Al had overestimated my thinness. Dave said that I may just get through if I took my clothes off. Telling them to close their eyes to protect them from the glare of white flesh, I stripped down to my underpants. I passed all my clothes, light, helmet and everything else through the squeeze to Dave. Then I set off into the hole that seemed very undersized for my body, flesh biting into the cold wet rock. My underpants came off as I pushed through out of the constriction. What an awesome sight. I was stark naked in the cave, apart from my black wellies, much to the merriment of Dave and Al.

Dressing as best I could in the confined space, I knew there were more horrors in store for me. I now felt confident and strong, ready for anything. 'Stemple Squeeze' was passed with comparative ease but still with trepidation and before long the cave started to enlarge. I now felt very much happier and well pleased with my performance. We quickly found ourselves wallowing in 'The Wallows' before reaching the large chamber in Link Pot and our previously rigged rope hanging down. Climbing out of this 20 metres pitch into the cool evening air and daylight was a relief, although the final few feet were somewhat snug. I was very pleased with myself grinning from ear to ear. I was grateful for the huge amount of support, encouragement and banter from Dave and Al. Later, on other trips into the bottom of Pippikin, I went in via Mistral, which at one time was a very tight piece of caving. Unfortunately explosives were used to enlarge the very tight passages shortly after it was discovered.

Richard Mercer and I went on a visit into Mistral in March '98 intent on finding the 'Ciglaere' series. Visiting 'Gour Hall' and 'The Hall of the Mountain King' on the way, we dropped from an extremely liquid mud floored chamber into a wonderful fresh, fast flowing stream. We followed this up with the passage getting smaller until suddenly the passage reared up. There was a most wonderful 22 metres high waterfall crashing down from the roof passage above us. A fixed, but twitching rope indicated a climb. It looked too wet and the dubious nature of the rope precluded an ascent. Richard and I did many trips together often in the company of Bill and Kirky.

Richard and I went to Illusion Pot, a recently discovered

hole on Wackenburgh Hill in Kingsdale. The entrance of the cave is quite difficult to find as it is hidden in a boggy shake-hole. It was quite filthy to start and after a short length of passage we came up against the duck which on this occasion had very minimal airspace. There were a number of bailing items to help increase the airspace to an amount that we felt happy with. After an hour of sloshing water we had the airspace required. We entered the water and spluttered our way forward for 20 metres to where the passage rose up into a much larger one. We explored 'Expressway', 'Vandals Passage', 'Rushton Chamber' and on to the 'Final Rift' and sump. This had been dived from Dalebarn Cave making possible a through trip from one side of the hill to the other. There were many fine formations including some that looked like streaky bacon.

In 1992 Richard had been able to book a trip into the far reaches of White Scar Cave. Bill, Kirky and Krysia plus Richard and I were the party. Arriving by 10.00 we wandered through the show cave until it was possible to climb over the railings to enter the deep, cold, black looking lakes. Part swimming and part traversing, a scaffold pole being very useful at one stage, we reached a boulder choke, 'Big Bertha', after what seemed an eternity. I started off and climbed steadily up through the choke as I thought, mistakenly as it turned out, that was the way to pass it. I suddenly came across a very still body clad in a wet suit looking very ashen. I shouted down that I had found a body and needed help. Suddenly lights went on above me. I felt very silly and sheepish. I had entered the 'Battlefield', a new and quite pretty part of the show cave tour. The 'body' was a dummy emulating a caver for the tourists.

Backtracking I found the correct way to be at stream level. Crawling through in the water, we entered a large and quite spectacular stream-way. After a short swim, we climbed up cascades and followed the fine passage with water filled potholes in the floor. Further upstream we traversed along ledges above the water and passed below the climb up to the inlet of the 'Sleepwalker Series'. We did not bother with this but instead continued through another swim and up onto more ledges. From these we found a very greasy climb up into a very pretty grotto. Continuing, we climbed some more cascades but did not enter the lower and very wet passage ahead. White Scar Cave was a really enjoyable and great trip.

During the Foot and Mouth restrictions of 2001 we were lucky enough to be able to explore beyond the show cave in Ingleborough Cave. This cave, linked by diving into the Gaping Gill system, was gloomily black, very wet and cold but with some dramatic and impressively large passages. These either had deep water as in 'Lake Avernus' or deep gravel to reach 'Giant's Hall'. It appeared that the whole cave beyond the show section filled to the roof. The water was bitterly cold so we turned round after attempting the swim along the joint controlled passage of 'Lake Avernus'.

In September of that year we were blessed with a particularly fine spell of weather. I was in Kendal for a Kendal Caving Club meet. Richard, Damian Teal and I went to Box Head Pot. The entrance is crowned with a conning tower of pipes. Getting into the tower was very awkward much more so to get out of when we returned. Once through the oil drum and pipes the cave quickly enlarged into some magnificent shafts with not a drop of water anywhere. We were very lucky. Apparently they become unpleasantly wet for some time after rainfall. Our route was the 'Kendal Flyover', the better of the two options available. From close to the bottom of the shaft it is possible to enter Lost Johns via a fairly tight passage, but we did not attempt this that day.

Next day we ventured into Notts Two. The entrance shaft had been dug out and secured by miles of scaffolding, blocks and concrete through 40 metres of vertical boulders, a fantastic feat of engineering. At the end of the boulder choke there is a very slippery and awkward 5 metres climb down, especially so on the way back. Thankfully there is a conveniently placed scaffold tube in situ that aids the climb. The short length of passage beyond leads to a junction. From here we firstly went to the downstream sump past an area known as 'Kleine Scheidegg'. On this occasion low water prevailed allowing us to go further than is normal. Returning to the junction, we then wandered upstream into Inlet 5 and 'Curry Inlet'. Both these inlets had phenomenal formations the like of which is rarely seen. Thinking that we were the only ones with a permit that day we heard a commotion in the distance. We hid behind various boulders waiting to see who it was. Lo and behold it was 11 Cave Instructors undertaking a trip to revalidate their C.I.C. award. Knowing most people we had a talk and then left them to carry on with their trip.

Having done Cherry Tree Hole some time previously, Richard, Bill, Kirky and I returned to the shake hole where this is located, with a view to doing Darnbrook Pot, having just done a wet trip into Out Sleets Beck Pot. The entrance was a wriggle down for some 13 metres to where we reached a narrow rift passage. We followed this downstream until we entered a small but high stony chamber when I suddenly noticed movement. What the hell was that? It was quite large and furry. When it moved again I noticed that it was a fully grown rabbit. Feeling sorry for it and its lack of rabbit friends I placed it in my tackle bag and headed out. Back on the surface I released it. Where did it go? Yes, you guessed right. Back down the hole we had brought it up. Needless to say I didn't go back for it again.

Steve's next trip in 1984 was the descent of Jib Tunnel in Gaping Gill. Well, not on the first occasion. It was a glorious day in early May. The walk up through the Ingleborough Estate was very pretty and walking through Trow Gill was a lovely prelude to the day. Having put on suits and attached our S.R.T. kits I wandered along the short entrance passage attached to the rope I had fixed around a huge boulder on the surface. The huge baulk of timber once used for the winch descent was still lodged in place. (This has now gone). Fixing the first hangers Steve joined me at the edge. Asking if he was OK I set off down. What a tremendous place. The water issuing from 'Spout Tunnel' was avoided by several deviations and at 50 metres down I reached a small ledge. I looked across to the other side of the shaft to 'Birkbeck's Ledge'. This was first reached by John Birkbeck in 1848. The first complete descent of the 110 metres deep Gaping Gill main shaft was made by the prolific French cave explorer, Edouard Alfred Martel in 1896!

I was by now so totally wrapped up with the rigging that I had not even noticed that Steve had not yet set off. I rigged the final and very dramatic 35 metres drop from the lip of an overhang and descended to the floor of the chamber. It appeared as I set off down that I was going to abseil into a bottomless pool of water. After a tentative landing the water was found to be only a couple of inches deep! Where was Steve? I heard a very faint plaintiff shout from somewhere far above and could just make out Steve at the top. I set off back to the surface and found that he was very annoyed with himself for not committing to the descent. Telling him not to worry about it we started to wander slowly back, wondering how I could rescue the day for him.

I knew that Christmas Pot was near and by way of compensation we descended this as far as 'The Drainpipe'. On the way back to the car we talked about 'Jib Tunnel' or 'Lateral Shaft' as it is sometimes called. Steve said he wanted another attempt. We arranged to come back one evening the following week. In fact it was only 2 days later that we were once more gearing up for this. Steve finished his evening surgery around 20.00. After an evening meal at his house we drove up to Clapham and walked to Gaping Gill on a lovely cool night.

This time there was no problem. He was right behind me all the way, enjoying every minute of the descent. We arrived back on the surface just as dawn was breaking. After a lovely walk down to Clapham, we drove back to Buxton arriving for us both to start our days work in plenty of time.

I was at Gaping Gill again 4 days later with Tim Allen and we did a trip to 'Farrer Hall', quite a remote part of the cave. This time we descended the 'Main Shaft', a descent through history. Although not as dramatic as 'Jib Tunnel' it was still a fine way down. I will always remember going through 'The Font' in the far reaches of the cave. This is a tight miserable hole almost full with liquid mud and the key to the rest of the trip. The continuing passage became quite pretty with some small but lovely formations. After much crawling we passed a tight squeeze over a hump to reach the end at 'Farrer Hall'.

Steve's next visit to Yorkshire was to the fine open Alum Pot with a stream entering from the surface. He was by now really enthusiastic and keen after his descent of 'Jib Tunnel' to go and do anything. First we went down the north end of Alum. This I found to be an amazing way in. The re-belay for the main hang was in a most dramatic and airy position. Almost on the lip of a huge overhang I began to worry about Steve again. Was it the fact, like 'Jib Tunnel', that these drops were in daylight? I need not have worried. He followed straight after me. We then did Diccan Pot in fairly high water conditions. It was very draughty and cold but we managed to keep dry and warm in our new yellow PVC over-suits. These oversuits seem to be a kind of uniform for caving in Yorkshire! A glutton for punishment we did several small trips the same day, Borrins Moor, Upper Long Churn, Wilson's Cave and Selside Cave. What a great day out.

We had another trip north before I set off for the Untamed River Expedition in October 1984 doing a 'Jib Tunnel' to Stream Passage Pot exchange, some Eldon members were doing 'Jib Tunnel', and Hurnel Moss Pot on one day. I rigged Stream Passage Pot whilst they set about rigging Jib Tunnel.

On my return from Papua New Guinea, Steve was desperate to shake off withdrawal symptoms and cabin fever. We drove north several times and did many classic holes with one memorable day doing Diccan and then Ireby Fell by the 'Ding', 'Dong' 'Bell' 'Pussy' and 'Well' route. On another occasion we descended the fine 'Shadow Route'.

Having never visited Nidderdale we decided to see what the caves were like in that area. In July '87 we had a 'caveathon' visiting Low Eglin's, Goyden, Manchester Hole, New Goyden, Tom Taylor's and How Stean Tunnel. We had a couple of days later in the year on successive weekends caving on Leck Fell. On one of these we did Rumbling Hole and Death's Head both really great trips especially Rumbling Hole. On the other we decided that Lost John's was the one we wanted to do.

It was a miserable November day, dull, windy, misty, cold and wet. This was a day that should have seen us at home by the fire or somewhere other than Leck Fell. That did not deter us, however, and even though the water level was high a descent was made to Groundsheet Junction and continuing from there in deepening water, that ultimately reached our chests, to the sump. On exit darkness had fallen, in fact it had been dark for quite a while. The wind was blowing everything (apart from sheep, sensibly sheltering in the lee of a wall) horizontally, rain and cloud included. We were wet through and had to change. The prospect was not very enthralling. Stripping off with naked flesh in abundance a sudden gust of wind took my underpants bowling down the road. Streaking after them was not a sight to behold. The more I chased them the more the wind played games with me. Light became an issue the further I went away from the car. Sod it, I thought and hurried back to put on the rest of my dry clothing before jumping with relief into the passenger seat. Driving down the road I picked up the sodden pants and put them with the rest of the evil wet mass.

Amongst many others the main caves we descended later were, Little Hull Pot, Out Sleets Beck Pot, Long Kin West, Long Kin East, Rift Pot, Hunt Pot, Juniper Gulf and Nick Pot, not via 'Vulcan' as this was reportedly very tight, but by the 'Traverse in the Gods'. On exiting from Juniper Gulf on one of many trips' an excellent varied pot which ends with a superb 70 metres pitch we found that the entrance pitch rope had frozen solid. Snow had fallen too. By clever use of a Petzl Stop and warmth from my hands I was able to de-ice the rope to allow our jammers to grip. Thankfully, we exited into the cold, snowy and misty darkness.

As a youngster in the 60's I had climbed on occasions

with a character called Ken Wood. He was perhaps one of the best in the country in those days, a very quiet and unassuming person with a very dry sense of humour. I moved away from Kendal and did not climb with him again. Eventually Ken also moved away from climbing into caving. Not only was he of the 'right build' for this, he had done many of the nasty tight holes. On one occasion Steve, Pete McDonald and I met Ken in Kettlewell. I had met Pete whilst working for Whitehall. He was an instructor there and we ended up climbing and caving together a great deal. This was a good arrangement because his wife Elaine was really friendly with my wife Carol.

I had arranged with him for us all to traverse 'Dowbergill Passage'. It is a passage that has had more than its fair share of rescue callouts, mostly from getting lost or becoming overdue with subsequent failing lights. The survey gave me no clues as to where to go. It was a straight line. Fortunately Ken had done 'Dowbergill' some time ago but had an inkling of where to go. What a bewildering place. Setting off from Providence Pot we quickly reached the start of the 'straight line' passage as shown on the survey. From there we climbed up, we climbed down, we traversed, continually going up and down or traversing the rift until 'Hardy's Horror' was reached. An intermittently appearing phone wire was of absolutely no use as a guide whatsoever in this perplexing 20 metres high vertical maze.

I set off into the tight slot of 'Hardy's' and became well and truly jammed. With the judicious use of the travelling rope which we had fortuitously brought along Ken, Pete and Steve managed to pull me out and up. Phew, I had to think of another way. So stripping off totally for the second time in my life on a caving trip I eased my way through, but this time not losing my pants! The boys had not relished the thought of retreating as we were very close to the end. It was then a formality to wander out of Dow Cave. It was a fast trip of 3¾ hours but would have been much quicker had I not become stuck.

Having done nearly everything I had wanted to do or could get into it was now a question of repeating descents. Most of my future Yorkshire trips were done with clients. Steve had packed up caving to concentrate on his running. My life was changing too as work was more demanding and I became based in South Wales. I was leading treks worldwide, running caver training and assessment courses along with giving advice to various centres and organisations. As well as visiting the Vercors region of France frequently for holidays, I was also organising and running caving trips abroad for clients, mainly to the Vercors, on a regular basis.

Chapter 5

The Vercors Years

I had mainly been caving with the Eldon with trips to Nettle Pot, Robinson's Pipe a mine near Matlock and the recently discovered Streaks Cave in Stoney Middleton Dale. Nettle is an excellent vertical hole with a tight entrance shaft becoming much tighter just after the 'Sentry Box'. This had a choice of ways from the bottom of the entrance shaft, either by the fine, dry 'Elizabeth' pitch, or by the much more difficult, deeper and damper 'Crumble' and 'Biza Pots'. Streaks Pot, another good trip, was a horizontal tight hole where we did a through trip from the lower entrance and ultimately climbing up to the high one through 'Telescope Aven'.

Early in 1983 I had been asked by Geoff Blair and his wife Maureen, members of the loosely formed North-west Pothole Club, if I wanted to go to the Gouffre Berger. They asked if I knew of anybody else who wanted to go to help defray the cost of buying the necessary rope. I said yes, as I knew Dave Edwards wanted to have a trip there. He had been a few years earlier in winter but did not get very far in the cave at all. Each member of the trip was asked to contribute karabiners as we needed around 150. I had heard much about this iconic and wonderful cave and the invitation to go there was a dream, come true.

Whilst visiting AG one night to obtain first hand information about the Berger he suggested that we should climb Mont Blanc afterwards. Not only would this be fun it would be totally different way to end a trip to France. AG had bottomed the Gouffre Berger before and it was great to have an insight to what was involved. Dave was to meet some of his friends out in the Dauphine after the caving trip as well, so the idea of climbing the Blanc seemed pretty good to me.

I had had a good warm up to the trip having worked for Whitehall Outdoor Pursuits Centre, I was not a C.I.C. or even a Local Cave Leader in those days' helping out on a specialist caving week in Yorkshire. This was the week in fact, I did Pippikin! We did many classic trips with an enthusiastic group during that week in glorious weather, abseiling through Swinsto to exit from Valley Entrance, County Pot to Lancaster exchange trip on ladder, County Pot to Pool Sink exchange, again on ladders and finally Bull Pot of the Witches.

Dave, his wife Caroline, Carol and I set off earlier than the rest of the team for the Berger in my Ford Cortina Estate with the rope, all 1,000 metres of it in 5 bags along with the 150 karabiners. We also crammed in our camping gear not to mention climbing gear too, with a view to start rigging the cave as soon as we arrived. We crossed the Channel and drove to Grenoble and up to the Sornin Plateau where we camped for the duration. Nowadays camping on the plateau is forbidden but it was the traditional base for every expedition to the Berger, becoming known as 'the wood of a thousand turds'.

The day after we had arrived Dave and I set off, ably supported by Carol and Caroline helping to carry our kit. We had 7 bags to carry to the entrance! Our wives bade us a fond farewell as we set off on the greatest underground adventure I had done at that time. The seven bags comprised 5 of rope and metal work and our 2 personal bags. Dangling these from our harnesses we abseiled the 15 metres entrance shaft to the head of the 27 metres deep 'Puits Ruiz'. Ruiz, one of the original explorers had fallen down this! Fortunately he survived. The rotting wooden platform at the pitch head looked as though it would collapse at any second, and send us too plummeting ground-wards. Continuing, we descended the 15 metres series of small drops called the 'Holiday Slides' to the 35 metres 'Puits du Cairn'. All was going well. From the base of 'Cairn' we commenced the dreaded meanders, a narrow but high, twisting rift passage. Fortunately wooden stemples had been wedged across the rift at strategic points that helped us to traverse higher up in the wider sections. The stemples were quite old with several gaps and several long steps were needed at times. This made bag carrying strenuous. Trying to do the journey once with 6 bags proved to be far too difficult so we did the journey twice! At the far end the 38 metres 'Puits Garby' descended to the continuation of the meanders. Finally after more cursing, pushing, shoving and generally sweating we popped out at the head of the 28 metres 'Puits Gontard'. It was great letting gravity help once more with getting our burdensome bags down the cave. From here three very short pitches called the 'Relay' took us to the head of 'Puits Aldo'. This superb pitch is one of the deepest in the cave at 42 metres excepting for the aptly named 'Hurricane' pitch, the last on the journey to the bottom which was also renowned for becoming very wet when it was raining on the surface.

We started Aldo's by doing a long traverse out across the left wall of the shaft. Dave rigged the rope that would, hopefully, keep us dry in case of bad weather outside. At the end of the traverse a fine clear drop found us at the bottom. A very short pitch down followed and we had reached what had been nicknamed 'Telephone Boulder' adorned with masses of abandoned telephone wire. We had arrived at the start of the 'Riviere sans Etolies' or 'Starless River'.

Walking downstream in the passage, known as the 'Petzl Gallery', I was really impressed by the sheer immensity of it. I had not dreamt that anything could be so big underground. We passed 'Lake Cadoux' very easily as it was dry and remained so for the whole trip. Often this is a 60 metres long lake necessitating the use of a boat to cross. Huge fantastic formations decorated the roof of the passage, the 'Salle Bourgin'. After climbing up a short way we dropped down a 10 metres pitch known as 'Petit General' to where the river arrived. Here we traversed a wall above a deep pool, the 'Cascade de la Tyrolienne' and continued along the huge passage circumnavigating massive house sized boulders. This is 'The Great Rubble Heap'. In a crack between boulders I noticed a pram frame, complete with wheels. Ummmm, I wonder who had been walking babies down here!

We reached the start of the 'Hall of Thirteen'. This was a most magnificent sight. Huge gour pools stretched off into the gloom at the end of which we saw massive rocket sized stalagmites. Our load of bags was now somewhat diminished having offloaded 2 on the way. Dumping the remaining 3 rope bags of rope and metalwaork at 'Camp 1' we returned to the surface with just our personal bags. These had food, spare clothing and a shelter along with extra carbide.

We soon reached daylight and back in camp 9 hours after we had left, tired but well pleased with our work. The following day was one of rest and sunbathing. Some of the team had already arrived. Next day Dave and I along with Colin Davies set off to bottom the cave. Quickly dispensing with the entrance series we arrived in Camp 1 some 2 hours after setting off. How wonderful just to have one bag to worry about through the 'Meanders'.

Picking up the burdensome bags again at Camp 1 we set off. It was good to have help. However, somewhere between Camp 1 and the 'Enormous Cascade', a hollow stalagmite with a dribble of water amplifying the noise to what might be a Niagara sized waterfall, Colin found that he had lost most of his S.R.T. kit. Sensibly he decided to return to 'Camp 1'. It was disappointing not to have his help with the bags but Dave and I continued to 'The Canals'. Our first pitch of the day was the 15 metres 'Balcony'. Some calcite slopes followed taking us to the 15 metres 'Vestibule' pitch. This dropped us into the start of the 'Coufinades' or canals. This is where, if we had them, we would have changed into wet suits. However, we were confident that we would not get too wet. I always felt much more comfortable caving in a fleece under-suit and PVC over-suit. This often feared section had traverse ropes about a metre above water level that helped to keep us out of the deep sections as we did not wish to get our fleece suits too wet. Although very frayed and battered the ropes did their job keeping us dry above our waist.

Passing the 5 metres 'Cascade Abelle' the cave changed character and became active. We now had to be much more careful with our rigging. More wading and traversing took us to the head of the watery 17 metres 'Cascade Claudine'. It was fun avoiding the deep plunge pool at the base of this pitch, the 'Cascade des Topographes' follows. We soon reached the top of the huge descending gallery known as the 'Grand Canyon'. Grand, no, steep, filthy and very slippery, yes! Slithering down this steep slope we reached 'Camp 2' finding it in a jumble of boulders. This section I found to be the most unpleasant part of the cave. We clambered down many boulders. A greasy, muddy hand-line helped slightly at one point.

Leaving the 'canyon' we continued along a dry passage to the 20 metres 'Puits Gache'. The descent of this pitch is awkward, initially against the wall it abruptly became free hanging. At the bottom we rejoined the river.

I was having an amazing time. This was very akin to doing a long alpine climb except that Dave and I were abseiling the vertical pitches. Ultimately the hardest part was yet to come because we had to climb back up all of them to the surface. We quickly reached the top of the fine 'Grand Cascade'. At the bottom of this another cascade demanded we rigged it differently to the others as the descent would have been in the full force of any flood water. Dave rigged this wet descent. At the bottom he tensioned the rope diagonally from the top of the pitch to a belay point some 10 metres away from the base of the pitch. I belayed another rope to abseil down but this time I clipped myself to the tensioned diagonal rope. This thankfully, kept me dry, certainly drier than Dave.

We were very lucky that water levels were low. This pitch must very be serious when water levels are high. By now, having been absorbed in the technicalities of rigging, time had simply flown by and hunger suddenly made itself apparent. We tucked into some of our many chocolate bars and dried fruit. I ate so much chocolate on this trip that I very rarely ate it again for a considerable time after. We were soon at a mass of ropes, of very dubious reliability and vintage, adorning the right wall. This was 'Little Monkey'. Using these ropes we traversed across the vertical wall to a point where we could abseil 10 metres to the short tunnel leading out to the head of 'Puits de l'Ouragan',

Hurricane. I felt 'Little Monkey' was perhaps the most serious part of the whole trip and I was very glad when we reached the solid floor leading out to 'Hurricane'. I had heard stories of a caver being stuck at the end of 'Little Monkey' when the cave started to flood. Fortunately for him he had his dry clothes and emergency supplies with him for his 3 day enforced bivouac.

Managing to keep dry on the 44 metres descent of this aptly named pitch we reached the extensive and extremely windy chamber below. All we had to do now was to walk to the sump. Passing the huge '1,000 Metres Inlet' up to our right we clambered over boulders, down short cascades and traversed deep pools until a dry oxbow was entered on our left which avoided a small pitch. Back in the stream again we waded and traversed around pools until we reached the 'Pseudo-siphon'. This is the turn around point for most people. The next bit is THE wet bit. Twenty metres ahead we reached the true sump where we scrawled our names in the mud on the wall after a cold swim 1,122 metres below the entrance and some 4 kilometres from the entrance.

All that remained now was to return to the surface. We were both wet but warm from our exertions. We set off very pleased with the fact that the pair of us had carried all the ropes for the trip, our own personal survival food and equipment and had rigged the whole cave together. Camp 1 was reached 27 hours after leaving the surface and the bottom of the cave. Here we had food and a well earned sleep after which we arrived on the surface into glorious sunshine 41 hours after leaving. I was pleased as punch and I wanted more of the same. Celebrations in camp that night were, to say the least, lively as the rest of the team had now arrived. AG did an early trip with another mate, Bulmers who sadly died in 2013. After they had exited AG,

Bulmers, Carol and I set off for Chamonix for the ascent of Mont Blanc.

After discussions we decided to do the ascent by the long way and wished we hadn't. The weather was not kind. We caught the telepherique to the top of the Aiguille du Midi and descended into the Vallee Blanche. Turning to our right we made our way to the Cosmique Hut on the lower slopes of the south face of the Aiguille du Midi below the Cosmiques Arete. We set off early but by the time we had almost reached the top of Mont Blanc du Tacul the weather had really turned nasty so down we came. It would have been good to reach the summit of the Blanc but it didn't really matter. What did matter was that I had done my first 1,000 metres deep hole and I was well pleased.

My next visit to the Vercors was in August 1985 with Pete McDonald with whom I was doing a lot of climbing. I had just bought a new Ford Fiesta and although small it managed to take all our camping and caving gear. The Eldon were going to be in the area and had booked the Berger for 10 days commencing in the second week of August. Pete wanted to go down it as well as explore other caves in the area. We camped in the Bourne Gorge at a small, cosy site run by Madame Lattard. She was a lovely, quite elderly lady. Although there were few facilities, it was situated on the bank of the river, useful for rope washing, and was a lovely peaceful site. It came complete with a vegetable patch and boules pitch! The French are addicted to this most traditional of games and is played everywhere where a ball can be rolled, dropped or slid.

Our first trip was to the fine Grotte de Gournier, close to the Choranche Show Cave complex, the Couffin/Chevaline. The show cave itself is well worth visiting to view some remarkable formations and straw stalactites. Walking on past the show cave we reached the entrance in a further 10 minutes. Beyond the fine entrance porch was a black and very cold looking lake. This had to be crossed. Fortunately I had brought an inflatable boat, one that we had used in Nare on the Untamed River Expedition. I fixed one end of a pull back line to the back of the boat and the other to a convenient boulder and put on a buoyancy aid. Using my hands as paddles in the icy water I set off across this Stygian lake. Grotesque gargoyle like formations dangled absurdly from the roof. I reached a point 50 metres away where there was a break in the wall on the left rising from the black water where I could land. After nearly falling out I grasped a hold and clambered out. After fastening another pull back line to the boat so that I could help Pete in his crossing he pulled the boat back and quickly joined me.

Our next problem was a short 5 metres climb up to reach a ledge to begin a traverse across the vertical wall to where it was possible to climb up over some deep gour pools into a huge gallery. The climb was made easier because a piece of metal had been bolted to the wall allowing me to reach an alcove where there were a multitude of thick mini columns to fix the end of the traverse rope and to dangle an end down to enable Pete to climb up using his hand jammer for protection. Although easy the 30 metres traverse was spectacular as it wandered across the wall above the black waters of the lake below. The roof above was adorned with grotesque, gargantuan stalactites as though we were in some fairy hall. I was able to re-belay the rope several times. This ensured that if either of us slipped we would just dangle a few centimeters below it.

From the entrance into the gigantic gallery we walked and scrambled over huge boulders past some fine formations for about an hour. At a depression in the boulder floor we found the point where we could drop down through the boulders into a fantastic stream passage. Alternating wading in and traversing above the blue crystal clear water was a delight in this marvelous passage. The traverse was protected by bits of thick fencing wire or tatty bits of rope to which we clipped our cow's tails to for protection. We reached a point where the fencing wire and tatty rope ended. Turning around we made good time back to the entrance. Pulling ourselves back across the lake we reached glorious sunshine. How wonderfully refreshing and different the air smells after several hours underground.

The following day we went to the Grotte de Bournillon. To the left of the entrance porch, the largest in Europe, is a magnificent waterfall plunging down over 300 metres, the Moulin Maquis. This makes a fine abseil descent from the plateau above. Descending waterfalls and canyons is called 'canyoning' or to put it another way 'caving with the lid off'! It is great fun. The Bournillon is where the water resurges from all the caves in the plateau above. In times of flood the flow of water is in excess of 80 cumecs. It is not a cave to venture into in times of wet weather. Pete and I were very fortunate because it had been sunny and warm for a few weeks and we were able to reach the far end where the passage splits to enter the two sumps. This was the only time of many visits to the cave that I have been able to reach the terminal point.

After visiting the interesting Grotte Favot with its remarkable pentagonal shaped phreatic tunnel, we went to the Berger and had a fun trip down to 'Puits Gache' before turning around to come out. During our trip we helped Paul Deakin create a photographic record of the Berger. We rested the following day and then visited the Scialet de Malaterre a magnificent hole in the middle of the forest.

This has a very substantial metal bridge spanning the bottomless looking shaft. We fixed our rope to the metalwork above the floor of the bridge then lifted the middle section of the platform out. This allowed us to thread our way through the girders below to descend the spectacular 120 metres to the chamber at the bottom of the shaft. We did not explore further as the way on looked extremely muddy and very miserable.

Visits to the Gour Fumant and Pot de Loup on off days preceded a descent of the 273 metres deep, Scialet de Trisou. Steve Dickinson (Dickie) who was in Papua New Guinea with me had been part of the Berger contingent. He had now joined us for a few days of relaxing caving. The Trisou is a very fine hole having several deep shafts along with many smaller ones. We reached the first of the deep shafts half way through the trip. This, the 'Puits de la Douche' is 56 metres deep and has, interestingly, a tide mark about a third of the way down all around the shaft wall. This indicated to me where the water backed up to in times of flood! A sobering thought. As it was a beautiful day outside we were not too concerned. Gloomy caving followed as the cave became wetter and the rock a foreboding black colour. The final deep pitch is the 46 metres 'Puits de l'Infini'. Here the rock bristled with chert, a hard flint like rock, at the top. The volume of water descending on top of us greatly increased as we reached the bottom. A short drop followed to where we reached the sump.

The following day we headed to the show cave of the Grotte de la Luire. I had heard that the Luire was a really good trip and I wanted to do it. During the Second World War the large dry entrance porch was used as a hospital for the French Resistance injured during their skirmishes. Unfortunately it was found by the Germans who summarily killed the patients!

I began talking to the cave owner and asked if it was possible to explore beyond the show cave. "Oui, c'est pas de probleme". We had to arrive before 10.00 the following morning before the tourists arrived. However, if there was any chance of rain he would not allow us to descend. The cave is an epi-phreatic system where the whole known cave fills from the bottom up! In times of flood, water exits the cave at around 40 cumecs.

Fortunately the day dawned bright and sunny. It was a 'spot the cloud' day ensuring that it was going to be another scorcher. We arrived in good time and not too tired after the 3 minute walk from the car park. Having donned our caving gear we set off. We were not going to encounter any S.R.T. pitches but we did have a Petzl Stop and jammers for the descent of the 'Grand Scialet'. We descended the 96 metres of fixed ladders and rope of extremely dubious quality to the base. From there we explored this very complex system down to a depth of around 350 metres, the lowest point achievable without diving. There were no signs of vadose development anywhere, but amazing phreatic features were everywhere. On setting back to the surface my mind was recalling the picture I saw at the entrance of the show cave. It depicted a caver sitting in a boat rising up the 'Grand Scialet' at a rate of 1 metre per minute!

Our next venture was to the Trou qui Souffle. For the first pitch of this cave it was possible to fix hangers from the seat of our car! In reality though, we parked the car easily on the far side of the road, crossed it and set off down. The hole could almost have been a drain in a gutter apart from the strong draught of air being forced out of the slot. This too was an amazing trip to the sump at -220 metres and was one I regularly used on all my guiding trips.

At the end of the trip we made a visit to Annecy and the Parmelan Plateau. I had heard that there was a superb 613 metres through trip descending from the Tanne de Bel Espoir down to the Grotte de la Diau. We decided that it would be good way to finish off the holiday with this on the way back to England. The entrance is found on the top of the plateau. We camped in an orchard at Thorons Gliere close to the Route de l'Anglettaz forest road that would lead us to the Chalet de l'Anglette. This was the starting point for the walk up onto the plateau. Checking out the Diau was a very important precursor before attempting a through trip. We planned to do this the next day as it was necessary for us to determine the water level and to ensure that it was low enough for us to exit. Knowing where we came in to the Diau from the Espoir would also be very useful. We would be pulling the ropes down after ourselves. After we had pulled them down having descended the first pitch we would be totally committed to the trip.

The trip into the Diau went without any problems. Interestingly new flood water resistant ladders had been placed on the short climbs leading into the main river passage. This was huge and obviously took a massive amount of water. One of the side passages we entered to avoid deep water was so windy that our carbide lamps were constantly blown out. Wandering up this magnificent river gallery we were amazed at the sheer size of it. We were looking for the 'Affluent de Grenoblois'. This is where we would emerge into the river gallery when we did the through trip. Ninety minutes after leaving the entrance we easily found the 'Affluent' and entered the smaller passage. We followed it up to the base of the pitches coming in from the Espoir. Water levels were low meaning that the trip would be possible the following day.

The 1 hour walk to the Espoir was very picturesque, but hot with heat from the sun reflecting back at us from the lapiaz. After we had gained the plateau great views were had of the snowy Mont Blanc area. We blundered around trying to locate the elusive entrance, eventually finding it below the plateau rim suitably signed Tanne de Bel Espoir. There was even an arrow pointing down! Here we donned our caving gear and set off. I rigged the 36 metre first pitch for S.R.T. just in case I could not find the window I needed to pendulum into. Whoever would be last would rig the rope so that we could pull it down after he had descended the pitch.

At the point I thought the window would be in the shaft wall I locked my descendeur so that I would not descend further. I could not locate the window at first but once seen I managed to start swinging across the shaft as though on a giant swing until I grasped the floor of the window and pulled myself in. Phew! That was quite a pendulum. Pete came down next and intimated that a thunderstorm was beginning to make its presence felt. Desire to go further waned immediately. The thought of being flushed out of the Diau was not appealing. Out we came. That evening there was a violent storm. We would, possibly, have made it through but there was always that chance that we could have become lost or the storm started earlier. It was the best decision in view of the potential for a major catastrophe. Caves will always be there another day.

My next Vercors visit was again another holiday. This time I went with Steve who was keen to experience different caves. It was really good to be caving in a country where exits are generally made into sunshine and warm air. Changing out of wet gear is far more pleasant rather than fighting off hypothermia in the UK. We camped as I had on the previous occasion at Madame Lattard's. She had remembered me from my visit of the previous year and was very pleased to welcome me back.

Our first adventure was to the Gournier. Once we reached the stream I was determined this time to reach the first upstream sump. I had decided to take some 'tat', (spare rope) for gaps in the traverses above the stream. Water levels were lower than on my visit with Pete. Having reached the end of the fencing wire and tatty rope I was able to climb across, albeit somewhat airily, and fix one of the spare bits of 'tat' that I was carrying. This eased the situation for Steve and we carried on in this superb steam-way until we were stopped by a 12 metres high cascade. This I climbed fairly easily and brought Steve up. We entered the 'Salle Chevalier' a short distance ahead. The way ahead looked difficult as it involved a 40 metres climb up to reach the 'Salle Gathier' and upstream sump. Having no rope or climbing gear to scale this we sadly turned around at this point. I was not disappointed at all as I had really enjoyed the trip and very pleased that I had overcome the problem with the missing wire. I asked Steve to leave the 'tat' in place for others as we came back down the stream-way.

Our next venture was thwarted by the threat of a storm. I had thought we could go and do the Trou de l'Aygue. The entrance started off as a long, flat out crawl in a very wide bedding plane. I could hear stones rattling above my head or was it rattlesnakes? I rationalised that rattlesnakes were only found in the US of A so we continued. I weaved snakelike this way and that way looking for the widest part for ease of movement. By the time I reached the stream I had become somewhat disillusioned with the cave. Steve had too, so we exited. Rumblings were heard in the distance as we changed our clothes and I was glad we were out. Perhaps the cave was speaking and telling us to get out by giving us the eebie jeebies with the rattling stones. By the time we had reached the car a storm was in full force. Phew I could well imagine the water rising quickly and making the bedding plane a very unpleasant place to be!

The storm was thankfully short lived and we made a visit to the Scialet de l'Appel the following day. This is a delightful cave with many short pitches, although at one point, after a traverse, a difficult climb up to a pitch head had its moments! We then visited a different type of cave, the Grotte des Ramats. On this occasion the cave was bone dry but it obviously took a great amount of water in wet weather. We entered where the underground stream would resurge and followed a heavily eroded and rough passage upstream to where it was blocked by a sump. To avoid this I made a difficult climb up of 11 metres to reach a squeeze at the top. I entered this head first. This I thought to myself would be very entertaining on the way out. It was! We continued to the 'Galerie de la Verna' before turning round. Exiting feet first from the squeeze at the top of the climb was made easier by rigging a retrievable rope to aid our exit which then enabled us to abseil back down the difficult climb.

Our last cave on this trip was to be the Glaciere d'Autrans. We had set off to do this the previous day but had difficulty finding the cave. We eventually found the entrance in a deep snow filled shake-hole. Thinking that we did not have enough time for the Glaciere we opted for the much shorter but still interesting Patinoire d'Autrans. The entrance to this was just a few metres away to the left, almost hidden by the hard neve. There was a frozen lake as smooth as an ice rink in the very aptly named 'Salle de Glace' just after the very short entrance pitch. We also found a passage that took us to where we could overlook one of the main pitches in the Glaciere, the 'Puits Englace'.

The following day we walked straight to the entrance where we geared up. Clutching bags I fixed a rope at the start of the entrance passage which is known as 'The Toboggan'. It was not named 'The Toboggan' for nothing. It was very slippery and the downward slope became steeper as I reached the head of the 'Puits Englace'. Here, I climbed up 3 metres to find the hanger placements buried in the ice for me to fix the rope for the 32 metres descent. Steve's light shimmered through the translucent ice in a wonderful orangey glow. This would have made a superb picture if either of us had thought to bring a camera. Thick ice was frozen to the wall for the length of this amazing pitch. I was impressed. Ice pinnacles littered the floor of the ensuing passage. Two short pitches took us to the head of two long pitches that totalled 51 metres. I ran these together as one making a tremendous descent, very glad that they were dry. Two further but smaller pitches took us to where the character of the cave changed dramatically. From being one of spacious shafts, a sharp and very rough meander continued to where 3 small pitches took us to a squeeze and the bottom of the cave. After thrutching back out of the squeeze and rough menaders I was glad to be back in the beautiful shafts prussiking back out.

Although I had been guiding clients here in 1988 my next 'fun' visit was not until July 1992 with my mates from Kendal, Richard, Kirky and Bill. Kirky had broken his arm a few days before the trip but did not want to miss out. He had a fiberglass cast from his wrist to his elbow but he is a tough lad. We had a miserable drive to Madame Lattard's. The French lorry drivers had completely blocked many roads in France so our journey involved going through Belgium, Germany and Switzerland. What a drag that was. Instead of going to the Vercors straight away we camped at Thorons Gliere as I had in the past, near Annecy, in pouring rain. The following day I thought that we would take a look at the Grotte de la Diau. We looked but only managed to reach the water level marker not far from the entrance due to flooding. A day later we were ensconced in Madame Lattard's campsite thankful that the rain had stopped.

Our first excursion was to Les Saints de Glace. This had been connected to the Trou qui Souffle in October 1989 and was reputed to be a good hard trip. The entrance was easy to find being only 5 minutes from the road immediately beyond the Trou qui Souffle. We were soon at grips with some tighter sections. At one place it had been enlarged from 23 centimetres to rescue an injured caver but it was still quite snug. The journey to the 'Salle Hydrokarst' was a great trip and possibly the first time that an English party had descended to this. The idea of doing the through trip to the Trou qui Souffle grew but by the time we had rigged the TQS the following day this idea had dissipated. We went on to do the Glaciere d'Autrans, always a favourite. Grotte Favot was explored when it was pouring down and the Goule Blanche which was in a state of high flood after 2 days of heavy rain being viewed from a safe distance, a small layby on the roadside. The Glaciere de Carri was a great little trip where we stopped at the tight bit close to the bottom. I decided that the classic 'trouser filler', the Scialet de Malaterre should also be descended.

We arrived at the bridge spanning the shaft where I rigged the rope and attached myself to it. I then lifted the grid from the floor and asked Kirky for my 'large yellow' bag. Now this bag is large, extremely large, as it took over 360 metres of rope to fill it. Whilst today there was only 140 metres stashed inside, the bag still did not look small and commanded a presence. I kicked the bag through the gap in the floor and, ooooooops, I had forgotten to attach it to my harness. The rope snaked out shivering quickly as the yellow bomb flew through space to land with a large thud on to a sloping shelf fifty metres lower. Unfortunately the rope slid out of the bag and slithered on down the remainder of the shaft, leaving the bag stranded and somewhat out of reach.

We all arrived safely at the bottom and then one by one we set off out. Fortunately there was a re-belay about half way back up. Kirky not wanting to be thought of as being nursed volunteered to rescue the now empty yellow bomb. He came up last. On leaving the re-belay he was able to swing around. After many futile launchings and much cursing he managed to retrieve the 'bomb'. It remains in service to this day much to the horror and cursing of many 'carriers'.

We did the Grotte de Gournier as far as the steam-way before we went over to the Font d'Urle area to do the Reseau Christian Gathier. The French guide book description was not very encouraging as it mentioned a series of 'etroitures', meaning tight squeezes to me. This was a difficult cave to find but once found, the small entrance descended a sloping 35 metres snug rift to a chamber at the bottom. At this point Bill decided to leave his watch as he had forgotten to leave it in the car so he hid it under a stone. We continued through some magnificent formations but only went as far as the 'Salle de Tenebres' where we decided to exit. Driving back to Madame Lattard's, Bill realised he had left his watch behind in the cave. Not only had he left it behind but he had set the alarm to go off every hour. Anyone entering the cave would wonder what the hell the beeping sound was. No doubt if not found the alarm would be beep beeping on the hour every hour for many months to come. Having two cars the boys left for England and I left for the Cueto Coventosa through trip in the Cantabrian Mountains.

A short climbing and caving trip to the Vercors in May 1997 was done with Dave Halstead and Michael Forest. This was not the most successful caving wise due to the high water conditions prevailing and bad choices of cave. Not only were they difficult to find but they were tight too. The Scialet de Gay Bunny and the Grotte de Enveribard could only be penetrated a short way before my body size prevented further progress. We did, however, reach the severely flooded stream in the Gournier. This was a very impressive sight indeed. We also had a memorable view of a flooded Grotte de Bournillon. Here we climbed the stony slope to the right of the entrance and explored the cave on the right hand side of the huge passage as far as we could via high ledges on the right, well above the raging, booming torrent.

A fun holiday in August 1999 resulted in a solo trip to the far end of the Goule Verte, a short but interesting excursion, a fun trip to the Brudour Sump in the Scialet de l'Appel and at long last an exploration of the Goule Blanche. Janice Smith came with me and although a character and caver from South Wales she was more interested in seeing the sun than the darkness in the caves. I met up with some friends from Kendal, Rose and Paul East and Julian and I suggested to them that we did a trip into the Goule Blanche. This was for two reasons. One was to find out what was beyond all the pipe work adorning the entrance and the other was because the French guide intimated that it was pretty at the far end. It was. 'The Salle des Roses' being especially so.

After the easy entrance a short climb up above a small lake and behind a pipe took us into a higher gallery. This ended in a huge and seemingly impenetrable boulder choke. Finding the way through this long complex mass of boulders was taxing and perplexing. Occasional sooty arrows on the wall and short lengths of rope draped down awkward climbs indicated that we were on the right route. Eventually we reached a rough crawl which sported foam adhering to the walls. This indicated that the passage had flooded quite recently. The crawl took us to the start of the climb into the 'Salle des Roses'. Before climbing up to this we continued to reach some deep looking water in a wide rift. Although the traverses to keep out of this water were easy, a fall would have had serious consequences. The end of the cave was marked by many extremely fine cauliflower type formations. Returning along the traverses we climbed up into the 'Salle des Roses' and ensuing chamber to view the remarkable formations. It was a serious climb where a rope was necessary.

A couple of days later after walking up the Grand Veymont with Janice one day and the But de Neve the following day I ended the holiday by having a couple of days on my own although Janice came for moral support to find the entrances to the Clos d'Aspres system. We caught the telecabin from the Balcon de Villard to the top station at 1,750 metres. Here there were great views of the surrounding grey limestone mountains. I found a path across several pistes and followed this to where we joined up with a path that took us to the ruins of a bergerie, shepherds hut, and the start of a large area of lapiaz. Just beyond this I found the lowest entrance of the system, the Brumes Martinales. Following the obvious fault line I then reached the Scialet du Blizzard and finally a little further the Scialet de Silence. All these caves are named in red paint at their entrances.

The Scialet de Silence is reputed to be one of the best trips in the Vercors and was one I had wanted to do for a while. I was pleased that I had now found it. I had an S.R.T. kit with me and a 50 metres length of rope, enough to see what was what. I set off down the small diameter shaft with Janice guarding my rope on the surface. I descended what seemed to be a devious route until I reached the end of my rope as I landed on the floor of a small chamber. With no more rope I headed out.

That was the last time I did a 'fun' trip to these wonderful caves. In between all the above trips I was guiding clients and after that last 'fun' trip I continued taking clients there until the last one, to date, in May 2005.

Chapter 6

European Caving

My first experience of European caving outside of the Vercors was on a trip to that very popular holiday isle, Mallorca. Carol and I had split up and I came here for caving and walking with a new girl friend, Brenda. She loved walking, in all weathers, and was keen to visit this isle for a break. We secured a 2 week package deal staying at Cala san Vincente and hired a car. We were to meet other friends and they had arrived earlier, Ian Wolstencroft (Grum) with Geoff and Maureen Blair who had invited me to the Berger in 1983. Our first trip was to the Torrent de Pareis. Whilst this was not a cave it was an exciting trip down a deeply incised canyon. We all ended up on the beach where Jason and the Argonauts had been filmed.

The first cave that Geoff, Mo, Grum and I did was the Avenc de sa Miranda, basically just an 85 metres deep shaft. We then drove on to the Formentera peninsula where we descended a roadside shaft, the Avenc Terrasa. All five of us then visited the Cova del Cal Pesso in Pollensa the following day. This was found quite easily after a fairly steep walk up the hill. It was a warm cave, very pretty inside providing us with an easy and good trip.

Finding the Cova de Campana the following day was somewhat more difficult. We eventually found it a kilometre up from the road on a steep and craggy hillside. It is the deepest cave on the island at 304 metres. Below the second pitch in a vast chamber there were some very fine formations. Some artistic person had conjured up some quite remarkable and erotic mud statues. Leaving a candle burning at the top of the slope we descended the chamber admiring the many helictites on the way, some of which were over 12 inches long. An arch at the bottom of the chamber led to the top of the shorter third pitch. This took us into another large chamber, where most sensible people turn back. On the second trip into the cave a week later this was the point where we did turn back, however, on this particular occasion we were intent on reaching the bottom.

We found that the character of the cave had now changed somewhat having become much more serious. The fourth pitch, which I found to the right of the chamber, followed the line of any dislodged stones, and there were many, from the ledge above it. To avoid denting the helmet of anyone who was below, great care was needed. After three re-belays I landed on a huge rubble slope, which confirmed the looseness of it all. Hanger placements became non-existent so natural belays had to be utilized for hanging the ropes. However, I did find a bolt for the head of the final drop. It was a difficult take off, having to literally launch into space. The bottom was reached where a red paint inscription confirmed we had reached the lowest point.

Other trips followed. We descended the Avenc S'Aigo, Avenc Llorer and the 'cave under the green house', the Cova des Diners. We explored the local cave to the hotel, the Cova des Rodes until Geoff, Mo and Grum returned home. Brenda and I did some walking and I did the excellent Sierra Caval Bernat Ridge. This was a mini Skye Ridge, an excellent, extremely airy excursion along a narrow limestone ridge some 300 metres above the sea.

One night towards the end of our stay we met up with some people from Skipton, Eric and Ruth McKenna-Parker. They, too, were also taking advantage of the 'get 2 weeks for the price of 1' deal. After many G and T's they accepted my invitation to the Campana for a short intro into caving. They enjoyed it and over the next couple of years Eric and I occasionally climbed together.

My final trip was to the Avenc Travessets. At 145 metres deep, it is one of the deepest shafts on the island and I wanted to do it. Finding it was difficult but eventually I was geared and ready to go. It also appeared that it took a huge amount of water when it rained. Belays at the head of the pitch were difficult to arrange and even more so the deeper I went. I set off with much trepidation as the walls were composed of breccia. As soon as I reached the bottom I sped back up the ropes as I was getting nervous in this foreboding, austere place. I was glad to reach sunlight.

I had met Nick Eve a caver with whom I worked with on occasion at the Leadership Trust, a management training company based in Ross on Wye. He was a member of the Hereford Caving Club and I was invited to their annual dinner and I was asked if I would give them a talk in January 1987. This I did on the Untamed River Expedition. We caved in Ogof Fechan and the wonderful Ogof Craig-a-Ffynnon, where I marvelled at the formations in the 'Hall of the Mountain King'. We ended up in the 'Promised Land'. On emerging and whilst changing I asked Nick if he wanted to go to County Clare in Ireland in April. He was very enthusiastic about this. John Cliffe and his girlfriend at that time, Jan, came too, all travelling in John's old Vauxhall Astra. John also worked at the Leadership Trust with me at that time. He also knew Ogof Ffynnon Ddu very well so I did many trips in there with him visiting Smith's Armoury on several occasions amongst through trips from Cwm Dwr Quarry Cave to Top Entrance and vice versa.

We were picking Nick up at the Leadership Trust and driving to John and Jan's who lived in Abercraf in the Swansea Valley, where we were leaving my car. Brenda and I arrived to pick up Nick. He was in a dreadful mess. Not only did he have a huge white patch over his eye, he was obviously in great pain. Nick wore contact lenses and somehow he confused his lens solution with a dettol solution. This obviously did not do him any favours. He said it would be better if he stayed behind but we said that he would be OK in a couple of days and persuaded him to come with us.

After picking up John and Jan we continued driving to Fishguard to catch the ferry to Rosslare. We arrived quite late in the evening for the journey to Clare. After an overnight drive we arrived at the Outdoor Centre in Lisdoonvarna, quite tired. Although we did not cave that first day we caved for the next six days with, perhaps, the first excursion as the best trip. This was the through trip in a downstream direction from St. Catherine's to Fisherstreet. Firstly, before walking up to St. Catherine's, the start of the traverse, we had to place a ladder and double safety line down the exit shaft to Fisherstreet so that we could climb out when we reached the end.

The weather was perfect the whole time enabling us to do trip after trip, Pollballiny, Faunarooska and the superb through trip from Poulnagollum to Poulelva. We needed to rig the 40 metre exit shaft to Poulelva, as we had Fisherstreet a few days earlier, to allow us to escape. Poulnagollum would be a very serious place indeed if we were to be caught out in flood water, so we were very glad of the settled weather. We also did Cullaun 2 and Poll-an-

Ionain the cave with the aptly named 'soggy dishcloth', a huge stalactite, reputedly one of the largest in the world. This is now a show cave!

The most serious cave we did was the Coolagh River Cave where the entrance swallows the River Coolagh. All the passages in the cave flood to the roof after heavy rainfall. Although it was drizzling slightly when we went in, the forecast was for a fine day. The long bedding plane some two thirds of the way through was very thought provoking being dark, gloomy and not very high. Our final trips were in Poll na gCeim, a vertical system and in Polldubh exiting from B3.

In February 1987 together with Dave Edwards and Mike Wooding I set off with the intention of descending the Jean Bernard. This was then the deepest cave in the world. We had found out that the best time to explore this cave was in the winter when water levels were much lower, or perhaps non-existent, as it would all be frozen solid on the surface. Along with mountains of gear we set off on the drive to Samoens our base for the trip. On the way we did a quick trip into the Grotte de Balme, situated between Cluses and Magland, just off the A40 Autoroute on the Route de Flaine. The reason for choosing this cave was that it was on the way to our base in Samoens and Flaine as well us allowing us to stretch our limbs. It was also quite good fun and with a great view of the Autoroute below from a huge window within the cave. Huge icicles dangled from the porch of the window like monstrous Swords of Damocles. After this short excursion we continued our drive to Samoens through some deep snow where chains were needed. We now knew that the approach to the Jean Bernard would be diabolical if not impossible.

The following day we set off for the Jean Bernard. The car lurched from snow drift to snow drift as it slithered and skidded up the access road to a point where we could drive no further. Even chains didn't work and we became bogged down in the deep powder snow. Donning much warm clothing, snow shoes and heavy bags of caving gear we started the long and what turned into an incredibly laborious plod up the hill. The snow was waist deep. Even with snow shoes we sank down into the powder. At each step we thought that cross country skiing would be really good fun instead of this torture. We wove our laboured way through interminable pine trees gradually gaining height, seeing nothing of our surroundings as they were shrouded in a cold grey mist. After two hours of misery we gave it up as a bad job and stumbled and fell back to the car and returned to the gite where we were staying.

It was decided that we would only be able to cave in ones that we could find closer to the road. One of these, the Grotte de Ermoy, sounded great. The intro in the guide book was encouraging and one that we could do as the French description said that, "l'exploration n'est possible que lorsque gele a pierre fender dans le vallee". Only to be explored when the frost is cracking the rocks in the valley!! Well, it translates as something like that anyway and it was well below freezing.

We did this cave down to the terminal sump at -110m. Our exit using ice climbing gear was into loose unconsolidated snow. This was fun, as too was finding the next cave we did, the Grotte de Riviere Enverse. The entrance to this was excavated through drifted deep snow where we found a grille of ice columns barring entry. We hacked these away with an ice axe and explored a jolly little cave to reach a point not far from the sump. Loose rock deterred us at -96m.

In July of that year John Cliffe and I visited the Charteuse region of France where we undertook some through trips, but these are described in a later chapter. However, John and I had designs on the Antro del Corchia which was part of the deepest cave system in Italy at that time, the Farolfi, Fighiera, Corchia at 1210 metres deep. (Currently the deepest cave in Italy is the Abisso Paolo Roversi at 1350 metres deep). As this was a holiday we decided on the more reasonable and much lower entrance of the Buca d'Eolo (also known as the Antro) and continue to the sump 670 metres down. We also decided to use the Serpenti entrance as an exit some 170 metres lower than the Antro entrance. Prior to my running a trip to Annapurna Sanctuary in February 1990 we decided to go in January.

Needing support we asked Nick if he wanted to come along to which he agreed. Another character, Tim Bancroft and his wife Pam came too. Tim is a comedian and great fun who gave us loads of laughs as well as a great booster of moral. He often used me as a caving leader for an organization he ran, the Derby Outdoor Pursuits Centre. He also had a dog called Gimmer although it was nicknamed 'Aardvark'. Why I don't know and I didn't know who was the daftest, Tim or the dog.

Deciding what ropes we would take was easy, as were the flights but how were we to get to Levigliani from the airport at Pisa? Car hire was duly arranged. We were going to be using carbide as our lighting source. We had heard that it was virtually impossible to obtain in Levigliani, the nearest town to the Corchia where we would be staying. Carbide is heavy stuff so I decided I would take some as hand baggage with the remainder going with the caving gear as checked in baggage. The others, sensibly, put all their carbide into their checked baggage. We all carried our S.R.T. kits with us as hand baggage. After checking in our main bags we ambled along to Passport control and security check. Our hand baggage was duly X-rayed. Picking up our bags on the other side of the machine mine was pulled out.

'Excuse me Sir' said one of the security staff. 'What is in your bag?'

'As we are going caving it is my rope descending and climbing kit, jammers and carbide' I answered.

'What are all these metal bits and what is carbide, Sir?'

I confirmed my answers by saying again that I was going on a caving expedition and that the metal bits were descenduers and jammers that are needed for descending and ascending ropes. The carbide I explained was to be used as a lighting source, saying that when water was dripped on to the rock, acetylene gas was given off. This was then lit to give a very bright glow of light so that I could see where I going. The officer was greatly impressed by all of that but he recovered and said 'Well, I don't know whether we can allow your carbide on the plane. Excuse me a moment I need a second opinion.'

He called his mate over. Again I was asked what I was going to be using carbide for. Once more I explained at length as the queue behind me lengthened considerably.

'Well', the second security bloke answered. 'I don't think we can allow that on board, sir, but I'll go and get my supervisor and have the situation clarified'

So off he went and came back with the supervisor. 'Well', said the supervisor. I was now beginning to think how many wells make a river! 'Explain to me what this rock does.' I was by now exasperated, so I opened up the inner tube full of carbide, pulled out a piece of rock and spat on it. The ensuing pong and sundry mayhem meant that I was not going to be allowed the inner tube of carbide on the plane as the supervisor ran off with the fizzing rock and rubber bag. None of us mentioned we had several more 'pigs' of carbide in the hold. The escapade had certainly brightened the day for the people waiting patiently behind us. As we were collectively over weight by 50 kilos with our baggage allowance we were charged £25 for this excess.

We arrived in Pisa to find that the car, a Peugeot 205 Junior, we had hired was obviously far too small for everyone and all our caving gear. John, Tim, Pam and Brenda volunteered to go by bus, so long as Nick and I took all their gear, as far as Pietrasanta which is not too far from Levigliani. Nick and I drove the 70 kilometres from the airport in timely fashion taking just over an hour to Levigliani and located a B & B, the 'Pension Vallechiaro' in the neat village clinging to the side of Monte Corchia. We were looked after by the proprietor, Signora Piera, a middle aged woman known by the Italian cavers as the 'Mother of all Cavers'. She was a larger than life lady. Having found our 'chambers' we emptied the car of gear. I then drove back to Pietrasanta to pick up the stranded rest of the team. They had arrived at the bus station not by bus but having caught the train and then walked the 600 metres to the bus station. Whilst I was gone Nick did a good job of securing a deal for a 'tenner' a night, so long as we used our own sleeping bags. Not only did we have B & B, we also had an evening meal each night with 3 bottles of wine thrown in for good measure. When we were all reunited and cleaned up we had our first evening meal and in the restaurant we met one of the original explorers of the cave during the 1930's. Unfortunately his name now escapes me. Although he spoke very little English and us even less Italian we had a jolly evening as tongues were loosened by much more 'vino collapso' than was advisable after such a long day travelling.

By 10.00 the following day we were driving up the quarry track. It took 20 minutes to the Buca d'Eolo entrance. It was a deadly drive made worse by our crushing hangover. Quarry wagons careered down the track towards us at breakneck speed. Avoiding them meant driving off the track on several occasions. We eventually ended up at the end of the week having ripped off the exhaust and severely dented a wing plus a few scratches. John and Nick decided to rig the lower, Serpenti entrance whilst Tim, Pam and I would rig the upper, Antro or Buca d'Eolo entrance hoping to reach Stalactite Gallery to meet up with John and Nick. It was only a short walk into the quarry where the Antro was sited and Nick helped to carry our gear to the entrance. Nick then went back for John and dumped the car off the track and out of harm's way hoping that wagons would avoid it. Fortunately they did.

An icy blast was roaring out of the Antro. After only 50 metres the passage became huge before developing into a canyon type of passage. I decided to install ropes on a couple of small climbs as a slip would have been unpleasant. A particularly difficult section had a very thick rope installed along it. After the 'Pozzachione' shaft another short pitch took us to a very large chamber. The 'Slickenside' descended from this and after a 23 metres pitch was descended we decided to call it a day. We dumped the bags and returned to the surface. There was still a little way to go before 'Stalactite Gallery' in the Serpenti. Route finding had been difficult at the start due to the many holes that descended from what I hoped was the correct way. Every hole had anchor sleeves at the head of the drop. We had entered around 11.30 but by 16.15 the thought of dinner being missed ensured that we turned round and headed out. We arrived at the entrance at 18.55. Walking quickly down the track we had a superb view of Levigliani lit up below a cloudless and starry sky. We hoped we would meet John and Nick at the Serpenti entrance. We did. Nick and John had emerged at 18.45 having reached 'Stalactite Gallery'. Good timing or what! It was another good evening with an enormous amount of food washed down with the three bottles of wine. A local came in and jabbered away in drunken Italian. As we seemed to understand everything being said, but understanding not even one word we were treated to a bottle of champagne, some grappa and a huge Italian cake. Our table was mess of crumbs, wine splashes and plates in total disarray. We had had a great day.

The following day whilst having breakfast two Italian cavers appeared. They gave us some carbide and asked if they could use our ropes to explore some passages below the 'Pozzachione'. I said that it was OK for them to do so. Nick drove John and me to the Antro entrance where we descended quickly to the low point of yesterday in under an hour. We made a few slight improvements to the rigging on the way by adding a couple of deviations. Picking up the bags we continued to the head of an amazing and beautiful 30 metres shaft. A long traverse out to the pitch head allowed me to rig a fine free hang. I landed on my name! John and Nick the previous day had placed pebbles to form Des at the base of the shaft to say they had been there. After a dubiously rigged 10 metres pitch, John and Nick must have climbed up this, we entered the beautifully decorated 'Stalactite Gallery' to find that very little if any damage had been done to the formations.

We made a brew with my new home made 'bivvy' stove. It worked well. After half an hour we set off again following an awkward rift passage which ended at a 30 metres deep pitch that was difficult to rig. I eventually found a couple of large flakes that seemed as though they were firmly attached to mother rock and provide a suitable belay. Unfortunately the descent was down with the water. I was glad that water levels were low. A red rope dangling from the roof looked as though the real way was a very airy traverse from where we rigged the pitch.

Another awkward rift followed and a further two pitches separated by more awkward rift traverses making bag carrying laborious took us to the head of quite a remarkable pitch. Two short pitches took us down to the head of this amazing 45 metres shaft. The descent of this almost perfectly cylindrical shaft was a delight, although the take off was difficult, down the free hanging rope. All too soon we were back in awkward rift passages. Suddenly the character of the cave changed and we emerged from the confines of the rift passages to find ourselves at the main downstream sump, a beautiful and impressive blue green lake. We turned sharply to our left to follow a river cascading down. It was great to be walking again. Deep pools were traversed around interspersed by short climbs both up and down.

We met the two Italian cavers who were able to explain to us that there was too much water after 'Lake Merika'. I think that all they wanted was a trip to the bottom without having to rig anything! We continued to the lake, another wonderful place, and although only a short distance from the bottom of the cave we reluctantly turned back. We had become somewhat concerned for the others as they were supposed to be following behind. Fortunately, or should I say unfortunately, we met the others quite soon in the narrow awkward rift passages. I was very relieved to see them. Nick then recounted a tale of how he had been 'bombed'. We manoeuvred past each other, John and I to go out, whilst the others headed off for 'Lake Merika' and then to return de-rigging as they came.

This very serious 'near miss' occurred on the second pitch. Pam and Nick had descended this to the floor and in those days people often carried their emergency kit in an old metal ammo box. We were not the exception. Tim had been given charge of this. As he was sorting himself out at the head of the pitch the box somehow became detached from him and bomb like it sped down the shaft narrowly missing Nick some 30 metres below. 'Bomber' Bancroft was apparently politely told to be careful in future! A connection with Nicks head could well have been fatal.

John and I headed out and made another brew in 'Stalactite Gallery' whilst waiting for the rest of the team. It was a long time before they appeared. In fact I was very worried as we had been waiting for two and a half hours before we heard them clanking upward. Fortunately we had our polythene survival bags into which we snuggled. They worked quite well in keeping us warm, infinitely warmer than the 'turkey wrap'.

Leaving Tim, Pam and Nick with the brew gear John and I set off out through the Serpenti. Finding our way was relatively easy and we were on the surface in an hour. Stuffing all the gear in the beat up car and then, as arranged, we walked down the track. Stars twinkled at us in the inky black clear sky above us as we headed down to the Pensione 30 minutes away. After a bite to eat and a wash and brush up tiredness was overwhelming but at the same time I was once again becoming concerned for the others as they had not arrived home. However, much as I tried to stay awake I couldn't. I awoke suddenly at 6.00 to the sound of church bells and quickly realised that the team still had not arrived. I was just about to set off back up the track when the car arrived. Phew. It transpired they had managed to lose their way out of the Serpenti.

After a day off walking over Monte Corchia we returned the next day to quickly de-rig the remainder of the cave before having a day trip to Pisa and, yes, we did visit the leaning tower amongst other places taking pictures with each of us in turn appearing to hold up the tower and stopping it from keeling over! This was a fun and very low key trip, although much of our gear went awol on the flight home. We never did get it returned either.

In 1993 I started to do some caving with Donald Rust as we worked together at the Leadership Trust. He was a keen caver and cave diver. We had done a small number of local trips together into Little Neath River Cave, Tunnel Cave, Pwll Dwfn and Ogof Ffynnon Ddu. This included the superb through trip from O.F.D. 2 up into Smith's Amoury in O.F.D. 3 and all the way down to exit from O.F.D. 1. This was a really fine experience. A couple of days before Don and I had recced the way making sure we knew where we had to go. After this I suggested to Don that we should do some foreign caving.

Don and I then visited the Parmelan Plateau and the Pierre de Saint Martin (P.S.M.) in successive years doing a variety of through trips of which more, later. In 1995 Don had set up Rhongyr Isaf Outdoor Centre at Pen y Cae in the Swansea Valley in South Wales but he still wanted to cave abroad. He asked me to become a director of the centre to which I agreed. We decided to visit the P.S.M. area again intent on doing some of the other caves in the area and invited some of Don's staff who worked there to join us. As in the previous year we made our base at Tardets.

My first choice of cave was to descend the Gouffre d'Apanice which had, reputedly, a superb 300 metres shaft called the 'Puits de Pirates' to reach the bottom of the cave. I had rigged to the head this pitch when Don and I had to abort the trip due to some members being unable to negotiate the first pitch. I was quite angry about this as I had been assured that they were competent at S.R.T. After a team talk it was decided that only Don and I would be descending the deeper caves. Our first trip after the 'discussion' was to find the 770 metres deep Lonne Peyret.

Setting off in mid afternoon we found the entrance quite easily so I rigged down to -84 metres, likening the 34 metres first pitch to Nettle Pot, above Castleton in the Peak District. The next pitch of 50 metres had quite a tight start through a slot but it quickly opened out. We continued via two small drops to the head of the 20 metres deep next pitch. On the way back up the return through the slot was quite awkward. The following day we quickly descended to the end of the previous days rigging and continued all the way down some amazing pitches, especially the final two of 54 metres and 47 metres. At the end of the 54 metres pitch I had to stand on top of a sharp flake to fix the hangers for the 47 metres pitch, gulp!

We had now used all our rope. It was great to have the freedom not having a bag to lug around. Very quickly after all the pitches we joined the water. Following this down a short distance we found another pitch. I had no awareness or knowledge about this 8 metres pitch when bagging the ropes. Ummm, what could we use to descend this obstruction? Cogitating, I said to Donald we could use our chest slings, foot loops, sack hauling sling, waist belts a bit of 'tat' we had along and go hand over hand down. Not exactly text book caving and certainly somewhat risky especially as we were approaching the 500 metres level. Anyway, we went down with the array of bits belayed to a single hanger! We continued along huge boulder strewn galleries. Route finding was helped by fluorescent markers. A short ladder helped overcome a short problem as did a nylon shoe lace on another. Eventually we reached the large Salle de Embarcadere at 500 metres down.

At 106 metres down the cave pinched in and being in

the front here was not where I wanted to be. I called Donald forward and told him, as he was the thin boy, to check it out for me. He said it was tight but I should get through OK. Taking my helmet off, I squeezed my way through this snug passage and popped out like a champagne cork at the far end. At least I knew I could do it OK on the way back. It's great having a thinny along. Possibly though, the tightest bit during the descent is the squeeze at the head of the 54 metre penultimate pitch. I found the Lonne Peyret to be an exhilarating 10 hours trip as we had not only to rig the cave we had to de-rig it as well.

Two days later we went to the Soum Couey Lodge. Once more we were armed with a lot of rope. I found this to be a much more demanding trip and the tight 350 metres long meander beyond the 20 metres pitch near the entrance was really snug and quite tiring for me. Another caving club had also rigged the cave but, as I observed, the cave was liable to flood and the already rigged ropes would be in a direct line of any flood water. By doing some quite airy traverses I was able to rig our ropes well clear of these in-situ ropes on all the pitches. As such we were able to descend a completely separate way down. Our way down would have kept us relatively dry in the event of water entering from high above.

At the bottom of the pitches a long and miserable meander, which would take all the water in wet conditions and possibly sump, took us to the 'Salle du Rechaud'. We took all the high alternatives to keep out of the water, just in case! These lower passages were often quite pretty but the caving was generally pretty boring and we had had enough by the time we reached the 'Salle Henri Brosset' at −440 metres. After a breather we turned around for the journey back. At the second pitch on the way in I had rigged quite a long traverse. On the way out this provided some interesting manoeuvres for Don. He had a large tackle sac dangling below him as I did too but I had the benefit of the rope behind me as well as in front. Now Don as already mentioned is much smaller than me so whilst de-rigging he slipped and carved a long wonderful arc through the air. Unperturbed he continued de-rigging and we exited without further ado. We were both very tired, much more so than after the Lonne Peyret, by the time we reached the surface after another 10 hours trip.

A final visit to the Gouffre d'Apanice a few days later was, unfortunately, aborted due to much water flowing through the cave after several days of rain.

Chapter 7

Through Trips

These are the ideal. Simple really, start at the top of the hill and come out at the bottom, pulling the ropes down after abseiling each pitch. Although totally committing, because once the first rope is pulled down the only way out is from the lower entrance, they are great fun. You do not have to prussik back out of the cave. As a climber I had wandered around Windy Ledge high up on Windy Buttress at Stoney Middleton and went through the Bossen Hole, a short journey through the buttress for a first 'through trip'!

My first real taste of a through trip was, I suppose, the very short, easy, but fun Upper Long Churn. The highlight of this trip is the 10 metres climb up the chute of water that plummets into 'Dr. Bannister's Hand-basin' to reach daylight after a short length of passage. Although only 10 minutes or so needed to complete it gives the essence of what happens on a through trip. This was followed by a much more serious excursion from Top Sink through to Lancaster Hole in the Easgill system. We rigged the 40 metres deep entrance shaft of Lancaster Hole so that we could exit before wandering up the pretty dry stream bed of Easgill to Top Sink. It was a lovely day, sunny and quite warm.

The only difficulty I remember was finding the way

through 'Limerick Junction'. Doing this early on in my caving experiences with Dave Edwards, Dave Draper and Pete McDonald I was confident that we would not get lost as they had all been that way before. They were looking for a jammed stone in a rift that they had placed a few days earlier to indicate which passage to take. Once this was spotted there was no stopping us. On we went visiting the wonderful 'Easter Grotto' and the other highlights of the trip, the large chambers of 'Cornes' and 'Monster', 'The Minarets' and the 'Main Drain'. In those days we were able to climb out from' Fall Pot' easily via the iron ladders. These have now been taken out and 'Fall Pot' needs rigging beforehand, although there is often a muddy, slippery rope dangling down an even more slippery but vertical tube off to one side. We continued along large passages and up 'Kath's Way' to find our rope, very thankfully, dangling at the bottom of Lancaster Hole with daylight filtering down from 40 metres above.

One abseil through trip that is always good fun which I have always enjoyed is the Swinsto Hole to Valley Entrance trip in Kingsdale. The entrance is found high above the exit dustbin of Valley Entrance and abseils through the hill down seven well watered pitches to reach the 'Kingsdale Master Cave'. This short but impressive stream-way is followed to a point just before the sump. Here a climb up is necessary. Although only 6 metres high it is best to have rigged a rope or ladder and lifeline prior to walking up the hill to the entrance. It is possible to climb up the right hand wall of the pitch but it is a slippery affair and not that easy. The downside of this is that whoever goes to rig the ladder or dangle a rope gets soaked before they even start. This is because of the deep water section close to the entrance of Valley Entrance. It used to be a duck but after much use the natural dam holding the water back was broken making the water shallower, but it is still a cold grovel through deep water. Another unpleasant side to Swinsto is that there is a 300 metres long hands and knees crawl in the stream immediately after the first pitch. Having pulled the rope down on this the crawl has to be done.

Heron Pot is another good introduction to the through trip repertoire although the exit, after a 60 metres long wet crawl, through some boulders is a bit snug. However, my favourite Yorkshire through trip is Simpson's Pot. Here, also, the exit is from the dustbin of Valley Entrance where again, the rigging of the pitch up from the 'Kingsdale Master Cave' needs to be done prior to the through trip. Starting off at the same height as Swinsto but 500 metres away towards Rowten Pot, Simpson's follows a stream down but does not have a 300 metres long crawl. There is a simple duck, according to the guide books, after the third pitch. I've never had to duck, only a simple flounder through the water. The highlight for me is the 'Great Aven Pitch' because I have always fought clear of the more normal way for people, the infamous and narrow 'Slit Pot', the scene of many rescues and epics.

Being somewhat larger than the average caver I sought to find the 'Great Aven' pitch the first time I did the trip. It was fairly easy to locate once 'Aven Pot' had been found. Returning a short distance upstream from this I climbed up easy ledges and into a small chamber where, at the far side was a colourful collection of 'tat'. I first went this way with Steve abseiling this marvelous 'clapper in a bell' pitch, happy not to be struggling with the confines of 'Slit Pot'. I have done this many times since. At the base of the pitch we descended an overhanging boulder to join Swinsto at the bottom of its final pitch. From here the 'Kingsdale Master Cave' is quickly reached and the climb up into the roof tunnel of Valley Entrance.

I have always thought of through trips as abseiling through a cave. However through trips of a different nature can be had in South Wales, notably in Ogof Ffynnon Ddu. Here the entrances in to the system are O.F.D. 1, O.F.D. 2 known as Top Entrance and Cwm Dwr Quarry Cave. Interchangeable trips between these entrances can be done without the need of any vertical equipment. My experiences in O.F.D. are Cwm Dwr to O.F.D. 2; O.F.D. 2 to exit from O.F.D. 1, but far and away the best trip I did was O.F.D. 1 up to O.F.D. 3 and Smith's Armoury coming all the way down through this very complex system to exit from O.F.D. 1. This has to be one of the best caving trips in Britain. I was fortunate to do this trip with Don Rust. He has an intimate knowledge of the cave and his route finding was faultless. I had invited some friends from Derbyshire along on this one as AG had not done this trip before. His mate Bulmers also came, along with another guy called Geordie who I had met on several occasions and knew as a good caver, although he stayed on the surface on this occasion.

The long O.F.D. streamway is a very fine part of the cave and one particular area of it is known as 'Marble Showers'. This aptly named place is streaked with white calcite contrasting sharply with the dark kimestone. Many different and varied trips can be done in the cave. These take a lot of patience to do as route finding is very difficult. Perhaps my favourite way of reaching the streamway was to abseil the 40 metre pitch in 'Swamp Creek' to the stream and then head off upstream to 'Top Waterfall', a marvelous place. To explore O.F.D. 1 everyone needs a guide but as a member of the South Wales Caving Club there was always a club guide willing to go on a trip there. There are many magical names associated with the cave, 'Bagpipe Chamber' conjuring up lots of leading off to God knows where, 'Frozen River', 'Salubrious Passage', 'Presidents Leap', 'Selenite Passage', 'Rose Bowl' and the very aptly named 'Gnome Passage' are just a few of many named features.

I really enjoyed these one way only trips. Not only were they easy with much less gear they were also much less strenuous. Coming back up to the surface again from a sump or impenetrable fissure is always the hardest part of any caving trip. However, I knew that there were very many wonderful through trips in Europe and I wanted to do some.

The first of the major through trips I did was in 1988 when John Cliffe and his girlfriend Jan, my girlfriend Brenda, Paz Vale, and I went to the Chartreuse. Anyone who has read 'Subterranean Climbers' by Pierre Chevalier will know all about the Trou de Glaz system. Most of the cave was explored bottom up from the low point, Guiers Mort. Stories such as how Petzl cycled 90 miles from Lyons during the war years for a weekend of exploration in the system are mind boggling.

We camped at La Martiniere very close to St Pierre de Chartreuse. Although expensive it had good facilities and had superb views of Chaumchaude, a needle pointed mountain. Our first trip was to be a virtually horizontal through the mountain trip, the Trou de Glaz to Grotte Annette Bouchacourt. Two others joined us, a chap called Al and Mike Wooding who said he knew the way.

Setting off quite late for the walk it took us only 35 minutes to get to the entrance to the Trou de Glaz. We entered the cave at 10.50 and the description of the trip from the Cerberus Caving Club worked extremely well, although we did go round in a circle at the base of the 'Puits Gnole' looking for the way on. One or two awkward squeezes during the trip found us at the exit by 16.45.

What an amazing view down from it. An exciting walk back round the hill had more than its fair share of exposure. We found many old names written on the rock, Petit Didier, Petzl, with some others dating back to 1883. It was a great trip even though Mike had mostly forgotten the way!

Two days later we were in for the big one, the 603 metres through trip from P40 to Guiers Mort. Only John, Paz and I were in for this. Al kindly took our car around to the exit, Guiers Mort after we had started the walk up to the summit of the Dent de Crolles. This would save us having to walk back into camp after the trip. The summit of the Crolles is an amazing place with breathtaking views. It took us a while to find P40 as there were shake-holes everywhere, but even so we were underground by 09.15.

Our journey started off in grand style with a superb 40 metres abseil! From the bottom a tight bit had me thinking will I fit down through this. I'd better because the rope had been pulled down the entrance! The ensuing gallery, 'la Galerie York' was straightforward until we came to a climb up. A ladder dangling forlornly did not encourage us at all. It had 2 rungs of serviceable use with rest either hanging off one wire or missing. Paz climbed up first. He was the lightest between the three of us, just. I was nowhere in contention. Paz took a short rope with him so both John and I had the security of this as we climbed the shredded ladder.

Very quickly after this we reached the head of the 45 metres, 'Puits des Trois Soeurs'. Now this was the tricky bit as we were unsure whether we had to abseil the whole pitch or part of it. After a council of war we decided to abseil all of it. How wrong could we have been? From the bottom we abseiled an 8 metres pitch and arrived at the head of a 13 metres pitch. Paz abseiled this to the start of what we found out later to be the start of the 'Reseau Polannais' an extremely tight and tortuous passage that would have lead us to where we were headed but not even Paz fitted down it. We reasoned therefore that we had gone wrong. Fortunately Paz had an S.R.T. kit so was able to climb back up the 13 metres pitch again.

How, though, were we to climb up the 8 metres pitch? All of us were climbers and our first attack was by throwing an end of the rope up to try and catch a projection. This was a pretty dumb thing to do and was obviously hopeless. Our next try was a human pyramid. That collapsed in a heap of unbridled nervous laughter. The floor man, me, could not keep balanced. The floor of the pitch was stony and uneven and as soon as weight was transferred to my shoulders I was staggering all over the place. Two hours after we had taken the wrong turn we arrived at the top of the pitch having used old climber's methods of placing chock-stones in the very fortuitous crack leading up the wall. We threaded slings around these small stones and pulled up on them.

That was certainly a huge relief. We found a way on. Whether it was the correct way or not we had no idea, but it was a way on. Part way along the tight meander my harness decided to snag on a projection. This had the result of immobilising me. I could not move backwards or forwards. As I was at the back it took quite a lot of maneuvering to free myself and catch up with the other two who were, by now, oblivious to my struggles. I was pleased to see them again and told them my story. They laughed. We reached a pitch. Which pitch it was at that time, we had no idea. Down we went regardless. More, but easier meanders followed until we reached more pitches. Again we had no idea where we were. On down we went, down three more pitches of 22, 16 and 20 metres.

By now I was concerned that we had not reached the 'Salle des Douches', the key to the whole trip. We had gone down another 20 metres pitch that was wet and I was hoping that that was the 'Puits des Douches'. Once we were all down we set about finding a way on. It was quite complex here. We poked in one hole and then another until I found what I was looking for, a red painted sign indicating that indeed we were in the 'Salle des Douches'. Phew, that was a relief. The way on into the Trou de Glaz and on into the rest of the trip was easy to follow.

Firstly down P36 and then across the tricky traverse across the head of the 'Puits de l'Arche' pitch. Long galleries continued until we reached a 41 metres climb up. This is the 'Cascade Rocheuse'. Although quite easy, for a climber, it could be a formidable problem for the less than competent. From the top of this we abseiled the 'Puits Banane' and continued through more easy galleries avoiding all vertical options by following the 'Galerie de Solitaire' until the final pitch, the 35 metres 'Puits Pierre'. From the base of this a tight passage, 'Reseau Sanguin' led into the Guiers Mort almost in sight of daylight. The 'Reseau Sanguin' is the sting in the tail. Consisting of some 250 metres of flat out crawling it can be dug out very easily and quickly for larger cavers as it is composed of loose gravel. A squeeze at the far end leads into the large chamber not far from the exit of Guiers Mort.

We arrived to see a magnificent red sunset framed by the porch of Guiers Mort, a fantastic sight and one we would have missed if we had not gone wrong. We had taken just under 12 hours after setting off. Not bad timing, considering we were marooned for two of those. I had found this the hardest foreign trip I had done to date.

We then fiddled around after that enjoying walks and sunshine until we decided to have a rematch with the

Tanne de Bel Espoir. A week later John and I were back at the Nantizel campsite in Thorons Gliere pitching our tents in a rainless thunderstorm, looking forward to a great trip.

The following day we checked out the Grotte de la Diau. Quickly remembering the way we were soon at the junction with the 'Affluent de Grenoblois' where the Espoir enters the Diau. After an early start the next morning we were soon at the entrance having no problems with finding it this time. I rigged the first four pitches as though for an S.R.T. in and out trip just to make sure I was on the right route. It seemed very easy to follow this time. John de-rigged these pitches setting up each pitch so that once he was safely down each of them he could retrieve the ropes.

On reaching the 'Toboggan' we found a very muddy hand-line in place which helped with the descent until it ended suddenly in a void. We were in the roof of the 'Salle des Rhomboedres'. Descending into this very fine chamber was impressive. The way out of here was easily found by following soot arrows marked on the wall that led us to the spectacular 'Puits des Echos'. It really did echo back to us as well! We descended this shaft in three stages 6, 20 and 39 metres.

At the bottom of the pitch is a place called 'La Jonction'. This is where the original explorers realised that they had made a connection between the two caves. We found the next pitch longer than anticipated but fortunately the rope we were using was more than long enough. After another short pitch we found ourselves in the Diau at the exit of the 'Affluent de Grenoblois' that we had been following. All that remained was to wander out to daylight 698 metres lower than when we had set off. We reached the exit after 8 hours underground. Again we were fortunate that we had a support team, Jan and Brenda, otherwise we would have had a grueling walk back at some stage to pick up the car.

We ate a celebratory meal in La Chaumiere a really fine restaurant and a fitting end to a superb holiday.

Back in Britain, other through or exchange trips were accomplished. Wretched Rabbit to Lancaster Hole and vice versa, Calf Holes to Browgill, as through trips. Long Kin East with Rift Pot, Stream Passage Pot and Jib Tunnel, Alum Pot with Diccan Pot or Lower Long Churn, to mention a few of the fun ones and the through trip on the Borrowdale Graphite Mine. However, I was still hankering after the deep foreign ones.

One such trip was the Sima del Cueto to Cueva Coventosa. After a working trip to the Vercors Nona, a non-caver and I drove for 12 hours to Ramales de la Victoria in the Cantabrian Mountains to meet up with Dave Elliot and members of the Bracknell Caving Club who had invited me on their trip. I met up with the group and set off for the Cueto. The long walk up the hill ended at some blades of grass blowing in an upward draught. This was the inauspicious entrance to the head of the 305 metres deep entrance shaft. A short slope led to the head of the pitch. Every 50 metres there was a re-belay. It was a spectacular, circular shaft often lined with calcite. At the bottom of this another series of shafts led on down. Much more shattered and broken they were not as pleasant as the main shaft.

Unfortunately I met a de-rigging team on the way out. They had taken the ropes off subsequent pitches. This meant that I could not make the through trip. However, once back on the surface and by way of compensation I went in to the Coventosa. Here I explored upstream where, on the way to the Lakes, I visited, the very beautiful 'Salle des Fantomes'.

The next foreign through trip, although we could only go for a week, was situated again on the Parmelan Plateau in 1993. I had persuaded Don to spend some time exploring caves in the area as there seemed much to do. There was, and one through trip we tried La Merveilleuse to the Vertige was stopped by my inability to get through a slanting squeeze at the head of pitch 2. It had taken two and a half hours not to find it. The following day we spent a further two and a half hours and we still had not found the bloody entrance! We stopped looking. Louisa, Nona, Donald and I tried to recoup sanity. Louisa quipped, 'woudn't it be funny if it was behind us'. After more diligent searching and finding a line of cairns we were totally at a loss for ideas. We then looked behind where we had been resting and what did we find? Yes, the Merveilleuse entrance!

After hurriedly putting gear on I set off down the fine 20 metres entrance shaft to the snow/ice at the bottom. A clamber up a ladder took us to a hole and tube dropping down to a small chamber. Going to the right did not look appealing in any way whatever. Anyone of more than very tiny build would struggle. Don managed it, just, and went down the second pitch an already rigged 48 metres shaft. On the way up the entrance shaft I noticed a black hole to my right. I mentioned this to Don. I carried on to the top but Don on his way up scuttled through this hole into a parallel shaft. Adjacent to the Merveilleuse was Entrance 4. A convenient tree allowed me to fix a rope and I descended to Don who was perched on a rubble heap. Fixing another rope and going over the edge I was confronted by a huge cataract of ice. A re-belay kept the rope free hanging to the next re-belay almost hidden under the ice. I thawed the ice with the flame from my carbide lamp. After another 10 metres I decided that as the rope was going to rub against a very sharp curtain of ice making further descent ill advised I came back up.

However, Don went for a look at this spectacular clear ice feature and reported back that he had found another re-belay and that the darkness beckoned. Unfortunately time was pressing so out we went.

However, on a return visit we entered the system again by entrance 4, the 'Reseau Glace'. We had a very spectacular trip down huge ice walls to the ice floored chamber at -149 metres. What a fantastic place. Although the entrance pitch was clear of ice the long second pitch was a complete ice wall of 40 metres. I had to exhume the spits for placing the hangers on this. At the bottom I entered a large chamber floored with glacier like ice cascades. We had chosen this cave because the water in the Diau was too high for us to check out prior to abseiling through our chosen through trip down the Tanne de Trois Betas. On the way back we attempted the evilly loose Tanne de la Poulie. The whole place was a collapsing mess so we gave up pretty quickly.

Having previously done the Tanne de bel Espoir I was now keen to do the 701 metres deep Trois Betas. This was reckoned to be far and away a much better trip than the Espoir and slightly deeper. It was infinitely better. After the Merveilleuse we checked out the Diau and found water levels were much lower than when we had first arrived. The through trip was now a possibility. Driving up to the Chalet d'Anglettaz once more we had two support drivers in Donald's wife Louisa and Nona my girlfriend, who would take the car around to the far side for us again. I always seem to have been lucky in that respect.

We had all taken a walk on the plateau the day previously looking for the entrance finding it fairly quickly. In fact it was easier to find than the Espoir. The following day I walked up in underpants and wellies in the hot sun to the cave. We were suitably armed with 3 long ropes, 73 metres, 60 metres and 55 metres just in case we managed to get one of the ropes stuck when pulling it down, I set off down the first stage of the 88 metres entrance pitch. I was perched on a tiny ledge waiting for Don to join me. When he arrived he clipped into the next pitch belay and looking that knowing look at each other we pulled the rope down. Well that's it. Once again we found ourselves committed to coming out of the Diau. By abseiling and traversing we reached a pitch that led in to the 'Salle des Rhomboedres'. From then on I was on familiar ground and 8 hours later we were outside at the entrance to the Diau. Our support team duly met us and after a photo call of the beaming duo in their squeaky clean yellow over-suits we returned to the camp site where Nona and I had a celebratory meal in La Chaumiere.

The following year Don, Louisa and young family, Nona and I plus a friend from Kendal, Richard travelled in two cars to Tardets our base once more for our explorations. It was a good camp site, flat, quiet and very close to a great restaurant, the Pont d'Abense. Richard and I did the Abime de Betchanka whilst waiting for Don to arrive. This was a really good 4¼ hours trip, very hot, so shorts and 'T' shirt under a thin over-suit were the order of the day. A wire spans the 70 metres deep entrance shaft with a belay fixing part way along the wire. Two more pitches and some fixed ladders took us past fine formations to the large 'Cathedral Chamber' from where a calcite ramp leads into 'Gour Hall' adorned with some very fine formations.

Once Donald and family had arrived we set about getting a description for a through trip in the Pierre de Saint Martin. We wanted to enter from high up in the mountains, the Gouffre de Beffroi (SC3), and exit in the valley from the E.D.F Tunnel. The only description we could get and ended up using was in Flemish! Not one of us understood this language at all but some caving words were approximately the same so we managed to cobble a description together that seemed to work, until we became lost. Prior to the trip we visited Ruben Gomez to purchase the all important pontonierres. These thin rubber suits with feet are used in deep water to avoid getting wet so long as the water does not rise above bib level. Ruben was one of the original explores of the cave.

The entrance was easy to find and we abseiled the 150 metres entrance pitches in several stages. These had been rigged previously by a local French team and fortunately for us guided the way down. This was especially so some half way down where the shaft becomes rift like and confusing. Finding the correct way on would have been more difficult for us without the rope in place. Strangely the French cavers seemed not to be in the cave. We learned later it was often the custom to leave this entrance rigged for the summer. Although the ropes looked somewhat dubious we used them anyhow!

The final drop, the 'Liberty Bell' was superb. I felt just like a clapper would feel hanging in its bell! Our way forward led through a tight looking hole which looked far too small, once again, to admit my body. Don again dispelled that thought managing to talk me through. We entered the narrow rift passage containing the 'Bassaburuko Stream' and followed it down as it became wider, walking along a lovely gravel floor.

Once we reached the 'Salle Cosyns' the cave became much larger, in fact, enormous. The more normal route from the Tete Sauvage enters this chamber. Just beyond 'Salle Cosyns' we became somewhat confused and ended getting lost for a short while.

We had gone too low and ended up in a deep, murky blue canal. I set off in the boat we had brought along to try and find a way on but the canal led nowhere apart from two sumps, one upstream and one downstream. I managed to fall out of the boat as I approached the bank after my voyage to nowhere. As the water was deep my pontonierre filled with water in this quest to find the way on. I became submerged in the pretty horrible water capturing what seemed like several gallons of water around me. I was hardly able to move and I could feel myself being dragged inexorably downwards. Fortunately Don and Richard duly dragged me out spluttering and cursing my bad luck. We discovered our mistake after we had climbed up again and turned to our right to find the correct way.

We made up for lost time speeding along the 'Grand Canyon' and into the 'Galerie des Marmites'. This was a passage with many circular pools of water, some deep and others not quite as deep. As we neared the end of the 'Galerie' we saw a blue, ethereal haze in front of us. We wondered what the hell it could be. Aliens from a distant planet, our lights playing tricks or what? As we approached the mystic light we saw two haggard and drawn looking faces which belonged to two Polish cavers who had been there for 48 hours. They had no spare carbide or any other form of lighting excepting of course for their gas stove although they had enough food for a month. Basically they were waiting for their friends to come for them!

Eating a hearty Polish meal of different meats, bread, cheese and pickles which barely dinted their supplies we asked if they would like to come out with us. No, they were quite happy to stay where they were and await their friends. We gave them a frugal supply of carbide to keep them going and bade them a fond farewell and traversed the 'Grand Corniche' into the 'Salle Hidalga'. After some shallow lakes we were almost at the serious part of the cave, the 'Tunnel du Vent'. Leaving the large and bouldery

'Salle Principe de Viana' we quickly found the 'Tunnel du Vent'. We inflated the boat once more and one by one sailed the tunnel. This wet bit has been the scene of many rescues as the passage quickly sumps in wet weather. AG had talked about this when he was involved in the rescue, whilst he was doing a trip from the Tete Sauvage to the E.D.F. tunnel, of some Polish cavers.

We were glad of our pontonierres although my clothing was wet underneath mine. I was warm, however. Once out of the wet canals and lakes we stripped off our pontonierres. Huge chambers now followed huge galleries in rotation, 'Navarre', 'Lepineux', 'Loubens' and the monster passage of 'Le Metro' and continuing we passed other huge chambers, 'Queffelec', 'Adelie' and 'Chevalier' until we reached the even larger 'Salle de la Verna', one of the largest in the world. The way through many of these chambers would have been extremely difficult to navigate, as their floors were littered with huge house sized boulders, if it were not for fluorescent arrows indicating the way forward at periodic intervals.

On the way we had passed the plaque to the memory of Marcel Loubens who died after a very tragic accident in 1952 whilst he was being winched up the 320 metres deep 'Lepineux Shaft during initial explorations of the P.S.M. This story is graphically told in 'Caves of Adventure' by Haroun Tazieff. Although the heavily barred entrance of the Lepineux can be approached on the surface access is not allowed.

We entered the 'Salle de la Verna' at some two thirds height above the floor where the lights of cavers below us seemed like tiny pinpricks. Traversing the right hand wall we entered a tunnel mined by the French electric company E.D.F. which took us to the exit doors of the man made passage 15 hours after entering SC3.

Opening these we exited into the cool night air and staggered, dream like down the track and the parked car at St. Engrace. It had been a tiring trip but a great experience and one that was steeped in history.

More through trips followed in Britain. One that stands out is the James Hall Over Engine Mine through to Peak Cavern although this has now been superseded by the Titan Shaft to Peak Cavern. I did JH as it is affectionately known, with members of the Eldon in March 1997. AG organized the trip. Fortunately the mine was rigged so we were not carrying any ropes. I was amazed at the amount of work that had been done by Dave Nixon (Moose) on the shaft known as 'Leviathan'. A complex series of pipes had been installed to redirect water away from the descent. One of the memorable things about this trip was the aptly named 'Colostomy Crawl'. I was glad to be going the way we were as the passage is body sized, slightly downward sloping but half full of sloppy liquid mud. What an appalling mess we were in after this. Even the wet bits afterward did nothing to clean us up at all.

One of the really good fun trips I enjoy greatly in Yorkshire is the very short but extremely atmospheric Yordas Pot to Yordas Cave through trip. This is especially so when water levels are slightly higher than normal. Starting off with a fine 25 metres fluted entrance shaft the way on is found at floor level. An initial flat out crawl in the usually cold, swiftly flowing water, gradually enlarges as the 'Chapter House' waterfall is reached. This is a well watered descent with the wet bit right at the end in the last 3 metres after which an easy walk leads out of Yordas Cave. Other very short fun trips I do on off days in Yorkshire are Thistle and Rûnscar Caves, Great Douk, Borrins Moor Caves, Rowten and Jingling Caves and many more.

One very impressive trip that can be made in

Nidderdale is Manchester Hole through to Goyden Pot, which I did in 2005 with Richard. All the passages within both of these caves are flood prone when the River Nidd flows. Huge trees can be found in Goyden illustrating that catastrophic flooding takes place.

Through trips to my mind are the most exciting of all caving trips, especially if there are lots of pitches to abseil. You don't have to worry about expending a huge amount of physical energy swarming up ropes, just mental energy whether the rope will pull down, are any passages blocked or even if you will pop out at the end! Two things stand out as important on the long abseil through trips. Make sure you have a survey and are able to find the correct way and to have at least one S.R.T. kit. All in all for me these provide the best in fun caving experiences.

Chapter 8

Nare – The Untamed River Expedition

Part 1 – Preparations and arrival in base camp

After the Berger in 1983 and the foiled attempt on Mont Blanc, Carol and I returned home to Buxton. Dave Gill was lodging with us at this time and a couple of days later he asked if Mike Boon could come to stay. It was fine with both of us. I knew of Mike but had never met him. He was a very hard caver and cave diver with many hair-raising exploits behind him. His book 'Down to a Sunless Sea' recounts his many hairy adventures, a must read.

Mike arrived and after several hours and wines he proposed that an expedition be made to Nare. This is a huge underground river reached by a hair-raising 300 metres deep free hanging pitch down a collapsed doline puncturing the earth. There are many others on the tree infested island of New Britain to the north east of Papua New Guinea. Mike had some satellite images of the area indicating that dense rain forest covered much of the island. It was to be a major trip and to finance it we would need sponsors. Nare had been explored by the French in 1980 but were stopped deep inside the cave by massive waves and turbine like water. In 1982 the Belgians mounted an expedition but after descending the main shaft called it a day, blaming water. They had decided that July was a good time to go. How very wrong was that decision to go at that time of year. They then tried to reach Ora but were apparently, lucky to leave the rain forest alive!

Dave pondered the idea and finally decided to undertake the task of leading the expedition. I was asked to be responsible for the climbing needed within this huge river cave. At that time it was the largest underground river in the world in the process of exploration. The French had encountered formidable problems. Not least they suffered with ill health as well as logistical problems underground amongst others.

The logistics were severe. How to get equipment down the shaft to support the push was perhaps the main one as several kilometers of rope were involved. Food and cooking gear had to be taken down. Hammocks and sleeping bags also had to go. Fresh food was of paramount importance. Unlike the French we had no medical urgencies due to our healthy eating. I do recommend tuna and mint jelly sandwiches though. Yum. Our surface support team made fresh bread for us every day and also sent fruit down. We even had a postal delivery from England. One day I received a letter from Carol nine days after it had been posted. I felt that that this was amazing service considering that it takes a day from Rabaul to reach Gonaile and a further two days from there to our camp, never mind how long it takes from the UK to Papua. How would we get someone out if they were injured and unable to move? What about communications? All these and more were preying on our minds.

A huge 302 metres deep entrance shaft guarded access to the 20 metres wide and dramatic river that flowed, in the dry season, at twenty cumecs. This had been crossed by several tyrolean traverses by the French who had an extremely difficult time fixing these. How could we make the setting up of these traverses simple? How could we survive underground without having to make a 302 metres descent and ascent after each day of, often arduous, exploration? How could we be comfortable in our base camp above the hole? How could we dry our clothes? What was safe to eat in the rain forest? How would we purify our water? How could we remain in contact with the outside world? It took two days to walk from base camp to Gonaile the logging camp by the coast, taking 24 hours by boat from Rabaul which was the major town on the island. Or you could fly into Gonaile in thirty minutes! There were so many obstacles and so little time, as the planned departure was for the end of October 1984.

Dave drew up his team. There were to be six members of the pushing team – himself, Tim Allen, Steph Gough, Steve Dickinson (Dickie), Alan Gamble (AG) and myself. All these had quite a reputation for difficult and often outrageous exploits. The other members of the team were, Dave Arveschoug who had done a great amount of cave discovery in Derbyshire, Dave Simms, Rod Leach as photographer, Doctor John Salmon seconded by the army, Jim Hook a geologist and Ken Kelly.

Our first job was to try and gain sponsorship. By this time Mike Boon had disappeared and untraceable. Dave took over the whole responsibility for the trip and approached the Royal Geographical Society for approval. Having filled in the huge application form, we were invited for an interview to plead our case and a few weeks later approval came. Although not quite a license to print money we approached several 'big name' companies for support. Lord Shackleton was the Patron for the expedition.

We were now well on the way with sponsorship and the amount of money we had to put in ourselves diminished almost on a daily basis. Phew. Steph approached the media and soon we were invited to appear on Nationwide. This national TV news programme invited us to 'appear' at the Royal Geographical Society in Kensington, London. Tim, Steph, Dave, AG, Rod and I went there to discuss the project and be filmed, as part of the Nationwide news programme, abseiling over the RGS building. To my complete surprise when we were in space leaning out over the building Patti Caldwell the interviewer shouted 'Stop" and asked us questions. The one put to me was, 'What does your wife think about all this?' AG, quick as lightning quipped, "she doesn't even know he's going'. Well that caused quite a laugh amongst everyone. So we bounced on down the wall to the applause from the many on-lookers. We even managed to appear in the Sunday Telegraph magazine – twice. Bridget Bardot was on the front cover of the second issue looking very demure and seductive! I have several copies!!

By March we were almost ready. We were extremely lucky to have many major sponsors without whom the personal cost of the trip would have been very high indeed. Kit was promised, flights arranged and the shipping of all our gear was to be done 3 months before we left. Steve Reay, a local family doctor, was enlisted as pre-expedition medical officer. He duly gave us the armfuls of injections required and provided suggestions and information for our own personal first aid kits. He sorted out what malaria tablets were needed for that area along with much needed medical background information. He was initially asked to join the expedition as the Doctor but due to family commitments he sadly stood down. At least he was involved and on our return was pleased to see us with our several ailments. It was interesting for him rather than the usual 'I've got a cold doctor, what do I do'? Scrub Typhus, Hookworm and Malaria had been caught by different members of the expedition and needed treatment. Another local doctor, Hugh Kidd, gave us use of his garage to store the huge amount of equipment. This was a fantastic help as our various houses were getting full of kit we had accumulated.

We also had to practice river crossing techniques. Not like the tame ones done on a Mountain Leader training course but across huge raging torrents. Ropes had to be fixed on each side of the river. Importantly we had to have a method for tensioning ropes so that they were as tight as possible. Tim adapted a 'Z' rig for this. After we all had an input into this we found it a very simple system. Seemingly, to all and sundry it appeared that as soon as the load came on to the rope it would slacken off. No-one could understand why it did not slip. This tensioning technique was used most successfully. I still use this set up when I do tyroleans during group activities on adventure weeks.

Before we had perfected the tensioning technique several of us nearly drowned. Eventually we learned. Whilst in Nare our 'secret weapon' had to be relied upon to get the rope across the river. Using a compressed air launcher supplied by G. Q. Defence, a government defence company, a grappling hook could be shot across the river where we hoped it would engage on a projection on the far side. Dave and I discussed the uses and after several practice shots we knew it would work for us.

To raise more money we organised a stomp. Now a stomp is a kind of manic pounding dance that the Eldon were masters of. Many tickets were sold for this. We also had some 'T' shirts with Untamed River Expedition printed on them. These sold like hot cakes. The stomp was a success and was held under the banner of a 'Tonic for the Troops'. I think this was where we gave the trip an acronym, M.A.N.U.R.E. (Men Against Nare Untamed River Expedition). My friends in Kendal held a farewell dinner for me just prior to departure at the Scafell Hotel in Borrowdale. Carol made me a special, partially hollow cake. This was amazing, as it replicated Nare, even to the extent of having a marzipan caver descending!

Dave Gill, Tim and Steph had set off a couple of weeks prior to the rest of us. Dave had put me in charge of making sure that the rest of us all arrived in one piece and not detained anywhere. October 31st our day of departure had arrived so Carol and I along with the rest of the team went to Heathrow for the flight out to Singapore. We said our farewells and boarded a British Airways Jumbo. British Airways had very kindly sponsored everyone's flight to Singapore. During the flight we were invited one at a time to spend time on the flight deck. An amazing place with a myriad number of knobs, switches, buttons, handles and dials. This could never happen in today's terrorist stricken world.

We arrived in Singapore where we had a 3 day stop over. Although lively and fun it did not appeal to me as much as Hong Kong. We had secured accommodation at Sandy's, a hostel on Rangoon Road. It was very comfortable and clean. During this time we visited the various obvious sights including the notorious Bugis Street where blokes dress up as women. They looked very convincing! It was fairly obvious to us though that they were blokes but I could see how some people could be taken in. The two Daves (not Dave Gill though, he was in New Britain) Jim and I visited a botanical garden where we met four really pretty girls, Alexis, Farrah, Celia and Suzanne. They showed us around and it was pity to leave them.

One evening we went to, apparently, the best traditional Indian restaurant in town. Although I have had better it was not bad at all. For a start I was concerned when we walked in that there was a long bank of wash hand basins along one wall and many hands and faces were being swilled down. We were ushered politely upstairs where we all sat at a long table. A giant banana leaf was placed on the table in front of each of us. What was that for? A place mat, I guessed and thought to myself. Next thing I knew was a man with a cauldron of rice behind me ladling much of the contents of this on to my banana leaf. He was quickly followed by another man holding a smaller cauldron. This was the Dhal Bhat man and was poured over the rice. Upon asking for a spoon or a fork I was told that they did not use such things there, using instead good old right hand techniques and definitely not your left hand as this was supposed to be used for wiping your backside.

I could see now why the wash basins were plentiful as the mess we were eating dribbled all over the place. Up my arms it went into my beard (I was 1 year in to a 9 year one). A series of baths might have been better!

A trip into Malaya was fun where we had an ice cream. It was ice yes, but cream no. The ice was crushed water and flavoured with condensed milk with fruit syrup poured over the crushed mess. Not as bizarre as an ice cream I had in China once. This was an iced lolly that I procured from a man with a green wooden box masquerading as a freezer on the back of a bike. There was no ice inside the box, just lots of newspaper. The frozen water tasted somewhat dubious but once I had given it some hefty licks I noticed what looked like kidney beans inside. I was right, they were.

The three days went quickly and we were soon on our way to Port Moresby. The 5 hour flight with Air Niugini was good and the meal chosen from a menu even better, with proper food, proper cutlery, served on proper plates. There was a bar on board the Boeing 707. AG and I made good use of this facility propping up the bar for an hour or so enjoying several G and T's. Although we were not too worse for wear as the plane touched down the exit from the plane into the heat of Port Moresby was somewhat blurred.

I was staying with John McGreavy and his wife Chris, really welcoming and very friendly, generous Australians, in their house in the town. The others were at various other residences locally as arranged by Dave through his contacts with friends in Derbyshire, having Australian friends in the capital. We all met up in the evening for a 'greeny' and 'browny' session. These were the nicknames for the dreadful bottled beer. The 'tinnies' were even worse! Sleep was preceded by unconsciousness followed by a short course in death. The following morning was deemed a rest morning prior to our afternoon flight to Rabaul. We were at last getting nearer to the hole and our reason for being in Papua New Guinea.

The volcano dominated town of Rabaul was a fine place with a spectacular landing strip. Walking the streets I thought that many battles must have been fought. Huge red stains on the pavement indicated that many people had lost copious amounts of blood. I could not have been further from the truth. They were caused by people spitting out betel nut juice. The red stained juice comes from a mixture of leaf, nut and lime being chewed. It is supposed to give a high but the only thing I reckoned it did was to give people bad teeth.

We were staying in a house some 7 kilometres out of town. Whilst waiting for a boat to take us to Gonaile we managed quite a lot of activity. In the 6 days we were holed up we managed to climb 'Mother' one of the mountains above the town, descended into the Matupit Crater and snorkeled on several occasions in the most wonderful warm sea. We were also lucky enough to have the use of a four wheel drive Toyota which greatly helped in our moving around to see these sights. One of the excursions we made was to look at a crashed Japanese plane in a tangle of palm trees. We also went on to view some Japanese gun emplacements sporting 6 inch guns. These were erected during World War Two. The local kids were very enthusiastic in showing us these. Our Doctor, John Salmon, arrived in the evening having travelled for 52 hours from Britain.

Another of our 'war excursions' was to view the tunnels which were used as the headquarters for the Japanese offensive. These tunnels took 8 months to dig by hand, having an extent of 370 miles. It must have been hell digging these from the pumice like rock. Three hundred British Prisoners of War were involved at the start. At the end 16 walked out and 2 were carried out on stretchers!

On November 12th the time had come to leave Rabaul. A boat had been secured, the Medea II. Boat, I felt, was a name that was being rather too generous. The S.S. Colander would have been more apt. Including the team there were 25 people on board. The first 4 hours were in daylight. Flying fish kept us company and some dolphins did a remarkable circus act for us. All this was very spectacular. As we passed close to the shore I noticed that the jungle looked horribly dense. At this point in time I was aware that we had a couple of days walk through this to reach our base camp. It appeared that we would have our work cut out just to get there. As darkness approached a storm gathered. The sea became rough and the night was pretty damn miserable. Sitting by the mast all night long, keeping eyes fixed on where I thought the horizon should be I was relieved when daylight slowly reappeared. This also coincided with calmer seas.

Some 20 hours after setting sail the Medea II docked at some logs purporting to be a pier at Gonaile, a logging camp. On landing I noticed that there was a rather large marquee adorning what was going to be shore base. This housed all our kit. Partially hidden by the marquee was a helicopter. I thought to myself whether we could get the use of this to ferry our gear up. It had already been arranged. A geological survey was taking place in the rain forest by a team from Cozinc Australia, a subsidiary of Rio Tinto Zinc and the helicopter was ferrying teams of geologists to various parts of the rain forest. Dave had met the consultant geologist Frank Hughes. He was an amazing man and extremely keen in our project. He kindly offered the use of his helicopter. This saved the Expedition thousands of pounds and many weeks of very hard labour.

Lindsay Telfer from the logging company met us and we went to our 'company' house by the sea. It was great swimming in the warm sea even though sharks were spotted below us a couple of times. They appeared to be reef sharks and not any real threat. Turtles also visited us and it was sad that the local population hunted these creatures at night. It was an idyllic spot but ... there were several 'horrids' to be aware of. On the shore were conical light brown and off white shells, ones that could kill you in minutes or quicker. They were not to be handled. Although only 2 inches long they were extremely lethal. Stonefish lurked but more disturbingly a crocodile was spotted. We had finished our evening meal and were taking the night air, as one does, clutching a 'greenie', when I noticed what appeared to be a couple of red marker buoys on the far side of the small bay. We were told that the 'red lights' were definitely not buoys but the eyes of an estuarine crocodile reflecting the light from our torches. It was purported to be 6 metres long! There were also many sea snakes. The lighter side of nature was the resident, orphaned hornbill. It ate all the fruit we gave it. As soon as whatever we gave it was swallowed than it was ejected out from the other end almost immediately. Hornbill crap was everywhere, but it did keep us amused with its antics.

It will get rather confusing with three of the team called Dave on the trip so to avoid this Dave Gill is Dave; Dave Arveschoug, became nicknamed Mango, although I'll call him Dave A and Dave Simms, Simmy.

Dave, Tim and Steph were at Nare establishing base camp, having been flown close to it by helicopter, lucky them. Our equipment in the marquee now needed to be sorted out. We were also starting our rations! Ken Kelly now joined us after a lengthy trip from Britain having flown into Gonaile from Rabaul.

Two days after we had arrived the helicopter took AG, Dickie and I for the ride of our lives. Flying over the canopy I saw that there was not a single break in the trees at all, until we flew over Nutuve, the administrative village for the area which also had a very basic hospital. This turned out to be a 2 hour walk from base camp. However, we were dropped off at Ire village, situated some 40 minutes walk away from our base camp near the cave. Suddenly our pilot Bill Wineburge flipped the helicopter over 90 degrees over on to its side saying that Nare was directly below us.

Almost speechless I saw a huge gaping black hole

puncturing the forest two hundred feet or so below me. All I could say was 'wow'. I was totally gobsmacked, what an amazing, mind blowing place. It looked absolutely enormous. There were no doors on the helicopter either which heightened the experience! Bill descended. We were just about to drop down inside the hole, when he decided it might not be a good idea! We flew back to Ire and landed at the edge of the village.

No sooner had we landed than the villagers swooped towards us wailing and whooping. They picked up anything and everything they could carry. Each load whether it be a heavy sack or a karrimat cost 1 kina – about a £1. Forty stumbling minutes later we were in base camp, our home for the next month.

Part 2 – Exploration

Our camp was situated virtually on the same site as the French expedition some four years before. Prior to our arrival the villagers, under the guidance of Tim, Dave and Steph, had cleared an area and erected a large awning over the area. It remained waterproof for the entire duration of our time at Nare. Dave had employed Camillus a local chap from Pomio to act as the expedition interpreter and was without doubt an indispensable part of the team. He fixed it for us to be supplied with 'vegetations' from the rainforest by the indigenous villagers from Ire village. Even from here some 10 minutes away from the hole I could hear the roar of the underground river.

It was good to see Dave, Tim and Steph. They had already started the exploration and had rigged the normal descent down the shaft wall to the river. Dave apparently had had a fright on the first tyrolean, Poseidon. (Most of the river crossings had been given names of sunken ships by the French!). During this review of the action so far, Camillus made us tea and dinner which he had partly gleaned from the jungle, ibeka, a spring green type of vegetable and Kau Kau, a sweet potato along with some tinned stewed steak. We all slept in our mosquito nets as there were a few buzzing around. Not only did the nets give protection from biting mosquitoes they gave each one of us an area of privacy, our own space.

After a fitful night's sleep listening to some fantastic jungle noises I awoke to the sound of a purring primus, the sun filtered falteringly through the canopy and Camillus lighting the daily fire. Camillus had procured a bunch of small but very sweet bananas. There were about 80 to the bunch. After several brews we set off to look at the cave. To reach the rim we followed a dry river bed to the rim of the shaft. Wow. Was this a big hole or what? You could put all of Yorkshire's shafts inside and still have room for more! Walking up to the left of the shaft there was superb vantage point where we could watch Tim and Steph descend into the depths. The roar of the river was quite pronounced as I watched the white torrent become engulfed by the huge entrance porch. It was certainly by far the biggest hole I had ever seen.

We wandered back for breakfast after which we all helped to build more bunks for the rest of the team for when they arrived. This done I sorted my caving gear ready for an assault on the cave the following day. Whilst doing this the villagers arrived with a fresh load of equipment dropped by the helicopter. The carry had been organized by the headmen of Ire village, Tome and Unaso. All in all there were 29 villagers. Camillus went walkabout for the nights' vegetables and came back with what appeared to be bracken as well as some Ibeka. As darkness fell and our 'street lights' were switched on huge fruit bats were seen circling in the clearings above us. A huge noise of creatures all vying for attention from their counterparts circulated the night air. Cane toads sounded like a series of football rattles! Dave, Tim and Steph arrived in camp as darkness finally fell having had a successful day. They had reached the start of the second tyrolean after traversing a ledge across a wall, 'Ledge Jo'. They reported that the passage beyond this was absolutely amazing with formations everywhere. The following day it was to be my turn along with AG and Dickie.

The day dawned sunny and after breakfast we set off

with two bags of kit each. We followed each other at 15 minute intervals to avoid waiting at re-belays. After nine re-belays and 2 deviations I reached the base of the shaft. The final drop was 90 metres. Gulp, what an astonishing place. Huge is a poor word to describe the enormity of the place. Looking up, the hole was ringed by trees 300 metres above our heads. Huge fruit bats wheeled around in the twilight of the porch. The river looked very inviting. Turbulent, but clear, blue water flowed through a tangle of jungle vegetation.

After a break and many drinks we all set off to the first crossing, 'Poseidon'. Quickly dispensing with this we found ourselves on the far side of the river. Picking up an extra sack apiece, each of us now having three, we walked downstream in an immense passage to where we could climb up 5.5 metres to traverse the 40 metres long 'Ledge Jo' using cows' tails to protect ourselves on the fixed rope that Dave and Co. had fixed the day before. I decided to place a higher line at the far end as the ledge was quite cramped and above the raging torrent. We fixed a ladder at each end of the ledge as I recommended this to make life much easier getting on and off each end.

Having descended from the ledge we made our way downstream again using cows' tails on a fixed line. The water was waist deep and I had by now become accustomed to being in it. The second tyrolean took a while to site. We found a large thread which was immediately opposite a very big stalagmite on the opposite bank. However, the river was quite turbulent here. Preparations were made as it seemed a logical place to make the crossing due to the exceptional strong belays for the tyreolean crossing. AG wanted first bash at this. Having donned two buoyancy aids he was ready. We managed to get a grappling iron across the water at the fourth attempt which had lodged securely between boulders. After tensioning the rope AG set off. We had secured two safety lines for him. One was belayed upstream and the other downstream. In the event of the traverse rope failing he could be brought ashore. A quick lunge was followed by a whoop of success. We were ready to rig the 'Python' tyrolean.

This done we were on our way back out. Night had fallen and finding the rope in the jungle was a nightmare. Eventually we found it and I set off first. It was a sweaty and muddy ascent but I reached base camp one and a half hours after setting off. I had really enjoyed the day. After a good wash and a hearty meal it was time for sleep.

I awoke the following morning once again to sunshine and our camp followers, the villagers who now seemed to visit us on a daily basis. The women wore virtually no clothes and day by day they became more and more attractive! By lunch time the rest of the team had arrived having walked in from Gonaile, a two day walk. We were now a full compliment. It was good having the surface team with us. They took over the running of the camp and began cooking and tidying up.

The villagers were really friendly. They bought us kau kau, ibeka, ferns, coconuts and Pomelo an orange flavoured grapefruit. We celebrated the day with a Sunday roast. Somehow Unaso had caught a wild pig for us. It was very relaxing being in camp as I was able to read, write, play chess or listen to my waterproof Walkman tape recorder. Camp felt like it could almost be England as we unfurled our Union Jack only to learn when we looked at the pictures back home we had erected it upside down!

All the pushing team went underground the following day. Dave and Steph were going to survey whilst AG, Dickie, Tim and I were to push deeper. In reality it ended up with AG and Steph rigging a phone line and to sort out where we could camp whilst the rest of went further. The rest of us crossed 'Python' and continued along the river bank through astonishing formations to a beautiful calcite wall. The river had become much more violent. It was my turn to lead. I climbed high above the river before I started to traverse across this encrusted calcite wall. After 50 metres I reached the far side. However, it was difficult not to linger part way across because there was a perfectly sized, smooth calcite breast complete with nipple, a very comforting handhold. Naturally this was known as 'Ledge of Bosom'.

After a brew we set off downstream past an awkward 6 metres traverse around some really frenzied water, fixing a rope in the process to where the roof lowered dramatically and the walls contracted. This was to be our third tyrolean 'Andrea Doria'. The river now had standing waves and the noise was cacophonous, quite an awe inspiring spot! We found the place where we wanted to cross and it was my hapless task to try and throw the grapnel iron across to the far side. Our 'weapon' was still not in service. Standing atop a wave lashed boulder I resigned my position after ten attempts and Tim had a throw and also gave up. Dave had a throw and managed to get the iron stuck in the middle of the torrent with no chance of freeing it. I thought that this was going to be a real swine to get sorted let alone cross. We gave up and headed off out.

AG and Steph had laid the telephone line from the bottom of the shaft to base camp. They had also had found a camp site at the base of the shaft in a dry shallow hollow. This was deemed to be a necessity to avoid a commute to the top after each day of caving. I stumbled in to base camp at 22.00 four hours after leaving the 'Andrea Doria'. The surface team fed and watered me as they did for Dave,

Dickie and Tim in the re-vamped base camp. What a great team. Cut branches had been fashioned to form tables, making eating much more comfortable. Folding chairs had been shipped from England. We now had a larger kitchen and storage area. My diary noted that at that this stage I felt that it was one of the hardest caving trips in the world but certainly one that is incredibly beautiful.

We now had a couple of days in camp to allow cuts to heal and regain our strength for the next push. Jim our geologist told us that the river bed next to camp was long abandoned and we discussed at length the geology of the cave. It was thought that as the river bed was composed of calcite considerably less water flowed at one time. There was a very distinct lack of faulting. We felt that once the roof of the cave collapsed millions of tons of rock stemmed the flow. The flattened pancake characteristic shape of the stalagmites was caused by water falling from a great height and with such a force the spray formed nodules on the ground. We agreed that our rope tightening technique was working extremely well. It was important for us to slacken the tyrolean ropes when we exited the cave to allow them to recover.

John was in charge of building the toilet and was being built along army lines. It was a raised dais above a pit. I was one of the first to use it and it was like being on a throne! The only trouble was that when I came to wipe my backside many eyes appeared out of the bush to watch. I wonder what they thought when they saw my white, bare backside being aired to the jungle air? We then constructed a modesty screen around the toilet to avoid further embarrassments. On another occasion I found that the inside of the cardboard roll had become home to some pretty large spiders.

After the two days in camp I was keen to get going again. Setting off with two bags I was quickly at the base of the shaft, filthy and sweaty. Tim, Steph and Dickie came with me. Simmy was erecting a 'lift' at the upstream end of the porch to allow us to have fresh food and any gear we had left on the surface. AG and Dave were sorting out our Advance Base Camp at the bottom of the shaft.

We were all at the 'Andrea Doria' looking at the twitching, violently swaying rope in the river some one and a half hours after setting off. This time we had the 'secret weapon'. With the right tools jobs are always easier. Our 'weapon' was the air launcher. It worked from a 4,000 p.s.i. fibre wrapped compressed air bottle and could fire a stainless steel grapnel iron 100 metres with only a 2000 p.s.i. charge.

A rope was fixed in no time at all but it was very low so we fixed another for security in case one failed. Tim went first and made it OK. I went second but became entangled in the violently twitching rope stuck in the middle of the river from our previous attempt a few days before. This forced me under the waves. Fortunately we were attaching a safety rope to everyone and I was quickly pulled back. That was quite an unnerving experience. Dickie crossed over but Steph did not. We did however manage to retrieve the jammed grapnel.

Tim and Dickie headed downstream to look at the next tyrolean. Thirty minutes later they were back unable to find a site so we all set off back to Advance Base. This was situated at the bottom of the entrance shaft some 30 metres above and away from the river. I felt a little uneasy with the fresh stone-fall debris surrounding the area. I washed or rather bathed in the river and my stinking caving gear in the lea of a large boulder. I felt a million times fresher afterwards. Hypnotised by the myriad of fireflies drifting in a carefree manner around me I quickly drifted off to sleep.

It was my turn to survey the next day whilst the others went on their explorations. Steph and I phoned for more gear which arrived spectacularly down Simmy's lift at the upstream end of the porch. Dave A had sent me a banana and written on it was 'Des, but don't tell the others!' We also received mail. A letter from Carol arrived 9 days after leaving Buxton. Our survey session was thwarted by heavy rain pouring down the shaft. We did, however, get a message via the phone to say that Simmy had built an oven and was making bread and pies.

As night fell Steph and I were treated to a spectacular display of bats leaving their roost to hunt in the gathering gloom, truly awe inspiring. It was dark when the team arrived back having had a very fruitful day having managed to avoid the next 2 tyroleans, 'Titanic' and 'Les Priapes' as named by the French, by traversing along the walls at water level. This became known as 'The Dirty English Sneaky Bit'. They had turned back at the base of what was to become 'The Flying Dutchman'. It was my turn the following day to climb up to the bridge and cross it, the key to exploring the rest of the cave.

However, it was not to be. I had the most horrendous of nights. A rock-fall from the roof area or side wall hit me. Fortunately my only injuries were of the sore nature and no major trauma. As soon as the stones rained down I kind of rolled down the slope several feet and shouted to the others to take cover. This was to no avail. Everyone had ear plugs in to deaden the noise of the river. Eventually everyone awoke and huddled closer to the wall.

Rather than risk another episode of falling rocks everyone decided to have a day off and to move camp inside the porch. I decided that I would head out. I phoned Base Camp with the news and to let them know I was on my way out. Ken who answered the phone asked if I wanted a pie. I said yes please and in reply Ken intimated that it would be a Desperate Dan Pie, but without the horns!

I slept well that night and ached only a little the following morning. On waking I saw that there were perhaps 50 villagers thronging the camp. They had bought bananas, pumpkin leaves, ferns, a live chicken and a dead rat! I was quite moved by all this generosity. Some were playing their musical pipes, a very haunting sound. Ken asked if I would go part way down the shaft with him to which I gladly agreed. I did this before heading off to a new cave that had been shown to us. It was called Kille, named after a yellow bird found there. Dave A, Jim and I were the gladiators on this.

A perplexing 2 kilometres walk through tangled jungle took us around 45 minutes to the hole in the floor. It was another amazing spot. A lush green gully descended some 80 metres to the actual cave mouth where another shaft 60 metres deep descended into a large chamber. This took us down a 9 metres climb and a 13 metres deep pitch, our low point that day. We had left our exit quite late and we realised that darkness was only 20 minutes away. Half stumbling we crashed through the undergrowth to arrive in camp just as darkness fell.

Two days later we were back at Kille. Nare had fallen into dis-favour. Dave A and Simmy had set off earlier whilst Tim, John and I set off at a leisurely pace much later. We arrived at the head of the big pitch to find Dave A at grips with it. Two short drops of 9 metres and 8 metres took us to the 60 metres big drop. This was a spectacular descent and landed in a deep pool. Further short pitches of 16 metres and 13 metres took us to a scramble over calcited boulders. Tim and I free climbed down to another large pool whilst Dave A, Simmy and John fixed a rope.

The very pretty passage continued for 150 metres past a sumped inlet to where it lowered. Unfortunately, 50 metres further on we reached the inevitable sump. There were very many bats in this last part and at the very far end there also some pretty sizeable crabs.

This was an excellent non-serious trip being pretty, fun and a 'virgin'. Another day away from Nare ensued. The caving team had a walk to Nutuve to get some sun. This two hour walk was pretty grim to start with as far as Ire village, being muddy and heavily forested. There were however great views from the village towards the Iso Gorge where we thought the Nare resurgence might be. The whole area was just wall to wall trees. Gradually the forest thinned as gardens were more in evidence growing a variety of crops, maize, taro, tapioca and kau kau. Passing through several much smaller villages we arrived in Nutuve under a perfect blue sky and hot sun. What a relief to have the sun burning on our backs. There was also a grassy air strip here.

As well as being the administrative centre there was also a very primitive hospital. In the hospital log we noticed that there were many machete injuries. Whether these were accidental or from disputes with others we could not make out, but, what was interesting there was a case of cannibalism registered from only 2 years previously. The many flies were most annoying, the price to pay for civilisation and sunshine.

One thing I noticed on the way back was that each village had small palm trees planted around it. They had large pointed leaves turned up. Apparently this is to ward off evil spirits. Each village too had a totem pole whilst Ire also had a burial ground and a huge totem pole. These recorded the names of the dead people. Around Ire too were coconut palms and breadfruit trees.

We were glad to get back to back in camp where to our delight we found that Simmy had baked some flapjack and fresh bread. There seemed to be no end to his capabilities. We all had a leisurely night talking, and on retiring I read and listened to my Dire Straits tape, 'Telegraph Road', my motivational but relaxing music for the trip.

Another day of rest followed. Many of the team were suffering from colds or cuts and needed to recover. However, the next day I was underground and quickly arrived at the new advance base camp just beyond the 'Poseidon' tyrolean in the twilight zone. Tim had decided he wanted to rig the direct way. This was the most trouser filling experience ever. The belay at the start was a stout tree, but the belay for the 230 metres totally free hang which gradually became miles from anywhere was a bendy old thing that swayed alarmingly when loaded but fortunately stayed attached to the ground!

The following day Tim, Dickie, John and I continued into the cave whilst AG and Ken went as far as 'Python' and then set off out. I approached the 'Andrea Doria' with trepidation but I passed it calmly and safely. At the far side the passage lowered further but enlarged as we approached 'The Dirty English Sneaky Bit'. Chaotic, white foaming water was our companion. We were just able to keep in slack water although it was waist deep. Another difficult traverse along a loose wall above some huge stoppers was heart clamping. Once past this obstacle easy walking took us up to a balcony at the low side of what was going to be 'The Flying Dutchman' tyrolean. We also had a great view of the 'bridge' spanning the high and wide passage. It looked like a picture I had in my mind of the bridge to Valhalla.

Dropping down from the ledge to water level I felt some trepidation. The river was plucking at my feet so roping up and belayed by Tim I started off by climbing up and diagonally across a flowstone wall until an awkward traverse took me to a calcite covered balcony below the vertical wall where I belayed. After bringing Tim up I set off on the start of a 20 metres section. I stepped across to the calcite wall, which had some small curtains and climbed up for 7 metres. A traverse across the wall, with 3 small stalagmite runners to safeguard my progress, took me under an overhanging prow on side holds to a final long step to reach the bridge.

I was now on the fabled bridge of jammed boulders. Although the climb was mentally absorbing and difficult I was more concerned about the bridge collapsing. The noise was unbelievable as the river below crashed and boiled its way downstream. I fixed one of the ropes across the bridge for Tim to clip into as he came across whilst I belayed him on the other. We reasoned that the tyrolean was the only feasible option to rigging the climb with fixed ropes and across the bridge.

Once we were both on the far side we walked in a downstream direction up in the roof along a wide ledge through a glittering array of amazing formations looking at what lay ahead of us. We were both somewhat impressed. Returning to the bridge we walked along the wide ledge in an upstream direction to where we could throw a rope over to Dickie and John. The rope was securely fixed on our side whist the tensioning system was rigged on theirs, the low side. Once rigged, we set off down. The tensioned rope was at quite a steep angle so as to avoid a fast descent we fixed another rope which we abseiled down whilst attached to the tensioned rope by our cows' tails. On the way in it was obvious that we would have to prussik the slack rope whilst attached to the tensioned rope.

Whilst we were doing this Dickie had slipped and had

received a rather severe cut on his hand. Undeterred he patched it up and set off out. We had been 10 hours away from camp. It was good to be back where we ate a hearty meal with many brews and some of Simmys delicious bread.

Our good intentions the following day came to nought. We slept late and AG came in suitably impressed having entered by the airy direct way. Simmy arrived too followed by Dave. We read, talked and ate. Heavy rain during the day made the river rise 50 centimetres, increasing the flow by an estimated 5 cumecs. The noise was even greater than before and was mentally very wearing. It was an amazing sight as we watched the rainstorm tumble down the shaft from the dry sanctuary well under the porch. When we contacted Base Camp we were told that the river bed going past the camp, 'the one that never has water flowing', Jims immortal words when he first saw it, had flooded. He had thought that it was part of an abandoned river bed. Apparently there was a 1.5 metres high flood pulse down it!

After a good rest and having had an enormous breakfast AG, Tim and I set off down the cave again the following day at 11.30. I did the climb again over 'The Flying Dutchman' and continued to the 'Howling Ledges', an area of tremendous and huge formations. Having rigged these with a safety line we continued down an immense gallery. It was not particularly wide but it was very high. The calcite had a very rough coarse sandpaper feel to it as well as being intensely white. There were many large white cauliflower formations in this area. In fact the calcite was so rough it filed away any exposed skin.

We continued down at or slightly above water level to a climb up out of the water to a ledge. The climb down at the far end of this was an inclined ramp of 45 degrees.

Numerous inlets gushed from the wall along this 80 metres long section. We had just avoided another tyrolean, the 'Torrey Canyon'. Beyond a large boulder and shingle bank the cave changed character dramatically. Gone were all the fine formations, all that remained was just a black, vast hall appearing to have no walls or roof. Eventually the bank ran out so we took to the wall again and by traversing 'Ledge Tim' we avoided another tyrolean – 'Les Nutuveens'.

Ahead there was more roaring and our pace quickened over the next bank of shingle and boulders to where the French had stopped. We were at 'Apocalypse Now'. What an awesome and incredible place. The roar and violence of water was mind blowing in the extreme. It made the start of the cave look like a mere stream! Huge cataracts of water descended perhaps nine metres in nineteen. It appeared at one point that it would be easy to cross as the river was funneled into a narrow channel. How deep that channel was no-one had any idea but it must have been deep, extremely so. The distance was around 2 metres and the drop about six metres. A misjudgment here would have been fatal. We were at the furthest point the French had reached.

I was impressed by the French achievement and admired what they had done. Because of their expedition we had some idea what to expect. The French had no idea. The cave was now wide open for us to explore new passages, but what lay ahead was like a boiling, crashing cauldron of foaming white water as far as the eye could see. We chose to leave the next part for another day so we set off back to camp.

The following day was a rest day and we discussed the expedition so far. I was really chuffed when AG said that my lead on 'The Flying Dutchman' was a magnificent effort. Everyone seemed to think that that clinched it. We also realised that yesterdays achievements were the biggest progressions yet. Moonlight drifting into the shaft that night was a magnificent, if eerie sight.

So the day of the push into new ground dawned and AG, Dickie, Tim, Dave and I set off to 'Apocalypse Now'. Tim and AG went off in front. When we had caught up with them Tim had jumped the 'jaws of death', the two metres wide slot and pronounced this simply as irreversible. Dickie had a nasty turn when the 'weapon' he was carrying slipped from his shoulder. He overbalanced and was spat into the river but was none the worse for his wetting. I managed to throw a rope over to Tim whereupon we rigged 'Apocalypse Now' and crossed over to 'New Britain'! I went over last and perhaps due to the rope slackening I was dumped in the river but a strong pulling team soon had me on dry land.

The noise was by now ear shattering and it was difficult to communicate with each other. We covered some 80 metres of new ground to where the river was squeezed into a very narrow tunnel. It was perhaps 6 metres wide and 3 metres high above the boiling torrent. Water lashed the walls of this space but there was hope of passing this along the wall we were on. My diary of this says it all '... *in this totally and utterly terrifying place. I have never (and neither had anyone else) seen such turbulence. It was a spectacle of unutterable violence*'.

Starting from a sheltered alcove we fastened the rope to a large thread and drilled an anchor point for the rope on the corner of the passage. Being chest deep in water and being flung around like a rag doll in a dog's mouth in the turbulence was quite unnerving. Any mistake at all would mean certain death. Two more threads allowed us to fix the rope to reach a ledge just above water. The small ledge dwindled as we progressed to where there was no hope of passing further. Waves constantly hit the roof. White foaming water crashed steeply down into what appeared to be a sump in the distance. We had reached the end of Nare and called it appropriately 'Armageddon'. It was a hollow victory. The Nare River remained Untamed.

Part 3 – Aftermath

Nare was the most spectacular, fantastic trip that any of us had ever done. Back at Advance Base it was most surreal. Moonlight filtered down the shaft along with tiny wisps of cloud lending a surreal air to the surroundings. I don't know who scripted this last part but it was so peaceful after the turmoil at the end of the cave. The following day we set off out AG first with me coming up second. Back in Base Camp I found AG still in his caving gear, tired but elated. Dickie came in 1½ hours later closely followed by Dave. Dave A, Steph and Jim had gone to Kille to de-rig. Rain was falling so we hoped that they would not have a flash flood. They did and said it was very impressive. Simmy made us all a huge meal and rice pudding. What a star. He must be the best Base Camp organiser anywhere.

After resting, a trip to Nutuve again for sunshine was mandatory. It was lovely just see the yellow ball in the sky let alone bask in its warmth. Inevitably the rain came so back we returned to Base Camp. Several more days of rest and getting plump on Simmys steak and kidney pies were followed by Tim, Simmy, Jim and I taking a walk to find the Ora resurgence. Our tour guide, Camillus had never been there before so we were quite relieved when two villagers who knew the way decided to come with us.

The walk was sweaty, steamy and a real grind. It was like walking through a six hour forest maze. Trees were to the left, in front, behind and to the right as well as above us. I have never walked through so many trees. The jungle floor was booby trapped with sharp irregular and coral like limestone. We tripped and stumbled behind our guides as we blundered on our way. When we thought we had arrived we hadn't. The empty huts were long abandoned in favour of a higher site. Begonias gave some colour relief to the pervading greenery whilst the dreaded 'chainsaw vine' ripped us apart. Just as total darkness descended we entered the village some 10 hours after setting off from Base Camp. We were wrecked. The village womenfolk gave us water but did not tell us where it was to be found.

Ora village would not have been out of place in a desert. Trees were all around the clearing but the earth was dust dry. We were given a guest hut, very sportan but great to be horizontal even though the base of the bed was only .5 metre off the floor. This was a bamboo pole mattress atop a wood framework. Our hut roughly measured 5 metres by 2.5 metres and had 3 beds. Simmy slung a hammock up which greatly impressed the villagers. Their only wealth was 4 pigs and 2 piglets. They also had a well fed dog. A pig would sell for around 300 kina (about £300).

In the morning we were shown the resurgence. We set off steeply uphill on a good path. This was followed by a long diagonal descent which we hacked our way through using our goloks to reach the base of the very fine waterfall issuing from a gaping cave mouth some 55 metres above our head. The force of the water issuing out from the hole was strong enough to create some pretty hefty waves in the plunge pool. We estimated that the rate of flow to be around 5.5 cumecs. Tim tried to reach the cave by clambering up a grassy gully on the right before attempting to traverse out but unsuccessfully. He did not meet with success. The rest of us bathed in the warm water for a couple of hours before heading back to the village.

Rain started to fall keeping us hut bound. I was dosing away after a bowl of soup when Tim staggered over for his cigarettes as they were behind me and let out a blood curdling scream. There was a snake a few inches away from my head. I could feel the blood draining from my face. I shot outside in a nano second and so was the snake. Tim was being harassed by it so he had picked up a long handled axe on his way out of the hut and deftly beheaded it. The snake was called by the villagers a Moran. Is this the same as a Taipan I ask myself? I believe it is!

The excitement over we had dinner, kau kau supplied by the villagers, Camillus supplied the ferns and we produced the stewed steak. The following day Tim and Jim decided to try and find the Ora uvala. Simmy and I were to walk back. Views from this idyllic spot were quite remarkable. Stretching out as far as the eye could see there was green. Just varying shades of green. Trees cloaked every hillside.

Simmy and I left with our porters while Tim, Jim and Camillus set off on their adventure. We were really pushed to keep up with our guides who had a habit of trying to scare us by throwing sharpened sticks, just missing our heads in the process, into the soft bark of some of the trees. I was quite relieved to arrive back in Camp and totally impressed how these people find their way around. No tracks just a wonderful sense of direction. I thought I could at times discern some vague paths but these disappeared just as soon as they developed.

There were a couple of characters who visited our camp most days. One was a porter who had a foot missing. Apparently he had caught his foot in a fire while cooking his kau kau. He then proceeded to walk to Nutuve where he had the affected part amputated, a hard man who still carried heavy loads. There was another man who only had one leg who visited with his wife. He had a small command of English and was very friendly.

Tim, Jim and Camillus arrived back from their adventures totally wrecked. Ora cave was only 2.5 hours away from the village but their journey back to Camp was an ordeal. They managed to get disorientated and had to bivouac overnight after bush whacking for 11 hours. They arrived in Camp after another 7 hours bush bashing session.

I had now decided that I needed to be back in the UK in all fairness to Carol to some earn money. After Simmy and I set up a hauling jib at the head of the upstream porch and ferrying gear around the base of the shaft for a couple of days I set off on the long journey back to the UK. Tome and Unaso guided me to Gonaile. Such honour indeed, the two headmen of the village. Walking back through the damp jungle I managed to attract 15 leeches in the process, one of which had fastened itself to my cheek. Unaso said I had snake on my face! We waded across the wide, very clear but fairly shallow Kiage River. I was very glad that my guides had my two heavy rucksacks as the humidity and heat was almost overwhelming.

The clearly followed track was very muddy and eventually reached the limit of the logging operations near to Gonaile. What an absolute mess they had made of the jungle. Bits of machinery, wire ropes and abandoned tyres littered the floor. Seven hours after leaving base Camp we reached the roadhead. We managed to cadge a lift for the first 4 kilometres in a four wheeled drive vehicle and for the rest of the journey we travelled on a large tree carrier. It is really sad to think that the encroachment of tree felling could seriously impact on the lives of people at Nutuve and Ire.

Back in Gonaile I dragged myself and my gear over to the house that we used when we had first arrived. Steve and Barbara were there and I was given two wonderful ice cold orange drinks. They tasted marvellous, after which I had the most refreshing shower. Steve having returned from work offered several beers. Wow, what a home coming.

We went night snorkeling along with some of the local villagers looking for turtles and crayfish which we found. I was very conscious of a lurking crocodile and the sea snakes wriggling around in the warm water. The locals managed to catch five crayfish which they were very pleased about. Whilst we did that Tome and Unaso were absolutely glued to the television. They were totally and utterly mesmerised by the moving pictures.

I slept well that night so after breakfast I packed three bags, one for travelling home with and two for shipping back to the UK. When Steve returned from work we set off to find the elusive Iso River. We found it and also visited a resurgence called Sibuli a deep blue crystal clear pool. There were no visible signs of water entering. A short length of cave adorned with roof pendants led up from the far end of the pool ending after 20 metres. We returned for beers and relaxation to find Brian Bennett had arrived. He was suitably impressed by our exploits and pleased we had succeeded.

The journey back started with a memorable flight from Gonalile International Airport! Well it wasn't really as it was just a wooden shed alongside a coral runway. The not so very spacious five seater plane belonging to Talair did not inspire confidence, even less so when the pilot asked me to hold the door shut while we took off. It was an uneventful short flight to Rabaul. Here I made my confirmations for the flights to Port Moresby, Singapore and finally London.

John McGreavy met me in Port Moresby and took me back to his house where Chris had cooked a really lovely meal after which we drank too much Aussie beer. The following day was a day of visiting people. Paradise magazine wanted the story and on to the British High Commission where I borrowed a video called 'First

Contact' a film about the Leah brothers' explorations of the Papuan Highlands. This is a fascinating story and well worth watching. Eventually I managed to procure a copy. A continual round of visitors at John and Chris's for the next few days was virtually a haze of good food and beer.

It was with a sad heart that I left Port Moresby for home. The last two months had been the most amazing of my life and in a way shaped the rest of it. I had been with some amazing friends and the camaraderie was very special. I was sad too, that some of the team were still exploring new caves although half of them did return within a few days of mine. The remaining members explored further remarkable caves for another couple of months. A lot of hard work for almost a year paid dividends as this was a very, very successful expedition to the largest underground river in the world explored at that time. Back home again and the media once more were in touch and I did an inevitable TV interview for Look North.

Perhaps the most daunting part of the return was giving a lecture at the RGS. Along with Dave we went down to London along with my wife Carol, Steve Reay and his wife Viv. I have never felt so nervous. We had several trial runs with the slide projector ensuring that the slides were all the right way up and in the correct order. This is because standing at the lectern we would be well in front of the screen only turning to it occasionally. The time came for the talk and Steve seeing my nervousness produced a small hip flask and said have a swig of that. The brandy seemed to calm me down and in we went to start the lecture. The front row was full of dignitaries including Lord Bishop and Sir Vivian Fuchs! I commenced the talk and fortunately all went well. Half way through Dave took over and then it was done. Dinner was served and it is was all very convivial.

Chapter 9

Sumatra '87

Two years had elapsed since our trip to Papua New Guinea and some of the team became restless for another adventure. I had heard that there were some caves in the northern tip of Sumatra so I set about finding out further details. I read from a 1984 Cambridge University expedition report there that there were resurgences and caves in a big block of limestone close to Banda Aceh in Aceh province. They were there to study the fauna of the caves so we decided that would be a good place to visit. Their expedition report also intimated the possibility of a large river cave as well as a number of cave entrances that they had not entered. It sounded all quite promising for our exploration. A base needed to be secured close to Lhok Nga a coastal village 16 kilometres south, south west of Banda Aceh. A study of the geological maps did after all reveal that there was a very large block of limestone there.

This was to be a much lower profile expedition although we did receive approval from the Royal Geographical Society. I managed to secure discounted flights with Garuda the National Airline of Indonesia and had secured accommodation in Bogor, Java whilst we secured the necessary permissions from various government bodies. I contacted Dr. Robbie Ko, the President of FINSPAC the

Indonesian Caving Federation based in the town. He was very helpful in securing maps and information on the area. Our main help in Aceh came from the expatriate population working at P. T. Semen Andalas.

I wrote to the company and received an enthusiastic reply from Pat Gorman who was very keen for us to visit the area. Without the help from the company, Ken Kemsley, Martin Wilkes, Clare and Tony Parvin, Cut Soraya, Morny our Indonesian cook and Nazir Dahlan our van driver we would have had a very much harder time sorting out accommodation, transport and of course the huge, inevitable amount of red tape.

The team consisted of six members of the Untamed River Expedition, Dave Arveschoug, Alan Gamble (AG), Steve Dickinson (Dickie), Jim Hook, Ken Kelly and myself with the addition of John Middlemist (Mouse) and Bob Cockeram, a well known Yorkshire caver. We were also asked to take along two Indonesian cavers from FINSPAC, Cahyo Alkantana and Edie Bratawidjaja. They were invaluable as interpreters, advisers and the go-betweens for the bureaucrats.

Because the expedition was of a purely sporting nature we obtained our permit from Robbie in only 6 months but only for the Gunung Leuser National Park. This, however, was 500 kilometres from our base!! Other permissions had to be obtained from the sub-province offices in Banda Aceh, notably in Takengon and Langsa. Robbie had done much work on our behalf. To this end it was agreed that Dave and I set off two weeks prior to the others to sort out all the paperwork that seemed to be accumulating.

We arrived in Jakarta on the 28th of July after a 19 hour flight into almost intolerable heat. Customs formalities were, most surprisingly very quickly finalised especially so in view of the paperwork. Our concern on leaving customs was would our reception committee be there to meet us.

They were. Three members of FINSPAC two of whom were Edie and Cahyo and another called Suwesta bundled us on board their truck. Edie skillfully managed to miss the mayhem of the frenetic streets taking us straight to a boozer! They perhaps thought with us being English we needed a beer. How right they were. We were then taken to FINSPAC which was also Robbie's home in Bogor. Here we discussed our plans with him, before being taken to our residence at Cisarua 10 kilometers from Bogor.

The following day I telephoned the British Embassy to make an appointment with the Ambassador. We had been told that this was an important step. The day was spent relaxing and exploring the local markets. They were dirty, very crowded with thousands of flies but the food was cheap. The evening was spent at FINSPAC watching a video on glacier caving in Switzerland.

We paid a visit to Bandung, a long and tiring drive of over three hours. I had expected that the roads, once away from the cities, would be quieter. Not so. They were just as busy and noisy with constant horn blowing and were even more dangerous. Vehicles seemed to attack us from all angles. The road was lined with little stalls selling anything that could be sold if only for a few rupiah such as bike parts, a variety of foodstuff and building materials. As we drove along the road there were fine sculptured paddy fields on each side and views constantly changed.

Our purpose in Bandung was to obtain geological and topographical maps of Aceh from the geological museum. Although they were cheap they were not particular helpful. Before setting off back we had lunch, very different to say the least. We stopped at a market stall and I fancied the crisps and twiglets. They were packaged and seemed safe to eat. The crisps were indeed tasty. When I had finished them I started on the twiglets. They were tasty too. I commented on this to Robbie who said that it was amazing what they can do with bird lungs and intestines!

Our visit the following day to Jakarta started abruptly. We were dumped at the bus station in Bogor. There were literally hundreds of people milling around and busses clamouring to be off on their journeys. Eventually we were pushed on the bus to Jakarta, 50 kilometres away for which we paid the princely sum of 750 rupiah each. That was about 35 pence. It was a relief to be in an air conditioned environment but stepping outside in Jakarta was a severe shock.

We had several jobs to see to in the city. Firstly we had to confirm our Banda Aceh flights, then sort out flights and boat journeys for our Indonesian friends and finally to visit the British Embassy. The heat was stifling as we flagged a yellow taxi to Thamrin where fortunately all three of the offices were sited. Having confirmed our flights we visited the Ambassador, Alan Donald. He was a great chap and extremely helpful. We had been trying to get hold of Pat Gorman in Banda Aceh on the telephone for several days whilst in Bogor to no avail. Contact was at last made and we were able to speak with him directly from the Embassy. Alan also gave us the names of several more contacts and helped with extending our visas.

Our final task also went without a hitch as we managed to book our Indonesian cavers on to a boat on August 8th for the journey from Jakarta to Medan the capital of Sumatra. We could not afford the flights for them! Even the boat trip cost the expedition £160 for the pair of them. We were able, however, to book a flight for them from Medan to Banda Aceh at a cost of £98. Two rest days of lazing around followed before Dave and I set off at last for Banda Aceh.

I had noticed on several occasions a sign outside hotels that durians were not admitted. I thought to myself that sounds quite prejudicial. Who were durians? Perhaps they were some kind of tramp, aliens from another planet or homeless people. Eventually I found out that durians are a fruit. The smell is perhaps the most obnoxious smell this side of a sewage works gone wrong. They are sold as a delicacy at many street corners. They are rugby ball shaped and about the same size but with spikes. I approached carefully as one was cut open for me. I could feel my stomach beginning to rebel but the taste of the white fleshy interior was a delight. Eating or rather tasting gingerly I had to pinch my nose before doing so otherwise I would have vomited all over them there and then.

By way of some light entertainment I paid a visit to the zoo in Bogor. What an amazing place. Lions, Tigers and all manner of other four legged beasts had much freedom to roam. I had one of my most fantastic and memorable animal experiences whilst there. Lion and Tiger cubs were being made available for people to hold. I wanted one of each to take home. They were sweet. Their fur is so soft and the lion cubs' feet were biffing me ever so gently on my face. What an amazing feeling.

Our flight to Medan and on to Banda Aceh was uneventful. We were met by a driver from P. T. Semen Andalas who took us to Patrick's office. The drive there gave us an insight to the problems we were to encounter during the expedition. Heavily forested hillsides seemed to have no easy access. Mosquitoes ruled, both day and night.

Patrick was a great guy. He had arranged for us to rent a house for a month for £200, complete with cook. We were taken there and on the way visited the Andalas Club, an oasis of western culture. Facilities included swimming pool, squash courts and of course a bar. Aceh province is a 99% Fundamental Muslim area. As such alcohol is virtually unobtainable outside of the 'club' or one of the Chinese stores in town.

We settled into the house, which unfortunately did not have air conditioning, mulling over the next problem. Where could we hire a vehicle large enough to transport the whole team? Fortunately a most remarkable and forceful lady in charge of travel and accommodation at P. T. Andalas, called Cut Soraya, came to our rescue. She had tracked down a bus after we had spent a whole morning drawing blanks. The bus came complete with driver as it was made apparent that there were no self drive busses available. A deal again for £200 for the month was struck over a drink of orange. Five litres of petrol per day were included in the deal. Petrol cost around 80 pence per gallon.

Driving around was just as mad as in Jakarta. Everything in front of you has priority, cars, vans, busses, trucks, bikes even people lurching down the road. Vehicles turning in front of us had the right of way. Signaling your intentions to turn right or left doesn't seem to happen! An accident is sorted out and a deal struck on the spot as insurance appears to be nonexistent.

Left to right: Jim Hook, Steve Dickinson (Dickie), Dave Arveschoug, John Middlemist (Mouse) and me at our rented house in Banda Aceh during the Sumatra expedition in 1987

We were now almost ready to go caving. Dave and I had finalised all the arrangements three days prior to the rest of the team arriving. All that was left to do was to locate carbide or 'karbit' as it is known locally. It was a fairly easy process and we found a 12 digit, ten fingers and two thumbs, vendor who sold it to us very cheaply.

Our intention was to find a river cave before the other members arrived. As such Tony and Ken from P.T.S.A. showed us a large resurgence. It was known as the Krueng Raba (Raba River). We parked the vehicle some distance away and had to walk across several paddy fields along a system of bunds (walls) separating the fields. The river issued from a 10 metre wide porch quickly enlarging to over 30 metres. We noticed a narrow passage to the true left of the river. I started to traverse above the pool that guarded access towards it, suitably attired in a life jacket. The rock was soft and crumbly. Six metres across and 5 metres up the wall I fell off making a resounding splash as I hit the salty water. Jellyfish started to swarm towards me which indicated a rapid exit for me before I was stung.

Another entrance was located by continuing along the cliff line. By now rain was falling heavily. It did not matter though as we were both wet anyway. We entered an incredibly hot passage, the floor of which was muddy and overlaid by knee deep water. A climb over a stalagmite barrier after 50 metres led to more water and more jellyfish!

The following day a visit was made to the eastern side of the hills looking for a waterfall that reputedly issued from a hole. It had been seen from the air but no-one knew how to get there. Four of us, Pat and Ken from P.T. Andalas, Dave and I set off in a Toyota four wheel drive to try and find it. Alas, after 20 kilometres of bumping and grinding we drew a blank realising that we could not find it. Even walking to the top of one of a thousand hummocks we saw that the secondary jungle ahead quickly led into primary and impenetrable jungle. The waterfall became a myth whilst we were in Banda Aceh. It had been spotted on a flight from Medan a few months prior to our arrival but during our stay was not spotted again.

On the day before the rest of the team arrived Dave and I found another entrance to the Raba River much further to the right. On entering there was an immediate smell of animal with claw marks in the clay floor. The entrance crawl enlarged to a large walking sized passage and a chamber with water on the left with, thankfully, no jellyfish. Going straight on and then right along a dry crawl led us to a three metres drop. We climbed down into another passage. Porcupine quills were everywhere. We followed this pleasant sized passage into a chamber with tree roots and a daylight pitch of twelve metres. Beyond this point the cave sumped. Not surprisingly we called this cave Porcupine Cave. Although we found some pretty formations, including a splendid gour pool, we could not detect any draught that would have indicated more passage.

We arrived 'home' to find that John, Jim, Ken and Bob had arrived a day early! It was good to see them and fill them in on the frustrations of our explorations to date. The news that Dickie was due in two days, Edie and Cahyo due in four days and AG in seven meant we had to wait for another week to become up to strength.

Our next trips were to caves associated with the cement works complex. This we undertook together. We parked our vehicle beyond the quarry next to the filthy entrance to Bat Quarry Cave. Continuing on foot through the jungle of vines, trees, lurking spiders and loose earth we arrived at the foot of a hundred metres high cliff. We climbed up easily into a huge twilight aven about fifty metres high. Daylight flooded in from another huge entrance on the left. The walls were an emerald green and some huge scallops had developed when the cave was fed by a river. Beautiful calcite formations hung from the ceiling with a massive stalagmite boss to the left. We descended to the guano covered floor to find that the cave ended before it had really begun.

I spotted a low crawl leading off to the right just above floor level so before leaving I entered this and found it full of debris. After a couple of metres I came face to face with a somewhat large spider fully 16 centimetres across. I do not know who was more frightened, it or me. I beat a hasty retreat. It is a pity that as I write these lines the beauty of this cave will be no more as it was on the destruction file at the cement works. In Britain it could, maybe, have been saved from Dr Nobel and his linctus, but here there are no conservationists. We called this cave Cathedral Cave (the Cambridge University team called it Jungle Quarry Cave).

Leaving this cave we walked a further 2 kilometres into the jungle on a very vague track to 'Through Cave'. Although only 100 metres long it sported a large formation and a large guano pit to trap the unwary. Emerging we dropped down to a small valley and river where we had been told it sank. It did. The cloudy water from decayed vegetable matter disappeared into miserable choked fissures beneath huge piles of rotting logs.

Disappointed we spent the late afternoon 'hashing'. This is a bit like 'Hare and Hounds'. We had been invited by Pat so that we could meet other people living in the area. Hashing is a non competitive run of an hour or so around the bush by the hounds i.e. everybody except the hare who laid a paper trail. At the end of the run penalty drinking takes place. Penalties can involve drinking as much as one bottle of beer in one attempt. Failure accounts for another 'penalty' beer. This means everyone gets very drunk as no-one escapes penalties. Accolades are also given to certain people but again involve drinking, but a smaller amount. Everyone has a 'hashing name'. Mine was Bedrock! It was jolly good fun and ideal relaxation. Dickie had arrived from Singapore just in time for the hash and appreciated stretching his legs. We were to be invited on several more hashes as this was a weekly event.

Pat had been waxing lyrical about a huge river sink in a valley above the cement works. This was to be our next major objective because a hydrological survey had revealed a large doline in the valley floor. However, our first need was to find a cave called Gua Iluh.

The van driver had become somewhat unreliable, compounded by the fact that we ran out of petrol on the way to the valley. Petrol obtained, we continued to where we could drive no further. From the bus we fought our way through swamps and bushes disturbing millions of mosquitoes in the process, to the Raba River. We followed it upstream for 400 metres to the cliff face where we found four entrances within 8 metres. These were entered with varying degrees of success and leaving leads for another visit. One entrance we named Spider Cave as it sported another giant spider.

Returning to the van we walked along the valley floor and our hopes rose as we crested a shoulder. Ahead we could see a huge river cascading down and although 2 kilometres away we could hear the roar. It was obvious too that the water sank in the valley. Due to the rainfall the upper end of the valley was flooded so looking for sinks was impractical. Pat had never seen the river here before or the large lake that had formed. We did not descend into the doline as time was pressing as well as the thick jungle.

On nearing the van we met an excitable Ken Kelly. He had found a cave entrance. He had found Gua Iluh. We vowed to return the following day. He noted that it had been the home

Where do I go now? John Middlemist (Mouse) swimming in the Raba River during the Sumatra expedition in 1987 looking for a way in?

for someone as he had found enamel eating plates, some cutlery and a rudimentary fireplace had been constructed.

Unfortunately we had to split in to 3 teams the following day as many jobs needed doing. Bob, Jim and Ken were the lucky three to go caving. Dave and I went to try and sort out an excess baggage allowance and to confirm our return flight as some people had time schedules. Dave and I also visited the cement works in an effort to try and secure some decent maps. A company called Binny apparently had some so we arranged to visit there the following day. On the way back we found our two Indonesian cavers fresh off the flight from Medan.

On our return home we found that the caving team had had a reasonable day. They had found 500 metres of cave. When I visited the cave a few days later I found that a farmer lived in the entrance with the kitchenware. Progress was mainly by wading or swimming in the warm water. Several bats whirled around and I noticed that water levels fluctuated greatly here.

I continued pouring over maps trying to locate possible cave sites. Ken had somehow negotiated a deal with a local to hire his scooter. This was useful and Edie and Cahyo really enjoyed having this almost as their own personal transport. Further explorations of the Raba valley did not reveal an awful lot although many sinks were found they were largely impenetrable due to the amount of flood debris accumulated.

The following days were somewhat fragmented. Various small teams disappeared into the jungle whilst others drove down the coast asking the locals if any caves were known in their area. John and I went back to the Raba resurgence determined to find a way on in what was possibly the best lead in finding a big cave. John displayed his cowboy techniques by lassoing a tree branch sticking outwards 6 metres up an overhanging wall. Prussiking up to this he continued with difficulty at first along an overhung ledge to where it widened and where he noticed a cave entrance. We were excited. Disappointingly the entrance turned out to be just a 10 metres deep depression. John looked really hot as he asked me to lower him down, so to cool him down I lowered him unceremoniously into the river.

As John scrambled to the bank Dickie and Jim appeared. They had completed a through trip on Gua Iluh. They were partly elated and partly depressed because the through trip linking the entrances had halved the number of caves we had found. Dickie noted in his write up that I was termed 'Big Bear'. Dickie and I went back to survey but found that the tape was less than useful as Dickie appeared to be drowning with the weight of it. We had to make do with scratch marks in the mud as Dickie slid down vertical walls into the fetid water. I guess we were able to do the survey with around 80% accuracy. We noticed on the way back that water levels had dropped by 80 centimetres. Clearly water levels were prone to very rapid fluctuations.

We were now thinking about another area when a worker from Binny's told us that he had heard about lots of draughting caves near Takengon at a place called Laut (Lake) Tawar. However, this was 480 kilometres away. I decided that 3 members of the team should investigate. I went to the Minister of Tourism to try and obtain the necessary permits for this but he was less than helpful. We would need another fistful of documents but he did give me a list of caves and also suggested the Sigli area.

The Minister relented and gave us guidelines for exploring these other areas. AG arrived as we were all about to go in different directions to find caves. John and Dave went off to Takengon reporting back 3 days later that there was absolutely nothing there. It would be a complete waste of time visiting the area.

By now I was feeling really ill as was Dickie. I missed the hash. Incessant torrential rain fell, streets were awash and the mosquitoes even more terrifying. Dave and John arrived back and were somewhat fed up. As I was feeling dead rough the team decided to go to Langsa. The house was packed up, cook, van driver paid and Dave and I retired to Tony and Claire's house as Dave was starting to feel rough.

The Langsa team again had very little success in finding caves but they did have, in AG's words, 'a cracking adventure'. It was confirmed that I had a dose of Dengue Fever not the dangerous sort though. Dickie, however, became very ill as he went down with the dangerous Haemorrhagic Dengue Fever. He needed 3 pints of blood in Medan hospital. All in all not a very successful caving expedition but while recuperating at Tony and Claire's I did learn how to water ski!

Chapter 10

Mendip, Forest of Dean and Soloing

Being a primarily northern caver Mendip and the Forest of Dean seemed a long way away. As such I only made one trip to Mendip before moving to South Wales but never to the Forest of Dean caves. However, when I started doing work for the Leadership Trust and based in Ross on Wye these two areas were on the doorstep. I always thought that the Forest of Dean caves were horrible muddy grovels little bigger than a badger sett! This remained the case even when I started work at the Trust as the caves we used at Symonds Yat were grovels. My opinion, though, changed soon after. The Forest does have some quite remarkable caves. The Slaughter Stream Cave is one such cave and starts of vertically before coming horizontal. The discovery of this system came about by sheer perseverance. Digging commenced at Wet Sink in the 1950's. After sporadic work at the site the big breakthroughs took place during April and December 1990. Although the cave is gated the key is easily obtained. Another good thing about this cave is the fact that there is a good pub nearby, the Dog and Muffler, making a fine end to an evening underground.

My first trip there was very soon after the

breakthroughs. It felt new too. Going in with Greg Jones, Colin Beechey and some fellow instructors from the Trust we ended up going to Sump 3 before retiring to the pub. There was only one snug bit and that occurred just after the locked gate. The fine 'Balcony Pitch' was very reminiscent of a Yorkshire pitch being big and airy but only 13 metres deep. Although it was only a three and a half hours trip it was a fine introduction to the cave. On another trip a couple of months later I went in an upstream direction to the large 'Flow Choke Passage'. Towards the end of the year I took Tim Nash, a son of my girlfriend Nona on one of his first caving trips to 'Sump 3'.

It was another 3 years before I went in again with Greg. This time we went into 'Pirate Passage' This was a very fine trip indeed with, at one point, a very awkward and tight climb up to enter the very long rift passage. On the way back I found a less snug bypass to this climb! Starting life large the rift shrinks to become a gravel crawl that becomes very wet and unpleasant towards the end. Once we were lying flat it was deemed to be the end of sensible progress as the passage ends very quickly after that.

Although I was taking groups into the miserable grovels of Symonds Yat it was not until August 2004 that I visited another of the Forest's gems, Miss Grace's Lane Cave with John Elliot. John is a very good caver, small and very thin he fits through the smallest holes. What he does not know about the caves in the Forest is not worth knowing. This was a caving trip through boulders with some solid walls on occasion! The entrance shaft has a fixed steel ladder. I was told that if we were to climb down the ladders the first set finished six metres down and a step to the side on to the next section of ladder would enable the rest of the shaft to be descended without further ado. I thought this a bit daft so we decided to abseil down but climb back up the ladders on the way out. It was easy to rig the rope in a 'Y' hang so that the rope hung freely down. Our trip ended quite a long way in at the beautifully sculpted 'Phreatic Causeway' a passage in solid rock!

Other than the various mines they were the only caves I did in the Forest although I did a couple of caving assessments in the squalid Seymour Swallet. Wigpool Iron Mine is an interesting trip especially the round trip from Meeks Entrance through to Steam Entrance. In one particular part there are some very fine pure white calcite formations that contrast sharply with the redness of the rock. Noxon Park Iron Mine was memorable for the huge lake that had flooded the lower levels. There were also many Greater Horseshoe Bats in the mine. The only other mine I visited on many occasions Old Ham Iron Mine. This became used by the Leadership Trust for their introductory caving trips in favour of the caves at Symonds Yat.

I had always been put off going to the Mendips due to the long distance to travel and the fact that access is often difficult. Many of the caves have gates and keys are needed. Forward planning is required as these trips have to be pre-booked often some six weeks in advance of any trip. Not only that but some landowners had closed many good caves forbidding any access. The access procedures are in place to try and reduce the amount of damage that inevitably gets done. Whilst the leader system ensures that formations are kept intact the best experience possible can be achieved.

In January 1986 I made my first visit to the area with Dave Gill and, I suppose as with many other cavers, my first trip was to the superb Swildon's Hole. The cave has a lovely stream-way punctuated by the usually very wet 'Twenty Foot' pitch. Just before reaching 'Sump 1' we climbed up into the roof to 'Tratman's Temple' and continued on to 'Blue Pencil Passage' via 'St. Pauls'. 'Blue Pencil' was not for me. It is tight! Fortunately we did not have this on the itinerary that day. Many of the Mendip caves generally tend to be much tighter than in other areas. They also gain depth very quickly due to the dip of the limestone bedding.

We had gone down to visit the late Tony Jarratt a very respected and experienced caver who lived in Priddy. He also owned Bat Products, a cavers shop in Wells. Having come back from Swildon's we washed and brushed ourselves up before devouring an excellent dinner. We then settled ourselves by the comforting warmth of an open fire and into our fourth bottle of wine. The fire gave out much heat as flames danced high up the chimney ensuring almost instant drowsiness when suddenly the phone rang rousing us into some sort of wakefulness. Our euphoria was about to be disturbed. It was the rescue team they wanted Tony on a difficult rescue in Longwood. Tony explained that he had friends visiting from Derbyshire. He told the caller we were three quarters cut and could not possibly get there. The excuse fell on deaf ears, so would we also go along and help!

We agreed and stumbled out into a wet and black night. On arrival at the cave we were told a young caver had entered the cave ealier in the day. He had also just bought a new wet suit that day. Having passed through the tight and awkward bit in the entrance series a boulder chamber is entered. A boulder had chosen that time to fall and hit the poor lad in the chest and killed him. The rescue team was having trouble extracting the body through the tight bit. However, this was quickly sorted out and the body emerged. Once the formalities were finalised we drove, sobered by now, back to the flickering flames of Tony's fire to sink some more bottles of wine. Rising late as caver's do we went in the early afternoon to G. B. Cavern, a fine cave with some pretty formations. I seem to remember seeing a crushed yellow mini in a boulder choke. I am not too sure where this was now but it did strike me as unusual at the time and wondered how it had got there in the first place. Perhaps I was halucinating?

I have had many trips into Swildon's as it can be refreshingly wet. It is also pretty and fun. On one memorable occasion I went there with Mike Davies the Head of Argoed Lwyd Outdoor Centre at Libanus near Brecon. It is one of the outdoor centres for Hampshire County Council. Rebecca (Becca) Smith one of Mikes staff came too. Mike was not too enamoured by caving, preferring instead to be out on the hill in the fresh air but he needed to do a few caving trips to gain his Local Cave Leader Level 1 award. It was a lovely warm day and we entered the cave. All went well until we reached the 'Double Pots'. These are shallow pools near the bottom and follow on one after the other. To reach them they are each descended by climbing down their left hand walls. This is where Mike became, in the true tradition of Mendip caving a fully baptised 'Son of Mendip'. Oh, and he didn't like water either!

On arrival at Sump 1 we all felt somewhat breathless and I thought that we had not rushed that much so why were we so out of breath? Anyhow thinking nothing more about it we started, what turned out to be quite a laboured climb back out to the surface. On the way out Mike became immersed in water cascading down the 'Twenty' as he climbed up the short ladder pitch, thus adding to his misery. On arrival into the glorious sunshine I said to Mike 'did you feel breathless in there' to which he replied 'yes'. Short on words but to the point being relieved to be back in daylight again. I had realised on the way out, when my mind became less muddled, that under certain conditions carbon dioxide builds up. I explained it was this that had made us feel tired and lethargic. The up side was, despite his wettings, Mike had enjoyed the experience

With a fortuitous move to South Wales the Mendips were much more accessible plus the fact Andy Sparrow one of the instructors at the Trust was an excellent caver and was keen to show me some delights of the area. Knowing my liking of S.R.T. he took me to the fine Rhino Rift, an unusual cave for Mendip as it is vertical! Although we did not go to the bitter end, as the final bit is very tight, we stopped at the bottom of the third pitch. On another occasion we did another vertical trip, 'High Atlas' in Thrupe Lane Swallet. This cave had defeated me previously as unknowing about Atlas I had tried to do descend the cave via 'Perseverance Pot', a tightish wriggle down. Atlas turned out to be a magnificent trip and our return was via 'Slither Pot'. So far Mendip caving had been a very pleasant experience.

We next did Manor Farm Swallet or as some wags say Manure Farm Swallet. It turned out to be a great trip and descends quickly down dip to 'Florence's Bathtub' the sump at the end of the cave. I had enjoyed both this and Swildon's so decided to solo them albeit on separate occasions when on my own in the area.

Solo caving is safe provided precautions are taken. Unlike solo rock climbing rescue after falling or becoming trapped by flood water underground is much trickier. It is important to have more than one light source and I always took three. Most importantly it is mandatory to tell someone where you are going and what time you will be out. I have enjoyed being underground on my own many times as well as greatly enjoying solo rock climbing.

Moving around on rock uncluttered by equipment gives me a great sense of complete freedom. Solo caving, however, still needs equipment such as ropes especially if doing an S.R.T. trip and survival gear so the feeling of complete freedom is absent as at a minimum two bags need to be lugged around. Although only soloing one cave a day when I chose to, on a climbing note I did manage to solo 100 rock climbs from Difficult to Hard Very Severe on Stanage in September 1983. A thoroughly amazing and euphoric day with much adrenaline flowing. I believe that anyone, who has the skill, experience and wants to, is able to solo at whatever standard they are happy with whether it is a cave, rock climb, high mountain or even a remote mountain walk.

The two prettiest trips I did on Mendip were firstly St Cuthbert's Swallet with Andy on a couple of occasions and secondly Shatter Cave with Chris Binding. This last was totally amazing with some of the most fantastic formations in any cave in Britain excepting, of course, for Otter Hole. That said there are some extraordinary formations in many of the caves in Britain.

On an instructional side I found that Goatchurch Cavern, perhaps the most popular cave on Mendip, to be a very agreeable and dry trip although the limestone has a mirror finish due to many thousands of people rummaging about. It has everything required for the first day of a Local Cave Leader Level 1 trip. Estimates say that some 36,000 people a year visit Goatchurch! Sidcot Swallet is another beginner's trip on the opposite side of the West Twin Brook valley to Goatchurch. At one place there is an awkward bit called 'The Lobster Pot'. It is easy to descend as lobsters know to their cost but devilishly difficult to climb out. The bell shaped and shallow pit is quite tight at the top and the walls are somewhat smooth. Much effort, cursing and perhaps some help from below are needed to exit. Even using a hand-line or a ladder escape is difficult but good fun nevertheless! Although the Mendips are not my favourite caving area I did have some really great times and trips, preferring instead the technical S.R.T. side of the sport.

One other thing about the Mendips I liked is the great social scene. A visit here usually ended up with a visit to the remarkable Hunters Inn at Priddy. Beer is served directly from the barrel, my favourite was always Butcombe which after only 3 or 4 pints my head started to spin especially without food. Here again the food in the Hunters is amazing and soaks up beer so that it is possible to drink even more! The cheese sandwiches are well over an inch thick with hand cut bread and the pie and peas are to say the least astonishingly good value for money. Traditional bar games are played here, bar skittles, dominoes, darts and shove ha'penny are the ones I remember.

Chapter 11

Instructed Caving

I had become qualified as a climbing and mountaineering instructor in May 1969 during a week long assessment in North Wales. This was a fun experience as we climbed every day. One of the candidates was called Ken Hosie and the other was Harvey Aspindale who met an untimely death on the Petit Dru. This qualification stood me in great stead as I gradually built up private clientele whilst undertaking small household jobs for people.

Geoff Arkless was our assessor. He was a genial chap and was a stickler for instructors climbing in the footwear that clients were going to be using. To that end we ended up doing a route called Diagonal a very fine Hard Very Severe on Dinas Mot in Llanberis Pass in boots. A few years later I did this again wearing rock shoes this time and wondered how on earth I had stayed on the rock. We followed this climb with West Rib an even harder climb. This I did again in 2002 and had the greatest difficulty on the main pitch not helped by a recent re-surfacing of my right hip.

During a visit to the Alps for 3 months in 1972 I was bivouacking outside the Argentiere Hut with Calvin Torrans in preparation for the North Face of the Aiguille de Triolet. Calvin was a really good climber from Ireland who had moved to Kendal to be nearer the mountains. He was a postman there and we often climbed together either in the Lakes or in Yorkshire. It was a cold and clear night and it was important to set off early as the forecast intimated that the following was going to be fine, warm and sunny. Also at the hut was Bill March. We talked outside before he and his mate went inside for their sleep in the warmth!

I was flushed with success having just climbed the difficult North Face of the Aiguille du Plan with Dick Renshaw. This was a serious climb and much more difficult as it turned out than the Triolet. We bivouacked at the start of the ice having climbed the rock intro. The climb was graded as a 'Difficile' but we both felt that 'Tres Difficile plus' would be a far more appropriate grade. The serac barrier at the two thirds height proved the most difficult where I was thankful that it was Dick who was leading at the time. To surmount the barrier he used 5 ice screws for direct aid. We had taken 13 hours.

The really pleasant thing about having climbed this north face was the ensuing ridge traverse from the summit of the Aiguille du Plan 3,673 metres to the Aiguille du Midi 3,841 metres arête in moonlight. The lights of Chamonix twinkled far below before grey cloud obscured the view. Head torches seemed superfluous in the bright clear night. Reaching the telepherique station on the Aiguille du Midi having come along a fine snow arête we found a friendly guardian who allowed use of a room. We caught the first cable car down to Chamonix where we feasted on lovely French pastries.

The 18 hour climb on the Triolet was superb. Lots of water ice with many stretches of 65 – 70 degree ice with a short steeper section of 75 degrees. We were, unfortunately, delayed for a couple of hours helping an

American climber who had fallen off in front of us. He had taken a 150 foot 'winger' ending up with a twisted ankle. The single ice screw he had placed for protection luckily held, otherwise I feel he would have been in a much worse condition. It was a graceful, slow motion fall as he swooped down without a sound and swung on the ice screw. We bivouacked on the descent near to Pointe Isabella

Back in Chamonix I met Bill again. He asked how long I was going to be in Chamonix and said I was staying another couple of weeks. He then asked what I was going to do when I returned to the UK. I told him that I had no idea whatsoever. His immediate words were 'come up to the Lodge and I'll give you a job'! (The Lodge is Glenmore Lodge). He was the deputy principal there. I went and he did. I learnt a great deal working there from the likes of Bill, Johnny Cunningham and Fred Harper, the principal. It was the first time I had worked for a Centre. After a while you know pretty much what you will be doing each Tuesday, Wednesday and Thursday on a regular adventure week.

However, the Lodge was different in that they ran far more specialist courses. I always remember Fred's words on a briefing before some Glasgow schoolgirls descended on the place 'You are professional people. As such you must always be professional with your clients and no messing around'. These words have stuck with me ever since in whatever Centre or trip I have been involved with, although at times, I have to admit it was difficult. It was a great place to work as all the instructors were keen, helpful and keen to share their knowledge and experience.

Living in Buxton was fun. My caving exploits had been noted and I became involved with instructed caving at Whitehall. It became apparent that to lend credibility to my taking people underground I needed a caving qualification. This happened, but as late as 1986 when I gained my Local Cave Leader level 2 award, as my experience had always been taken for granted, especially after Nare. However, being good at an activity is no guarantee that you have the soft personal skills needed to help others to achieve. Patience, I feel is of greatest importance, being able to encourage, support as well as being able to say that we will not do such and such a trip if conditions did not permit it to take place. Being knowledgeable about your activity is also very important and being able to relate stories about your adventures.

Too often people have the need to go out in unsuitable weather conditions not only putting their lives at risk but others too. Having paid money to a company, or whoever, they expect success no matter what. This applies equally to people going out for fun. Because they may have spent a fortune on petrol they often go out in atrocious conditions when it would be far more prudent to stay at home or go to the pub. Caves and mountains will be there long after mine and their lifetime.

It is often much more difficult to say no than yes. I believe that any instructor has the right to say no if they feel that conditions are not right, even it means deviating from a set programme.

There are increasing levels of caving qualifications. The basic level is Local Cave Leader level 1. The next higher qualification is level 2 and the third tier, Caving Instructor Certificate (C.I.C.). These awards were originally designed for cavers to gain a formal qualification to 'prove' they were experienced! This has now changed so that a person working for a Centre who needs a caving qualification goes through a process of training and consolidation prior to assessment. In 1997 experience seemed to go out of the window to become an instructor. The need for all instructors to have a formal qualification became necessary. Centres also needed to have a license and this was implemented by the Adventure Activity Licensing Authority. As such Heads of Centres had to ensure that all their staff had the right qualification for whatever discipline they were instructing and at the appropriate level.

This, to my mind is an anathema to the ethos of why many of us became instructors for whatever activity, whether it be canoeing, climbing, walking or caving in the first place. I along with many others of my peers became instructors because we loved being in the outdoors climbing, caving or whatever. The standards that are being asked at the lower end are ridiculously low. I cannot believe that a person can become a qualified caver, albeit at the lower level, after only 30 trips. This includes 10 different caves in two regions. How on earth can they have the experience to enthuse others? How can they have experienced all that water, route finding and objective dangers that caves can throw at them? In my mind there is no substitute for experience. Many candidates presented themselves with only the required basis for assessment but the trips shown in their log books were not what I would call caving trips at all being short very easy ones. Very few candidates showed real caving experience in big caves taking several hours.

The Local Cave Leader is as it says, local. By local I mean local to one particular caving area. The areas are Devon and Cornwall, Mendip, South Wales, North Wales, Derbyshire and Yorkshire. It is possible to have two or more 'local' areas as part of a Local Cave Leader award but generally only one.

However, the C.I.C. does ensure that candidates have a high level of skill and the people having this are cavers. A person with a C.I.C. is able to work in any area of Britain. I decided to go through this process after a discussion with Dave Edwards and having applied for exemption to parts of the assessment. I was fortunate to get exemption to 5 days of the assessment process and only undertook 3. This I did with Dave Elliot in April 1991.

Mines are used by some Outdoor Centres for their underground sessions. As such there are similar levels of qualifications as in Local Mine Leader at level 1 or 2, Mine Instructor or Cave Instructor with mines endorsement. Mines used for underground experiences take place in a variety of different types, including lead, slate, copper, iron and stone.

I was caving regularly at various Centres in Derbyshire from 1982 and whilst I only gained my C.I.C. in April 1991 I had been taking people on European adventures, relying on my skill and experience to ensure that nothing went wrong.

To have fun is important. On one occasion I had a group for an easy trip into the entrance series in P8. There was another group of people from another centre who were also going in changing into their oversuits and helmets at the road side. In a jocular moment I said to the group that this group had the lights on their helmets wrongly positioned. I told my group that lights needed to be on the back of the head and not on the front so that the person behind could see where they were going. The group swallowed this hook, line and fishing rod and duly put their helmets on back to front with their lights pointing backwards. The looks we received as we set off were ones of total disbelief, but it was fun. Fortunately I knew the leader of the other group who looked away and had a good laugh to himself. I was pleased that he kept quiet. Needless to say we did change the lights around once out of sight and before we entered the cave.

Another incident this time in Giants Hole was when I took a group of Youth Training Scheme youngsters there. We had admired the plunging water down 'Garlands Pot' and had returned upstream to 'Base Camp Chamber'. A 2 metres high climb up from here enters the 'Wet Inlet'. From the ledge at the top of the climb a high but very narrow sinuous section of cave continues and becomes tight after 50 metres. I had wriggled through this and pulled the larger youngsters through the narrower section before moving on. The passage became wider and much easier terminating in a wonderful black pool. Water appeared not to be flowing in but water was flowing out having being forced up inexorably and silent.

I was standing on holds above the pool when one of the girls appeared, her face covered in blood. My heart started to race and wondered what had happened to her. Had she slipped and banged her head receiving a severe wound? No, she had had a nose bleed and had smeared blood all over her face to wind me up. We laughed, but it felt very serious at the time.

One of the most memorable trips was in July 1988. I was working for Buxton Activity Centre at the time and had introduced some people from Warrington to the delights of the dark vertical world. The owners of Centre, Bill Mountford and his wife Wendy was enthusiastic for me to organise a Vercors trip. This was quickly arranged and at the beginning of the month 8 of us set off in the newer of the Centres mini-busses. Apart from Bill there was Dave Curry, Graham, Rick, Martin, another Dave, Myself and my girlfriend Brenda.

Our first excursion was the trouser filling descent of the Scialet de Malaterre. This proved a huge hit with the team. We chose this as rain was falling as we woke, as it had overnight, in torrents. The river running beside Madam

Lattard's campsite had risen and continued to do so all day. Luck was on our side because just as we arrived the rain stopped and out came that wonderful yellow orb in the sky. Although the walls of the shaft were wet it did not pose any problem to us.

We followed this with the equally fine and different Glaciere d'Autrans. I found that this year ice was much more apparent and I had to dig for the belays above the 'Puits de Glace' that were buried below the water ice. A wonderful, if slippery descent, was made to the base of the shaft where more ice lead down to the quick succession of large pitches where the ice disappeared but flowing water appeared! A damp descent ensued to the start of the nasty tight meanders below. Back on the surface we entered the Patinoire, the left hand entrance, and explored that. We found the passage that took us to overlook the Puits de Glace. Other passages took us along rough, almost like coral, snug calcited meanders that had water trickling along the floor.

Our next adventure was the normal trip in the Trou qui Souffle, the 'Reseau Bourgin' to the siphon at -220 metres. This too had more water than in previous years. For a party of eight I was impressed with how short the trip was. The first one out took 5 hours and the last 7 hours. It was a glorious exit into wonderful hot sunshine. As the entrance is actually in the road care needs to be exercised on exiting. Dave Curry nearly had his hand run over as a tractor rounded the bend and almost careered into the hole as he was pulling himself out.

No trip to the Vercors should miss out on the superb Grotte de Gournier. After all the trips I had done there I was still awed by the amazing entrance. I went on the boat first to rig the traverse. The others followed dutifully and we were all quickly wandering along the huge galleries. All that could be heard were the ooos and ahhhs of everyone goggling at the huge formations. I quickly found the right hole to climb down after an hour of walking in the vast gallery. Although water levels were still very high we all made it to the third wire traverse before I decided that this would be a good point to turn around and head out. After more oooing and ahhhing we reached daylight entering into a scorching hot sunlit world.

That is one good thing about summer caving in France. It is really pleasant to reach daylight and feel the warmth of the sun burning into your body making over-suits steam. There is always the fresh smell of air as daylight is approached, one of the most wonderful sensations that a caver feels.

I was very impressed with how the team was reacting to the trips. Not only was everyone coping well with the technicalities, but they were adept at keeping their carbide lights lit. In those days up to the early 2000's carbide lighting was de rigueur. They were difficult to get used to but my team was coping well. The problem being, of course, with carbide that it is a pollutant. In all the French caves grey deposits of spent carbide are seen. As the rock dissolves in the generator it shrinks to produce a grey, dry powder. Unfortunately many people just tip it out over the floor. Once all the rock is dissolved you have to replenish the generator with more. The advantage of course with a metal generator of the Fisma type is that the container becomes warm and makes a really good hand warmer or body warmer. Carbide lighting thankfully is replaced nowadays with much more cave friendly LED lights, so hopefully the spent carbide deposits in caves will disappear over time. Although LED's give a colder light they give a white glow rather than a beam giving a greater definition to passages.

I digress, back to the caving. After a day of walking in the mountains we went for the Scialet de l'Appel. Although the pitches are short they are quite awkward and we reached the 'Brudour' sump in double quick time. This allowed us to visit the Glaciere de Fontd'Urle on the way back. Not a great trip as it is over rather too quickly. Because the team was working well together I decided that Pot Deux was to be the final trip but before that shopping needed doing. I had not done this pot before and was eager to venture forth. After going to Grenoble, why, I don't know but we went there instead of shopping locally. On the way back we drove to the parking area for a look at the Grotte de Bournillon. Surprise, surprise, water was flooding out of the entrance and the normal way in was impractical. We entered high up on the right and went a very short way before heading back out.

Pot Deux day dawned bright and clear. I reasoned with the team that we needed a leisurely start as the trip would be an overnight affair. It was indeed leisurely. Ropes needed to be bagged, lots of them as the vertical shaft is over 300 metres deep. We did not leave Madame Lattard's camp site until 15.00. Armed with food, some sleeping gear and caving bags the walk to the cave was interesting to say the least. No worn path. We took the Darbounouse route as recommended by Marbach at Expe, a marvelous local caving and climbing supplies emporium not far from Pont en Royans.

It was hot and humid and as we approached the Pre du Rey rolls of thunder could be heard rumbling away in the far distance. As we gained height the way became rougher and more tortuous weaving between huge bluffs of rough, sharp limestone. We had entered the area known as 'le Purgatoire', a very apt name for such a chaotic place. Up and down small cliffs, stepping over huge clints and grykes following faint orange markers then red ones until I thought we had gone high enough. We were looking for a huge depression. It had become misty to add to the misery of finding the hole. There were so many depressions and so many trees. The guide book stated that the hole was situated in a huge depression by a tree. Well, not only were there many depressions that fitted that particular description, there were several thousand trees too! Each depression was looked at whilst one person stayed with the sacs to guide us back from the search in the mist.

The mist thankfully cleared and we soon found ourselves looking at a depression close to the Pas Morta. This is recognized by a huge white cliff facing east. There were the remains of a wooden hut in the depression. Ah, I thought we were close. Pot Deux is found some 300 metres west of the hut beyond the rim of the depression and close to a U.L.S.A. 82 sign (Scialet U.L.S.A. 1). We found the shaft as the guide book said next to a tree, one of thousands! Other pine trees ringed the shaft.

I was glad we had found it relatively quickly as I had heard that some people never find it and blunder all over 'le Purgatoire' for hours before giving up. The entrance to the shaft is of small dimensions and was surrounded by a decaying log and wire fence. It had taken us 3½ hours to reach the hole. We rested a long time before I began to rig the way down. It is such a large dimensioned shaft that there must be a way on somewhere. I almost made a mistake in the rigging realising very quickly that a bridge in the shaft needs to be rigged on the right facing the rock. I had set off on the left but almost immediately realised there were no spits to screw my hangers into. If I had continued down there would have been a serious rub point.

I reached an alcove where there was plethora of spits.

Most were useless being rusted relics. Below the ledge spits were very few and far between. It was still a long way to the floor. One hanger was placed 30m down below the ledge and another 15 metres below that. So that was it. One hanger for a 100 metre drop complete with a knot to pass 25 metres above the floor! That was interesting to say the least. I reached the flat stony bottom in 2 hours. Rick, Martin and Graham were the only other ones to join me there. It took me 1¾ hours for the journey out. Bill and Dave N reached the alcove and Dave C to the final re-belay. Seeing the others on the rope in various stages of descent seemed as though I was out in a starry night. I was sure the large dimensioned shaft must continue, but where is the way on?

The de-rigging team reached the surface at 07.50 emerging into a thick mist. For some it was a very painful walk back to the mini bus with the crossing of 'le Purgatoire' still just as difficult to cross as it ever was. We all missed the markers on the way back so we just headed straight down the hill until we burst on to the GR, (Grande Randonee). The following day we tidied and packed the bus for the journey home celebrating at night in the Auberge la Balme with a huge meal and too many bottles of wine. It had been a very successful trip.

Doing trips like this is the cream of being at the top of your sport. Much of the time it is repetitive stuff like going into Porth yr Ogof, Carlswark or Lower Long Churn, both heavily used novice caves in South Wales, the Peak District and the Yorkshire Dales. Being able to find odd ways of having fun is very necessary.

As I mentioned above instructing should be fun and not a chore. I have always been enthusiastic when taking groups out. I had no desire to return indoors for a 'proper' job being frequently asked when I was going to settle down and get a proper job, especially my mum who probably despaired of me for much of her life as I was always going off somewhere. If it wasn't climbing or caving it was taking groups trekking and climbing in Europe, East Africa, Himalaya or Karakoram. My 'proper' jobs always seem to tie me down. I left school and started an apprenticeship as a joiner. However, I stopped that after only a few months because the owner would not let me go to college and the pay was dire, £2.10.0 (£2.50) for a 6 day week. The second proper job was when I worked for the now long lost 'K' shoes as a pattern maker. I hated the clocking in and out 4 times a day. Towards the end I was very much on the wrong side of the department foreman as I was always out climbing.

It was always fun to run my own S.R.T. training courses and to take these clients to places that were dramatic and real. They were full of adventure. With caving there is a risk as too in rock climbing. I feel though that the risks in climbing are slowly being eroded away. Just note the plethora of bolted climbs that take much of the angst away from the effects of a fall. I am all for safety but it is being able to recognise what is safe and what is not. Experience is the only way to find out and getting in to scrapes and being able to find a way out of any given predicament. In a word this is called survival and lessons are learned from that experience. You don't get in to that one again. As more and more experiences are survived the chances of not being caught out are greatly increased. However, to have adventure there must be risk. Without that it is just a sanitised and cotton wool version. Accidents will always happen of course and I hoped that none would happen to me. A rogue stone falling from high, rock hold breaking, a slip, any of these that can injure people make for a difficult rescue if underground.

I have always thought the modern trend of having rope courses and on site activities moves away from the ethos of adventure or 'real' outdoor activities. Centres should remain places of Outdoor Education but insist doing increasingly more on site activities. OK, I agree there is a thrill in doing a trapeze jump or a zooming down a zip wire, but in real terms it is just a cheap thrill that can be had at any of the burgeoning rope courses springing up around the country.

Another very enjoyable trip was helping a friend of mine, Andy Sparrow, run a trip to Slovenia. Andy is well known for producing an excellent series of videos on cave safety. Called Cave Safe he made three. Each one dealt with different aspects of caving from horizontal progression without vertical pitches to the ins and outs of S.R.T. He also produced a great instructional book.

His clients were Peter Flanagan, Derek Thick and Graham Bazely. Our base for the trip was to be at the Speleo Camp near to Laze. The car Andy had hired was somewhat too small for our needs so I paid extra for a VW Jetta instead of the Yugo Koral. We were met by Franc Fucidj at his house. He showed us the recently completed bunkhouse which was ours for the week. It was, simply, superb. We were then entreated to a true Slovenian greeting, Schnapps and as much beer as we could pour down our throats. I for one was totally off this planet by the time we went to bed at 01.00.

Surprisingly I was up at 08.00 to find the sun shining. Franc supplied breakfast of bread and home made jam before he took us to our first cave, Planinska Jama. The entrance to this cave is huge being some 40 metres high and 30 metres wide. A walkway lead to the actual entrance before it continued to the locked gate barring the way in. The made up path was built by the Italians under

Mussolini around 1936. His idea was to go to the end of the cave and bore a tunnel into Postojna Jama so that he could transport tanks into Austria!

What a preposterous idea. We continued easily along the path in a magnificent tunnel with only one awkward step to the river. We crossed the shallow water to a 6 seater inflatable boat. A rip in the floor was quickly repaired. The next 1000 metres was delightful as we slowly paddled upstream. We noticed many 'Proteus Anguinas' swimming in the water. These salamander like creatures were a light pink in colour and totally oblivious to light. All too soon we reached the end of the main passage called 'Pivski Rokav'. Just before the sump at the end of the passage a landing gave us access to a narrow, low and muddy passage. This appeared to end but after a short 3 metres climb we entered a most beautifully decorated passage with sparkling calcite everywhere. Breathtaking formations followed more breathtaking formations. No wonder this is called 'Paradise'.

The trip into this cave took 5 hours. Having more hours left in the day we drove to Rakov Skocjan, after lunch in Postojna, to look at the very impressive natural rock bridges. Zelska Jama another river cave is found below these bridges in the bottom of the huge doline. Exploration of this cave necessitates a long swim or by using a boat. We left this for another visit.

The following day found us all, apart from Andy, at a cave called Logarcek which is very close to Laze and a 10 minute walk. The 20 metres deep entrance pitch is directly below a power line. A re-belay splits the pitch 6 metres down. It was difficult to find the way on from the bottom. I eventually found it by climbing up a stalagmite slope a short way to a ledge which we followed to reach a small hole and short crawl. Walking passage continued until we reached a steep, downward calcite slope some 30 metres long. I fixed a rope for this climb down. Facing up from where we had come we went right along an impressive but very muddy passage over a mud bridge to enter a rather large and impressive chamber full of mud with no obvious way on.

We returned to the climb and turned left. There were some quite good formations along the way but it was still grossly muddy underfoot. After a few hundred metres we beat a hasty retreat as there was an overpowering smell of diesel. Andy had agreed to meet us at the cave at 13.00 but by 13.25 there was no sign of him. This meant we walked back and we had just arrived when Andy appeared minus the car. He had had a puncture in the woods. The spanner supplied with the car did not fit so we borrowed one from Franc.

The puncture was quickly repaired so after a quick lunch we went to the Postojna show cave. What an amazing place this turned out to be but it was not, in my opinion, the best show cave we visited, although it was the most impressive one I had so far visited. The journey into the cave commenced with a 10 minute train journey through a veritable forest of stalagmites to 'Central Station'. Here we disembarked and walked through a kilometre of galleries with stupendous calcite formations. The whole trip took about 1¼ hours and was well worth the money.

On the way back to the entrance we visited an enormous chamber having chandeliers hanging from the ceiling. Yes, real chandeliers. Apparently they hold concerts in the chamber that can hold 10,000 people! On the train journey back we went past areas that had obviously seen some great explosions as the walls were heavily soot encrusted. The cave had been used as a plane fuel store by the Nazi Occupation. On the 23rd April 1944 a group of partisans who knew the system well set fire to it. The resulting fire produced a huge black cloud of smoke causing everything in that area to become black, walls, formations, everything. The fuel burned for 7 days.

Our next adventure was to Krizna Kama an extraordinary cave. Again we had to have a leader. Our guide for this trip was a girl called Martina a lovely girl who was studying geography but cave guiding in her spare time.

It was a 35 minute drive to Bloska Polica followed by a walk of 10 minutes to the changing rooms at the entrance to the cave where we were all given waders. I was impressed. The entrance gate was a very substantial affair. Beyond this a flight of stairs lead down into the cave and followed by a walk of some 500 metres to the river. Here we found a 6 seater boat (I'm glad there was no more of us as everything seemed to revolve around 6). On the way to the boat we were shown 'Bear Gallery' where the remains of Ursa Spaeleus are to be found encrusted in to the calcite. Estimates put these remains at 200,000 years old.

A short boat ride was followed by an equally short walk to where there were two, three seater rafts. They were fastened high up the wall presumably to avoid being washed away. Martina winched them down from their anchorage near the ceiling. Boarding these we set off to explore the rest of the cave by following the river which was not very deep. We were all very glad to be wearing waders as we had to get out of the rafts periodically to manoeuvre them over calcite dams. Formations grew in quantity and grandeur. After passing a formation called the 'Pirate Ship' the lakes became longer and we weaved in and out of many drooling stalactites and stalagmites to reach a place called 'Calvary'.

From here a lower section took us to even more spectacular formations. On a bend in the river the water continued but we climbed over some boulders carrying our rafts to rejoin the river. More lakes followed until we reached the end. I think there was something like twenty two.

Beaching the rafts we climbed up 75 metres. This was steep at first and followed by a climb up a short ladder to enter 'The Crystal Mountain' a remarkable and very pretty chamber containing some very impressive columns. A return through the lakes gave us a second chance to see these fantastic formations. I felt that this was, perhaps, the best trip of the week and we were underground 5¼ hours.

We drove back mesmerised by what we had seen. Having still more hours available to us Graham and I decided to descend Jama na Meji. This was a fine vertical descent with a very exposed re-belay. The hanger for this was only 100 centimetres above the lip of an enormous overhang, only two metres down. The descent to a bridge spanning the shaft was only twenty metres from where a further fifteen metres drop was deviated by a huge thread to keep the rope away from the rock.

Although I was not tired I could have stayed in bed much longer when waking the next morning. I was given charge of Graham again whilst Andy took his two novices to Jama na Meji. I decided to go down Najdena Jama. The entrance was a body sized chimney slot and dropped 6 metres into a chamber complete with toad and bats. I wonder where the witches were! We climbed up a stalagmite slope to where I belayed the rope to a peg and stalagmite boss for a twenty metres descent into a large canyon chamber. We then followed the rather pretty canyon passage steeply down to find a stalagmite boss 2 metres high and 1.5 metres wide.

Here we entered a hole on the left wall which gave access to short low passage which emerged into a huge but very muddy gallery. It was adorned by some fine mud statues!! Turning right at the 'T' junction in the chamber we entered a miserable muddy passage that went on a long way, certainly much further than the squelchy 30 minutes we went. We returned to the statues and headed left. Again we found a miserable muddy passage that was left unexplored.

Graham and I headed out to find Andy descending Jama na Meji. We picked up the bags and drove off to the recognizable clumping of a flat tyre. There was no spare. Andy was thinking that lightning does not strike twice, so I walked into Laze only to find out that we now owed for two tyres!! This was becoming an expensive exercise. I went back to the stranded car courtesy of Franc's motor bike. I hadn't driven one for years. It felt great. Franc arrived later and took me plus the two tyres to Logarcek for renewal. It cost a whopping 11,000 Tola to renew them. Fortunately Franc had a cheque book and paid for them.

We had just replaced the tyres when Andy arrived with his team. We found a stream and washed the horrible mud from all of our gear. We then set off looking for 'holes in the wood'. Firstly we went to Gradisnica a huge 75 metres deep pit and then on to Logaska beyond Logarcek. To reach this cave we had to negotiate a difficult level crossing. Three trains later we had worked out that someone has to stand on the lever by the track side to operate the barrier. If there is only the car driver I wonder what happens?

The following day was a free day so we all decided to go to Skocjanske Jama, a show cave close to the border with Italy. It was a pleasant drive. The 10.00 trip was the first of the day but there was a herd of screaming Italian kids. We opted for the 11.30 on the chance there were no more screaming kids. Views of the surrounding countryside were spectacular as we walked through fine pine woods. Looking down into the gorge we saw natural bridges and large dolines.

The show cave starts off very modestly until we reached the 'Great Hall' when the trip became increasingly spectacular until we reached the river gallery. Wow. This stupendous feature must make it the greatest show cave in the world. The river canyon is 140 metres high in places and the 'tourist path' wanders across the wall 70 metres above the river. At one place we noticed a marker where a flood in 1969 had reached 50 metres deep. This was a truly memorable spot. Walking out into daylight at the bottom of the doline was spectacular too. Here a tiny train took us back to the top of the cliff.

Continuing with our 'tourist day' we next visited Predjamski Jama. The entrance to this cave sported the rather fine Castle of Grad. Not many caves can say they have a proper castle of fairy tale proportions in their entrance porch! The castle is famous as it was lived in by a Robin Hood character called Erasmus way back in the 15th century. Although loved by the people the barons hated him. As a result his castle was besieged and Erasmus survived for a year to the consternation of the oppressors who began wondering how he was surviving for so long. In the cave (which for us that day was closed) there is a flue that leads upwards reaching the surface in a hidden hanging valley from where food was sent downt to him.

Unfortunately he was betrayed by one of his staff. Apparently, so the story goes, at a given signal a cannon was to be fired aimed at a certain point on the castle. This was the toilet block where Erasmus did what he had to do most days. The signal was given, a dropped handkerchief, and the cannon did its work and shot poor Erasmus to pieces. I wonder what he thought in those last few moments hearing the roar or whoosh, whether it was one of, wow, what did I eat last night or something quite different. Who knows? All we do know was that he was shot to pieces.

Needing some activity we returned to Rakov Skocjan and the natural bridge. I rigged an abseil over this for the decent into the doline. It was a fine forty metres drop. After a brief look into Zelske Jama and its river we walked out back to the car and drove to Laze.

The last day was spent initially in Logaska, we were OK now as we knew how to cross the railway tracks, which started life as a thirty metres descent. A pretty uphill then downward passage was followed before we headed out. However, the main event of the day was to descend the awe inspiring hole of Gradisnica. The seventy five metres entrance shaft landed on a scree slope. This was followed by a further 30 metres drop where we entered a huge but extremely muddy chamber. Presumably this is another large sump in the wet season.

It had been a grand week and without the support of Franc it would have much less so. We took Franc and his family out for a meal on our last night as a thank you for all their support.

Another good trip with clients was again to Vercors where we did the usual caves in July 1995. On the last day we went to do the Coufin – Chevaline through trip. This was arranged through the Groupe Speleologique Valentinois based in Valence. Bruno our guide from the club was quite a jovial and a big chap like me so I felt happy. Quite apart from the caving there were also some climbers in the group. It turned out to be a good combination, climb one day and cave the next. It was a pretty full on trip with the best climb I took people up was the Pilier des Nugues a great French 6b. My diary notes this as a mega steep and sustained route with a difficult second pitch.

The Couffin – Chevaline was a most remarkable cave and it was a privilege to be doing it as I had tried many times before get permission. The Couffin show cave is impressive with a magnificent array of straws festooning the ceiling. To leave the show cave is wet, very wet. Several low air space crawls, which obviously sump in wet weather, lead to a beautiful stream-way. We followed this upstream alternately walking and climbing up small cascades. The first of these was twelve metres high. Smaller cascades follow until the final one of 27 metres is ascended. Although not particularly wet it ascended a fantastic calcite wall decorated with rickety rusting electron ladders. This took us to a point known as 'The Dome', the 'summit' of the trip. It was all downhill from here.

A high, dry passage continued with amazing cauliflower like formations attached to the wall. At the end of this a descent leads to the amazing 'Galerie des Gours'. Not only did we have to swim these but we abseiled the dam walls. Gours I had seen in other caves were small by comparison. One gour had, fortunately, a scaffold tube partly submerged under the water. By a balancing act we all walked across. The water in this one looked deep and had the colour of blue ink. Sadly the amazing gours ended all too soon and were followed by a low, very cold and deep canal which, happily, was short lived. One of the team became very cold in this and I was glad to be at the far side where we could warm up again.

We emerged into the tourist section of the Chaevaline at the massive 'Salle de la Cathedrale' in darkness. What no tourists? All of a sudden dramatic music started and lights came on showing us the immensity of this chamber. On reaching the tourists we could tell they were impressed by our appearing, as if on cue, out of the darkness. An easy exit was made from the chamber via a blasted tunnel to the outside air. This was a wonderful 5 hour trip which I had enjoyed almost as much as the Berger.

In 1995 I became a Local Cave Leader trainer and assessor. This often gave me an insight into how little experience candidates had when they were coming forward for 'certification'. Caves recorded in their official N.C.A. (as it was until 2007, now the B.C.A.) log books gave it all away. As mentioned previously very few if any long caving trips being recorded, candidates had just fulfilled the criteria. Some of them were definitely not cavers. I was always gladdened when a real caver came along and over the years I noted that there were quite a few. At this time I was also the Technical Adviser for caving for many centres on caving activities.

My favourite cave for the Local Cave Leader Level 1 assessments was Llygad Llwchwr in South Wales. The cave has a snug entrance and several awkward rift passages. There are four river chambers of which River Chamber 4 is the finest as it has a myriad collection of wonderful formations. The stream issues from the sump adorned with diving lines for which an extension to the cave is sought. From where the water sinks high on the Black Mountain it is five miles in a straight line to this point so there must logically be much more cave to find. However, my chosen place for assessment was River Chamber 2. This has a vey overhung balcony overlooking the stream. One side of the stream is deep water but the far side has a sandy beach but no palm trees! Thr rigging of the descent of this and subsequent ascent was ideal for the level of ropewrok skills required for this level. I remember on one occasion, a fun one, taking an inflatable boat there and cruising down the short length of stream!

My favourite training courses, however, were always the S.R.T. ones, although I always enjoyed the Local Cave

Leader courses anyhow. The S.R.T. courses allowed me to share the delights of holes like, for example, Juniper Gulf, Rowten Pot, Long Kin East and Long Kin West with people who were keen and wanting to learn more. When teaching these courses in Derbyshire a day was spent above ground indoors either at Whitehall or in Dave Edwards' barn in Taddington near Buxton. A long day practicing all the techniques required for safe progression was followed by a trip down the south side of the gaping sixty metres deep hole of Eldon Hole.

Further trips to the Vercors followed. In 2000 I teamed up with Dave Edwards to help him run a course there. We spent some days in the valley exploring the likes of the Scialet Joufflus and the Scialet de la Fee Anglaise. Other days were spent on the high plateau exploring caves such as the Scialet de l'A.G. and an attempt on the Scialet de Silence which I had reconnoitered the previous year.

Unfortunately I did not get very far. The clients were unable to follow me into a draughting window due to the technicalities of this. I must admit I had reached it with not a small amount of difficulty. A pity as this has the makings of a superb trip. To reach this window I had made a wild 10 metres pendulum across the shaft and just managed to grab a loose hanger on the far wall which seemed a long way from where I had started swinging. Clipping in to this dubious bit of kit I traversed right across the wall fixing the rope to much more substantial fixings as I went to enter the window.

One of the more remarkable trips we did was the Scialet Michellier not far from Vassieux-en-Vercors. It was remarkable for the siting of its entrance. Situated in the middle of a ploughed field on the valley floor it had been discovered by the farmer of the land when his tractor almost fell in to it! Initially the rock on the shafts was very rough and cherty but the passages at the far end were very pretty but also muddy.

This trip with Dave's clients was a good one for me as we did caves that I had not been to before. This had also happened on some my previous trips as I sometimes took clients down something I had not explored before. This, I believe gives the idea of an adventure into an unknown system. For example, as I had mentioned previously I had not been to Pot Deux and that trip was really great fun. The uncertainty of finding the cave and whether I would find the way was always exciting. I suppose I was full of my own confidence and skills. All my clients appeared to have implicit trust in me.

My last guiding trip to the Vercors was in 2005 when I took a group from Usk College for a week in May. Fortunately we were not camping but staying in a gite close to Choranche. I have forgotten the name of this but it was a comfortable place with a large storage area in an old barn. The weather was particularly unkind and we were only able to do the Grotte de Bournillon via the right hand upper entrance, the Grotte Favot and the large dry passage in the Gournier. Even this was weeping water from everywhere that could weep.

An amusing incident occurred both on the way there and back. As we all know Passports are needed to leave the UK and enter the country again on return as well as the country being visited. We arrived at Passport Control in Dover, all 8 of us, when one of the lads informed us that he did not have his Passport. He'd left it home! We suggested that if he wanted to come with us he had better lie down on the floor and have gear placed on top of him. He complied. We presented the 7 Passports to the Officer. He counted the heads in the bus and waved us on. The same thing happened of course on the way back leaving France. The lad was hidden and the 7 Passports handed over to the French Officer who simply waved us through.

I fear for the continuation of instructed caving as it gets embroiled in politics. Long gone are the carefree days of going out and doing what seemed appropriate for the group. Centres seem to proscribe what cave is done to the extent that on the silly 3 weeks before the summer school holidays, for example, up to 27 mini buses have been observed in the car park at Cwm Porth above Porth yr Ogof in South Wales. These would have had a minimum of 12 people on board, making it well over 300 people underground with darkness difficult to find. The noise too, as screams are amplified throughout the cave made the experience extremely poor. Usually other caves that are equally suitable for groups are empty. Similarly other, shall we say 'sacrificial', caves in other areas are just as busy! These are Goatchurch Cavern in the Mendips; Pridhamsleigh Cavern in Devon; Carlswark or the entrance series in Giant's Hole, Derbyshire and of course that other well known honey pot, Upper and Lower Long Churn, (the 'Churns') in Yorkshire. Quality is, and must be the name of the game. What quality is there in visiting a cave with several hundred others milling around, shouting and screaming when cold water hits tender parts?

There is one good thing about all the caving qualifications. Each level of award has to be revalidated. The two Local Cave Leader awards every five years and C.I.C. every three. At least that ensures that 'Leaders' and 'Instructors' have to do some 'fun' as well as instructed caving at the appropriate standard, even though it is a miniscule amount. The climbing qualifications do not have this 'safety valve' of ensuring that everyone is aware of recent best practice. For instance a person gaining an S.P.A. need never ever climb again but still able to run a climbing session. I know several people who do not climb and still run single pitch top roping sessions. This to me is an anathema to the ideal of being an instructor or leader.

Chapter 12

Caving Nepalese Style

In March 1992 I was supposed to have been leading a climbing trip to Tent Peak above the Annapurna Sanctuary. Unfortunately I had pulled a ham string and could barely walk. As leader of the trip I could not just stay in England to recover as there were arrangements to make and documents to obtain in Kathmandu. Although walking was painful I managed to organise the paperwork whilst the rest of the group had a city tour. I decided that Pokhara would be a much better place to languish and spend a fortnight than Kathmandu, as the group was going there anyway to start their walk to the mountain. Whilst Kathmandu is extremely lively with much going on, it is noisy and did not have the restful atmosphere I needed.

After the group had left I read lots and became bored with just sitting. As my leg became more comfortable I decided to try it out and visited Nepal's only show cave, Mahendra Gupha. A short taxi journey took me to Batulechaur as I did not fancy the two and a half hours walk. On the way the taxi driver took me to the dramatic deep and wide Seti Gorge spanned by a road bridge. An attempt had been made to provide a suicide preventative fence across the bridge. However, it would be easily passed but severe lacerations would probably mean bleeding to death before being dashed to death on the boulders below.

At Mahendra Gupha car park, not really a car park as we know it just a place to stop the car, I asked the driver to wait whilst I explored. A gate barred access to the delights within as did an attendant standing in a stone booth demanding five rupees (about six pence). Having paid my fee I was asked if I wanted a guide but politely I refused his kind offer. The cave is now electrically lit but I was very glad that I took a torch with me. Electricity can be and often is, notoriously unreliable. Having the torch gave me the opportunity to explore the one and only side passage, which is unlit, to the absolute dismay of the 'cave guides' in the cave who seemed to be shadowing me. It also meant I would get out if the power suddenly failed!

The walk of a few metres reached the entrance where twenty five steps lead down into the wide, high porch. Although the cave is soiled by candle soot and inscriptions, it is quite good fun. The complete cave is developed below the coarse conglomerate capping rock with the main passage running north to south. It is trapeze shaped in profile, quite wide and high. Just beyond the main entrance I saw daylight to my left. I reached this by a short ascent over boulders to a second but smaller entrance. However, continuing down the main passage a very short distance I entered an opening in the right hand wall into a side passage. Passing a side chamber a short but low crawl in the broad passage took me to a roomier passage which, by the looks of it, is rarely visited by anyone. I suppose this is hardly surprising in view of the fact that it is quite loosely consolidated fine conglomerate.

Unlike the rest of the cave, which at one time must have been very pretty, there is no calcite here and the abundant breakdown is very loose. The north-west passage ended at a final breakdown. On the surface above this a hole at the side of the road, leading to Oderibuwan Gupha grew from a fist size crack into a half metre deep pothole. This was possibly entrance number three? It is now filled in.

Back in the main passage of the cave I continued to a pile of breakdown. The water which deposits the calcite on the ceiling does not trickle through cracks. Instead it seems to ooze through the somewhat sponge like texture of the conglomerate and covers whole surfaces. After rummaging around a while longer I then returned to the entrance and waiting taxi.

The driver had, as asked, waited for me possibly because I had not paid for the first part of the journey. He then drove me to visit the longest system in Nepal, once the longest in the Indian sub-Continent. It has many names, Devi's Fall (from a woman tourist called Devi who was washed into the cave when the sluice doors of the dam at the outflow of Phewa Tal, the lake at Pokhara, were opened unexpectedly); Devin's Fall; Fadke's Hole and Patale Chhango (meaning 'tight waterfall' in Nepalese). This last name is the most popular and generally accepted one. The Mardi Khola (River) flows through the cave.

Waterfall Entrance, signposted as Devi's Fall, is a place of tourist interest so the taxi driver had no problem finding it. I again asked him to wait, but paid for the journeys he had so far driven. He was having an easy day of it, sitting around in his car and getting paid for it, eventually! Situated a few metres north of the road, close to Tashiling Tibetan Camp, Devi's Fall is reached by following a small path between the Tibetan trinket sellers. I was aware that their persuasive talk and any weakness I showed would certainly mean I would spend many rupees. I passed a stone booth and, like Mahendra Gupha, paid the standard five rupees for peering into the depths below.

The meandering riverbed of the Mardi Khola

predominantly remains dry in the pre-monsoon period. However, during the monsoon and sudden rainstorms the riverbed overflows despite the fact that it is very wide and deep. Suddenly the riverbed plunges down through the more resistant capping rock into the underlying softer conglomerate as a spectacular and dramatic 38 metres deep circular shaft.

Having no rope or S.R.T. kit and unable to fly I could not, unfortunately, descend the fine looking shaft. To peer into it I climbed down a short way and made a long step over the narrowest part to a ledge on the far side. I noticed a huge thread which would have allowed me to make a free hanging descent to the passages below. An alternative entrance had to be found if I was to do any exploration of the system at all. I returned to the road and trinket sellers fending them away with 'thank you very much but not now'. A young, friendly Tibetan from the camp approached me and we talked about the cave. He knew where the other entrances were and, more importantly, he agreed to show me where they were.

A hole on the south side of the road was investigated as my 'Guide', who had never been underground before intimated that it connected with Devi's Fall. This was Entrance Four. The depression containing the hole was extremely smelly making me retch. This was due to the vast amount of decaying rubbish which had been deposited there. I started to descend a very loose chimney containing large boulders of dubious stability. Having descended a very short way I decided that discretion was the better part of valour so came back out of this mess before I was unceremoniously cast onto or into something I had no desire to be dumped.

I was then taken on a well worn path leading south and away from the smooth talking souvenir sellers to a large grassy balcony overlooking the Phusre Khola. The 10 minute walk to that point was along the rim of the dry, Phorke valley. Descending to my left, diagonally, across steeply sloping grass on a narrow track the valley floor was reached five minutes later.

This dry valley, a tributary of the Phusre Khola, is where I found Entrance Two, the easiest into the system. Huge boulders had to be negotiated to locate it. The key to finding the entrance was an ascent of a short but easy climb up a small cliff, the top half of which was buff coloured. However, I kept too far left and ascended through shrubbery and boulders to enter the narrow, heavily vegetated but impressive dry Mardi Khola Gorge. Here on the right is the huge cavernous Entrance Five, whilst lower down is a much smaller entrance.

Entering the cave by Entrance Five was a mistake. The huge chamber beyond, in the twilight zone, was very impressive indeed with many bats continually swirling around. I could only enter a short way before a 10 metres drop barred any further progress. At this point daylight was seen entering from what turned out to be Entrance Two. The chamber with all the bats is called, unsurprisingly, 'Bat Chamber' and is one of the largest in the system.

Coming out, I went into the smaller lower entrance. Phew, was it hot in there! The passage was very wide but of only stooping height with a firm but muddy floor. Shortly, ,after entering, on the left hand side, a low opening lead through a slot between seemingly loose boulders, some had calcite, to gain a miserable, low, muddy and loose passage. The heat was intolerable, even just wearing vest and shorts. What with the threat of imminent entombment and the heat I made a judicious retreat.

I then soon located found Entrance Two. It had a small pool of water just beyond the porch. Ascending over guano covered boulders we found ourselves back in 'Bat Chamber' at the bottom of the ten metres climb. My 'Guide' was now really enjoying his first caving experience. We were now standing on top of an inkasion hill. To the left of us 'Canal Passage' went underneath the drop. This was left unexplored on this occasion as I was aware that the taxi waiting for me would have accumulated mega rupees. I need not have returned so quickly as the driver had vanished into thin air. I went back with my 'Guide' for a drink at his house and to meet his family.

My leg was now sore so, unfortunately, more rest was needed. A week later and an unexplored cave beckoning I was back in action. I returned to Mahendra Gupha intent on taking some pictures and exploring Oderibuwan Gupha. I took one picture before my camera stopped working! Back in the car park I was engaged in conversations with many voices. One of these was with a local cave guide called Krishna Pariya (Deka to his friends). He wanted to show me Oderibuwan Gupha or, as it is known locally, Chameri (Bat) Cave.

We had a pleasant ten minutes walk following a track leading north-west from the car park to arrive at a huge, very old Banyan tree. Opposite this tree on the right of the track a climb over a stone wall lead us into a 'sinkhole meadow'. We found the entrance to the short Chameri Cave in the largest of these sinkholes to the right of a vague track. There appeared to be a smaller entrance to the left, but we did not investigate this.

An easy and short scramble down lead us into the first large chamber. At the far end of this we followed a short, low passage into a second larger chamber with abundant formations. This was a most pretty sight. Amongst the stalactites a number of bats were in their upside down mode.

One of the formations resembled Ganesh (the elephant headed son of Shiva and Parvati who are much revered Hindu Gods). Deka was intrigued by my Petzl Zoom as he only had a very quick burning candle. He had taken it out of a box at the entrance but it had now burnt down to his fingers in a matter of minutes. We exited into glorious sunshine. This was well worth the visit. The second largest chamber used to have an abundance of bats (Hipposideros Armiger) among the stalactites, but, strangely very few live there now. Before leaving Deka I had mentioned that I was going to explore Patale Chhango the following day. He expressed great interest in this venture so he agreed to meet me at Mountain Villa, the hotel where I was staying at 09.00.

The day started very cool but the heat and humidity soon increased and by the time Deka arrived forty five minutes late it was almost unbearable. We had a huge storm in mid afternoon. Fortunately Deka had arrived with a driver so off we went to Devi's Fall. Leaving the driver at the mercy of the souvenir sellers, Deka and I set off to explore. We entered, as I had done previously by Entrance Two and continued up into 'Bat Chamber'. This huge chamber is developed in the fine grained conglomerate with the ceiling consisting of the capping rock. Admiring the view out to Entrance Five from the top of the inkasion hill, typical of the conglomerate caves of the Pokhara Valley, we scrambled down to the west side of the chamber and under the 10 metres climb beneath the window of Entrance Five.

Here we entered the western north to south passage. This is called 'Canals Passage', a stream cave passage that was wide and high at the start. It became progressively higher and had a solid floor. All along this passage occasional round shaped, deep swirl pools occurred. In

France they would be called 'marmites' or cooking pots. Although dry they were a remarkable feature.

Walking up the passage we passed through a small breakdown chamber which contained large flowstone boulders. Beyond 'Bat Chamber' a small connecting passage took us into the eastern north to south passage. This is 'Lake Passage'. Further on in Canals Passage the ceiling rises into 'Road Chamber', another inkasion hall with its typical hill. This is directly below the road and the souvenir sellers. At the top of the 'hill' pieces of wood could be seen jammed into the cracks and niches 35 metres above our heads! A great number of bats (mostly Hipposidero Armiger and Rousettus Leschenaulti) swirl noisily around the chamber.

Climbing down in the north-east corner we reached the northern 'Canals Passage', which had one very fine swirl pool. A short distance further on we missed the very low connection with 'Lake Passage' in the eastern wall. 'Canals Passage' continued and joined the 'Main Rift' north of 'Road Chamber' which we followed out to daylight at the base of Devi's Fall. This is a most impressive spot. A conveniently placed scaffold pole enabled us to swarm up it to the base of the shaft. We had to be very careful here as stones thrown from the tourists above would have a soft landing, our heads! I suppose it is only human nature and most people who see a black hole are curious. This curiosity takes over the mind and a voice within says that a stone has to be thrown down it to see what happens. Does it splash, go thud or just squishes or even no sound at all if the hole keeps on descending to goodness knows where?

We came back the same way. Deka had enjoyed his trip and so had I. Proper caving gear was very absent but what the hell, we were having fun. Although we had made the connection between Entrance Two and Entrance One

(Devi's Fall) I was still intrigued about 'Lake Passage', the largest in the system, and I wanted to find 'South East Passage' as well.

My ham string injury seemed to have, more or less, resolved itself, so the following day I went back on my own to quell my curiosity. The torrential rain of the previous afternoon had had no effect on the ground. All it had done was to increase the humidity. On entering Entrance Two once more I climbed up the inkasion hill but instead of turning left to enter 'Canals Passage' I went across to the far, northern, wall. Huge boulders seemed to bar access to the obvious very large ensuing passage. Searching around, I eventually found a tricky climb down the boulder pile on the right hand side. This led to the first lake in 'Lake Passage' which I passed on the left without getting wet. At the far side I scrambled across boulders to the large 'Lake Hall'.

This chamber, a chaotic jumble of massive boulders, is the second largest in the system. Crossing this I had to be very careful due to everything being very loosely placed. Another scramble down at the far end took me to a deeper lake. This is a foreboding spot with a low dripping ceiling encrusted with twigs. It conjured up a picture of catastrophic flooding. Many rounded stones litter the floor. My mind panicked, was it still fine on the surface?

Beyond this gloomy place I followed a typical stream cave passage, which was interrupted by occasional pools, for a considerable distance around a long curve to the 'Main Rift' and the junction with 'Canals Passage'. I then returned to 'Bat Chamber' and set about finding 'South East Passage'. This I found at the topmost right hand corner of the chamber. It was a small square opening which quickly enlarged to a much more comfortable walking height passage. As I progressed along the passage bats were continually swooping around me in their dozens, a very interesting place to be. The heat became more and more oppressive but it was easy walking on a fine gravel floor.

I continued to the largest chamber in the system where I found some remarkable pure white, blade like, calcite formations resembling axe heads sticking out from the wall. A slope reared up in front of me and was not a pretty sight. It was fairly obvious that a massive roof fall had recently taken place as there was a very unstable pile of boulders and dust confronting me. Although I had wanted to exit from Entrance Three I decided to turn round and exit from the well known and reliable Entrance Two.

The total time I had spent exploring and poking around in Patale Chhango was around 5 hours in all. It was well worth the effort, not only for the unusual formation of the cave in the fine and coarse grained conglomerate, but also for the number of bats and fine formations. One thing I was very wary about was the possible release of water from the dam holding back the water from Phewa Tal. I had been assured that in times of drought this was not going to happen. Needless to say I saw that all the passages would fill to the roof.

In November 1996 I had returned to Kathmandu after taking clients on a trek to the Langtang region of the Himalayas. Rumours were rife, a new cave had been found under the city. I could not imagine anything quite so grim. You only had to look at the streets to imagine what filters underground! No, I did not want to explore it even if it was true. But, there might be caverns measureless to man waiting to be explored with no smelling, rotting or festering filth lining the walls or flowing through in a turgid stream. Returning in February 1997 from Chitwan where I had looked for rhino, ridden elephants as well as bathing with them I decided to follow up the rumour. Another of my favourite animal experiences happened whilst there. I was invited to stand on one of the elephant's trunk. I did as asked and then told to hold on to its ears. Immediately the elephant lifted me up and deposited me safely on to its bristly haired back. Wow. It then took me to the river where it showered me with a trunk full of water before rolling over and dumping me unceremoniously in the water.

Pasang, my agent in Kathmandu at that time, had arranged an interview with the Minister of Geology and Archaeology for me to find out where the cave was or even if it existed.

We arrived at the Government offices. The open ramshackle iron gates were not guarded so did not have to show passes. Having parked the car we set about finding the Minister. A wriggly tin roofed building looked the part as to his whereabouts. Doubling as a museum there was an interesting array of artefacts and the usual geological stuff one finds in these places but covered with eons of dust. Eventually we located the Minister's office. We waited patiently outside as one must in places like this. An office junior ushered us in and told us to be seated. We were made most welcome. Tea was served in cups, no saucers, just cups.

The Minister and tea arrived at the same time. He looked down on us imperialistically from a raised podium. Dressed in a dapper grey suit he sported a Dhaka hat that matched well with the grey/yellow wall behind him. He gave the air of knowledge, speaking English well, but preferred not to, conducting all the conversation in Nepalese. Pasang ably acted as interpreter. The Minister was obviously a busy man. Official papers stacked high on his desk were neatly piled, no sheet out of place. A bell placed conveniently behind his ear was pressed at regular intervals summoning a minion who knocked on the door firmly before entering. He either took a sheet of paper from the office or bought pieces in with him which in turn were neatly placed on the gradually growing pile. More tea was served by yet another minion.

Continuing with the conversation Pasang told me that, yes, a new cave had been found. However, it was not under the city but at a place called Chobhar. This is a picturesque gorge on the outskirts of town. I politely asked, through Pasang, whether I could be shown the cave by one or two members of his staff. I was just as politely refused. No one was available. A film, apparently, had been made of the exploration of this cave. The Minister trying to be helpful said he would give me the phone number of the film maker, but on reflection he would rather phone the film maker to contact me. Well, that was that!

We left, having taken an hour of the Minster's time and I was as much in the dark as I was before I arrived. At least I had substantiated the rumour about the cave, but I was still unsure whether it was a new discovery. On the way for an early lunch I suggested to Pasang that I might go and search for it anyway as I was having a day away from the clients. He suggested that I took Ngawang. He had been my Sirdar on the Kanchenjunga trek I had done a couple of years previously. Ngawang arrived at the hotel shortly after me and on hiring a taxi we rattled and bounced through the dusty, polluted streets for half an hour to the suspension bridge crossing the Chobhar Gorge. I'd visited this spot many years previously and had forgotten that the Bagmati River flowed through it. This is the river that flows past Pashupatinath where the cremations take place and the subsequent ashes swept into the river to join all sorts of filth to flow slowly to the Ganges. People do their washing in it and animals pollute the already stinking water as well as other perpetrations I dared not think about.

The bridge is thirty metres or so above the foul smelling foaming sewer masquerading as a river. Local kids harangued us. Did we want guiding anywhere? Ngawang assured them we did not want their services. They came with us anyway. I had forgotten to ask Ngawang whether he had a torch and on reaching the river I asked if he had light. No he did not. Oh. All we had was my trusted Petzl Zoom with the remaining battery life very dubious and definitely of unknown life. We were both dressed as if going for a walk on the beach rather than going underground. The only items that you might call sensible caving clothing were actually our walking boots. Our shorts and 'T' shirt pretended to act as a barrier against the cold and the sharp rock. The kids were very excited and wanted to show us 'their cave'. They guided us skillfully to the entrance in their bare feet. Ngawang had never been underground before and seemed excited by the prospect.

Scrambling to the entrance we entered the cave. I had my camera in a rucksack. Ngawang said that he must carry it. He felt responsible for me. I pulled rank and experience explaining that it was better if I carried it. A twisting rift passage of meagre dimensions took us past another, smaller entrance, after rounding a couple of corners. I kept shining the light back for Ngawang who seemed quite unperturbed whether he had light or not. Eight kids had decided to 'guide' us. One, not too bright, light for 10 people, was a real recipe for disaster. Passing the light to and fro I expected any minute for one of the kids to run out of the cave with it. I couldn't keep it with me all the time otherwise the kids would fall through one of the many holes in the floor!

On we went, climbing upwards now, twisting and turning in the narrow passage. Some leads off to the left were dead ends. The cave had recently been surveyed as Topofil cotton threaded its way through the passage. It acted as a good direction marker. Light was now becoming a serious problem as the battery was on borrowed time and threatened extinction any moment. I had only planned for a short trip and Ngawang had arranged for the taxi to wait an hour until we returned. Passing the light between us all was very time consuming. After what seemed a long time, flickering lights appeared in the narrow passage above us. Yet more kids were arriving. Wearing next to nothing they slithered down the rift with many candles. At last we could see much more as they scurried past us leaving us a few candles on their way. An exit was soon made into daylight at the top of the hill above the gorge, giving great views into it and towards Kathmandu.

I gave each of the kids some rupees for their 'expert' help before Ngawang sped down the hill to the taxi that was still waiting for us. The driver obviously needed his money for the outward journey so had waited very patiently for our return. He was somewhat dismayed by our disheveled appearance and asked many questions as to where we had been. Ngawang gleefully told him our story, in Nepalese, on our journey back into town. He had obviously enjoyed his first caving trip. Polite as ever, sensing that I needed to clean myself up, he declined the offer of a coke after we had arrived back at the hotel. I think he was dead keen to relate the tale of his adventure to his family. I later found out that this cave was called Twang Reng Gupha.

However, it was not the cave I had wanted to explore. That was on the other side of the river and looked difficult to reach as I did not want to cross the wretched Bagmati.

Twang Reng had been enlarged in a number of places in the search for and subsequent mining of malachite. This experience was a far cry from the structured caving as we know in the UK, but how enjoyable. It was fun being with excitable and happy people who were obviously very pleased to show us around 'their cave'.

Chapter 13

The Lava Tubes of Oregon, Washington and California

In March 1989 I was leading two treks to the Himalayas and had just returned to Kathmandud from the first having been to Kaire Tal on the western flank of the Annapurna massive with my group. They had now left for England and I was awaiting my other group to arrive several days later for an Everest trip. On the second evening of my wait a small group of Americans arrived at the Yellow Pagoda Hotel. This is, alas, no more and is now a bank! I was invited to play cards with them and one such game we played was 'Find the Lady' or Hearts. One of the clients was called Sandie to whom I was quite attracted. Playing cards again the following night I learned of their itinerary. They were going as far as Thyangboche Monastery and their return more or less coincided with my group's arrival at Sanasa, a little village close by, at a junction of ways. They were coming up from Thyangboche and then back to Namche Bazaar whilst we were heading into the mountains ahead towards Gokyo. Normally I would have stopped at Sanasa for no longer than 20 minutes, as it was an easy hour's walk from Namche, but for some inexplicable reason we stopped there for 2 hours having a very early lunch! Shortly before leaving, Sandie appeared with her group and after a brief, but close, reunion we exchanged addresses and she invited me to the States.

I had never been there before and this was an opportunity not to miss. So after writing a letter, before the days email was widely used, saying that I would really like to visit and see her, I left Derbyshire in early July and flew to Seattle. Sandie met me at the airport and we then drove down and across to the Pacific Coast at Manzanita to Sandie's beach house. Among visiting other places, doing lots of climbing and walking, we eventually went to Bend where I had heard there were some lava tubes nearby. I was very interested in exploring these. Sandie had never been to them either, having had no interest in what lay below the topsoil. She was willing to come with me as well as drive me there. After I had fried on the sunny cliffs of Smiths Rocks, a superb climbing area, for a couple of days of excellent rock climbing both Sandie and I decided to cool off out of the heat underground. Sandie was not a climber but was very happy to watch. I had met a couple of local guys and we alternate lead climbs.

As an appetiser we first visited Lava River Cave. This is a show tube situated some 12 miles south of Bend very close to Highway 97. The area and cave is managed by the Deschutes National Forest Service and only open during the tourist season as winter conditions make opening impractical. After paying our entrance fee we were then given a gas lantern between us. I took a head torch with me, though, just in case. We were then free to explore at our leisure. This was much more fun than being 'guided'.

Lava River Cave was a major distribution channel for flowing lava having no known branches and only one entrance, a long roof collapse. The north-west segment is the longer and passes under Highway 97. The shorter south-east segment goes to a point where breakdown and sand-fill block the passage. Strangely, Lava River Cave contains an incredible amount of sand which no other cave has in the north-west. This sand is actually airborne volcanic ash which came from the eruption of Mount Mazama (Crater Lake) about 6,800 years ago and subsequently carried into the cave by seasonal flooding or other natural event through contraction cracks in the lava. In some places, for example 'Sand Canyon', it is about 3.5 metres deep.

The cave was discovered by Leander Dillman who used it as a refrigerator, long before these were in every household. It is also probable that the Indians used it much earlier for similar purposes. As far as can be ascertained, due to the lack of historical records, the cave was discovered in 1889 and was known as Dillman's Cave until 1921.

Early accounts of the explorations reported that there were many lava pipe-stem stalactites hanging from the ceiling. Unfortunately these are now largely gone, destroyed by tourists and taken by souvenir hunters, a deplorable practise.

Before exploring other caves I had to find out how these phenomena were formed. Lava tubes are roofed over segments of lava flows or rivers. The tubes form only while the lava is very fluid during and immediately after eruption. It is called Pahoehoe (pronounced pa hoey hoey), a Hawaiian name and is the lava where the majority of lava tubes are formed. The high gas content in the lava makes it behave like water and it spreads in all directions if erupted on to a level surface, or a downhill slope. If the eruption is constant and prolonged, outer parts of the expanding lava field become static as they lose their velocity, heat and dissolved gasses, or even confined by the topography of the land, forming channels. These become rivers and, like rivers of water, can form meanders, overflow their banks, erode downwards and if their temperature drops sufficiently, 'freeze'.

Lava 'rivers' are the main mechanisms for spreading lava over wide areas. Their tendency to overflow their banks is important to the formation of the deep caves like Lava River Cave. They are formed from the ground up as each successive overflowing effectively deepens the channel. Under favourable conditions, crusts may form on the lava river's surface, very similar to the way ice forms on a river of water, beginning at the edge and spreading to the centre. If the lava river level remains constant, further cooling strengthens the crust. This continues until it is strong enough to support its own weight even when the level of the river on which it floated drops away.

Entrances to lava tubes are generally through a gap in the roof. This is often a place where the roof did not form or was an original or subsequent collapse. To sum up, lava tubes are roofed over segments of lava 'rivers'. They may still contain flowing lava (active), plugged with basalt (solidified lava) or empty. If they are empty they can probably qualify as caves.

Another type of lava, usually absent from lava tubes, is aa (pronounced ah ah). Aa is a flow that is extraordinary rough, jagged, clinkery and has a generally ragged surface.

Our next visit was made to Arnold Ice Cave. Its location is well marked on all maps of the Bend area with signs from all major highways and roads. The entrance is a fairly small opening at the base of a high north-west facing cliff in a dark, deep sinkhole. We could only manage to penetrate a few metres due to ice blocking the rest of the cave! Wooden steps could be seen leading down through the ice into what is a reasonably extensive system. It was really strange to encounter ice as the outside temperature was pushing 35 degrees C!

The ice found in Arnold Ice Cave is 'perennial'. This ice endures from one year to another, receding or accumulating a little each year. New ice is often clear unless, as in Arnold, the water running off is muddy. Perennial ice becomes cloudy with age. During winter cold, heavy air sinks into the collapsed trenches and on into the lower reaches of the cave. Here it displaces air warmed by the surrounding rock forcing the warmer, lighter air outwards. This exchange continues just as long as the air outside is colder than the cave air. Often the rock surrounding a cave reaches subfreezing temperatures. When water reaches this environment it is quickly frozen. The build up of ice was slowed during the time when it was mined for refrigeration.

Arnold Ice Cave was a favourite with the early Settlers way back in the late1880's being used for cold storage and recreation. It even gained international fame by being featured on postcards printed in Germany! At one time a logger had his cook house about 100 metres away from the cave and various individuals kept their whiskey cool inside! Ice even became the basis for ice cream making which was the highlight of many a weekend picnic in those days, although the ice at times appeared to be like frozen mud due to the impurities in the water. Humans used the cave as long ago as 1370, though probably not as a shelter due to the prevalent ice but possibly as a source of water and cold storage. The nearby Hidden Forest Cave may have been used as a shelter as this is considerably warmer.

In a lean 'ice year' before the advent of refrigeration an enterprising saloon keeper cornered the ice market and began charging an unprecedented 10 cents a pound. This created an unwelcome handicap for the other two saloon owners who overcame the problem by quickly building a road to the 'ice cave' where they established an ice mining operation. To consolidate their position a 'friend' filed a homestead claim to include the cave. The wooden stairway was installed in 1963 in an attempt to improve the cave so that visitors could safely negotiate the steep ice slope. There were only a couple of steps clear of ice when we visited so the content must fluctuate from year to year.

Our next exploration was to another part of the Arnold system, Charcoal Cave No 1. In 1928 Walter J. Perry discovered large amounts of charcoal here, but it was not until 1938 that a full investigation of the site was made when charcoal was found and dated to around 1370. This was determined by a growth ring dating process. Stone axe marks among the partially burned pine were also found. It is not certain why there were such large fires in the cave. There are many theories including a spiritual significance and the now discounted explanation of melting the ice for water. The roof of this cave is very thin illustrating the strength of the basalt.

We then moved on to Hidden Forest Cave, another part of the Arnold system. High entrance walls give a gorge like entry to the porch which we found in a large sinkhole. This, as mentioned above, appears to be the most habitable of all the caves in the system being ventilated enough to dispel cold night air as well as facing west.

The final cave of the day we visited, again part of the same system took much, much longer to find. Perhaps we were getting 'caved out'. Back in the car we drove along Highway 18 to the Highway 200 junction. Following this we found a track that progressively became so rough that we were forced out of the car and on to our feet. Not having much idea of where we were in relation to anything we ambled and stumbled around in the heat of the afternoon. We cautiously avoided several, very suspicious characters having an argument outside their Dodge pickup truck and waving bottles of beer around. I immediately thought that they were gangsters, drug dealers or something far more sinister and that we were about to witness a gang land murder. They would then realise that we saw everything and then chase and shoot us!! Silly how these thoughts happen but they seemed quite real at the time. I have always wondered whether they had guns on board.

Eventually we found the cave we were searching for without further scares. It was one that I was particularly interested in visiting, Pictograph Cave. Indian paintings and drawings, or Pictographs, depict scenes from everyday life from long ago. We saw these very clearly on the main entrance walls and they did look very old. The steep entrance slope descended into the large passage below. There is also a skylight entrance and a through trip was made to this along the boulder strewn floor. A crude wooden ladder allowed us to escape from the so cool interior to the melting heat on the desert floor above. This last part of the system is very impressive. The walls of the main entrance used to be a favourite haunt of ravens, but as visitors increased they went elsewhere. At the western end of the system we found a collapsed lava pond.

On the way back we made a short detour to visit Skeleton Cave. This is the most popular year round cave in the area and is accessible over all weather gravel roads and provides a pleasant excursion. We entered, as with nearly all lava tubes, through a roof collapse. The very short upslope section of the cave is extensively collapsed and its floor is 3 metres higher than the floor of the main cave.

Once we had entered it was easy walking almost all the way to the far end. Sand completely covered the floor except for the last few hundred feet which was clinker. Passages were generally wide and high. We found some small side passages off from the 'Junction Room'. The cave is relatively well preserved apart from having its sharp edges smoothed by visitors. Similarities may be seen here between the tube and rivers of water with cut banks, meanders and areas of rapid flow. At the 'Steep Slope' the tube is tilted at quite a steep angle for a lava tube and the rounded passage is characteristic of rapid flow.

The cave was discovered by Phil Brogan (later he became known as the father of Oregon Speleology) as a member of a party in 1924 at which time '...the entrance was odorous with a pile of must from a moonshiner's still just inside the entrance'. Originally known as Fossil Bone Cave it was Skeleton Cave that stuck, coined in a 1926 newspaper story by Brogan. Walter J. Perry mapped the cave in 1928. Perry being intrigued by the many bones, sent samples to the Smithsonian Institute and J. W. Gidley identified teeth of a Pleistocene bear one third larger than any other living species.

This was a long day out but thoroughly enjoyable. Our final trip to the lava tubes was a few days later where we decided to visit Lavacicle Cave. Tours to this cave were, in those days, usually on the third Saturday of every month during the summer as Lavacicle is a designated Geologic site and has a barred locked gate. So phoning the Lava Lands Visitor Centre I arranged a visit as well as a guide. After a 1¼ hour dusty, hot drive from Bend we met him. It was interesting to see that the gated entrance was small by comparison to other caves we had visited. Access into the main passage is by a small wriggle followed by a crawl. The cave is split into a longer northern section with the southern being a little shorter. Both sections are quite wide and fairly high.

The cave is characterised by a broad, smoothly arched passage with a jagged floor which is covered by light, fine brown sand, washed in through cracks as well as through the entrance blocking the cave at the far end. We explored the cave with ease. Ceilings and walls are mostly glazed, with little indication of the slowing down of the flow of lava.

Considerable areas of the walls and ceilings are covered with a white precipitate which is probably silica and is most obvious at points of high air movements. There is much of it on the floor where, depending on its temperature and the ambient temperature formed lava roses (cups), stalagmites or loose nodules. One of the larger stalagmites had stood over a metre high. Alas, these were either vandalised or stolen.

The cave was discovered in August 1959 by a firefighting crew. They were mopping up after a 9,300 hectare Aspen Flat fire. One of the crew, Dan Beougher noticed a column of clean air rising through the smoke and found a small vertical entrance. Three crew members entered the cave through a small offset passage. The profusion of lava formations they encountered became legendary. It became known as Lavacicle because of these. Fortunately, the Forest Service realised the exceptional nature of the site and promptly gated it. Many gates in the Bend area have suffered since either by removal or damage with the subsequent damage to the formations within. The access procedures whilst not ideal do offer a token of conservation for this remarkable cave.

Sandie and I 'lost' contact with each other for 18 years. On my return from a Duke of Edinburgh assessment trip to Morocco on September 1st 2008 I had the shock of my life. There in my email inbox was an email from her. This was completely out of the blue! I was feeling low having missed the last train back to Machynlleth, where I was living at the time, so had spent the night on Birmingham New Street railway station. This was certainly not a good place to spend any time at all let alone a whole 10 hours. Whilst I was doing the assessment Sandie had logged into Google and found me on the B.C.A web site. After only four emails she was winging her way to the U.K. We decided that as I had no family ties in the U.K. I would move over to the States to live. The long and drawn out process to become a resident ended on December 8th 2009 when I received a letter from the Department of Immigration welcoming me to the United States as a resident on a temporary basis for 2 years. A final round of form filling at that time would give me a 10 year permanent residency.

Whilst going through the process and living in Portland, Oregon I was looking for underground venues. I had little idea on where to start, other than the Bend area three hours drive from Portland. Other than the books I had from 20 years ago for the Bend area caves I needed information about the lava tubes in Washington. I looked in whatever magazines were available. Eventually I found a tourist one that focused on places in and around the Columbia River Gorge. This is a magnificent, heavily forested area of many dramatic and very high waterfalls, up to 190 metres, such as Multnomah Falls. The Gorge itself was carved out by massive ice age floods of which the most catastrophic occurred some 15,000 to 13,000 years ago. Called the Missoula Flood, it was caused by a huge ice dam, which had been steadily undermined, suddenly collapsing. Water from the enormous lake behind flooded out at a rate of some 2.6 billion gallons of water per second. This equates to an hourly rate of between 40 to 60 cubic kilometres of water per hour continuing for some forty hours. The result of this cataclysmic power was the scouring out of the huge river gorge known today the Columbia.

Flicking through the pages of this glossy magazine I found a reference to an ice cave although not exactly saying where it was located or even how to find it. This gnawed away at me. Where could I find out? I then bought a book written by a guy called Scott Cook called 'Curious Gorge' an entertaining and 'alternative' little guide which indicated fun things to do in and around the Columbia Gorge. There at number twenty, in glorious black and white, was the Ice Cave. Although there was no write up just some pictures and a how to get there description, I decided to check it out. Interestingly in the States, caves are just described but not how to find them, although G.P.S. co-ordinates are usually given. In 1988 the Federal Cave Protection Act was passed forbidding anyone to detail how to find any cave in the United States in writing. To go caving, or spelunking, as it is termed over there, you need to go with someone who knows where the caves are to be found, join a 'grotto' or caving club as well as, perhaps, joing the National Speleological Association (N.S.A) of the United States.

Sandie and I went to seek out this 'ice cave'. She had enjoyed the Bend caves years ago, but would she enjoy sliding around an icy floor?

In early May we drove along Interstate 84 to the town (it is called a city in the States as every large or tiny place is called) of Hood River from Portland, a world famous wind surfing paradise. Here we crossed over the Columbia River and headed for Trout Lake on Highway 141. The book had advised us to check with the Ranger office in Trout Lake whether the road was clear up to the cave. Having phoned before we left home and received no answer, we presumed that the Rangers were out and about. On arrival in Trout Lake we found that this was not the case as the office was closed, very firmly so, until two weeks hence. Ah well, what the hell we'll find out soon enough if the road was open. We continued up Highway 141 until we joined Forest Road 24 and followed this to a point where soft snow a foot deep completely blocked the way ahead. Parking the car in a 'Sno-park' we walked half a mile up the snow covered tarmac to a sign indicating a left turn to the ice cave. Walking another quarter of a mile down a snowed up forest track we arrived at a fenced hole and an information board as well as a plethora of signs indicating that this was the 'Ice Cave'.

A prodigiously stout wooden ladder descended into the icicle bedecked black void some 10 metres below, although little of it was usable as only the handrails stood proud of the ice. Keeping both hands on the handrail we slid down the 45 degree ice slope into the blackness below. Strangely, it seemed blacker than usual when heading underground. The sun that had been shining so brightly on the surface was replaced by a sudden and complete blindness that hid the ice from our gaze. It was there alright as I suddenly did the splits aka Bambi and ended up on my backside or butt as they say in the U.S. Once our eyes had become accustomed to the gloom we gingerly made our way into the amazing array of ice formations beyond the twilight zone. There were curtains, columns, stalagmites and stalactites. These fantastic draperies were of clear frozen water instead of calcite. We stumbled and fell through the passages totally astonished by what we saw. Little if any damage had been done by the few previous visitors. I thought to myself that what we were seeing was unique as the following spring all the formations would be very different.

On searching for more information I found that the name of this particular one was called the Guler Ice Cave and had over 200 metres of passageway. Although it is a seasonal ice cave the ice remains well into the summer. There are hundreds of other lava tubes in the area some vertical, some pretty and a few of them just miserable rough grovels. The guidebook to the area gives the co-ordinates of each individual cave but is not that useful unless you have a G.P.S. and know how to use it.

Guler Ice Cave has been known for centuries having being used by the Indians as a store for huckleberries. In 1860 a pioneer traveller R. W. Reynolds found that drinks served in Portland in the summer were somewhat warm whilst some distance beyond Hood River, in The Dalles drinks were served deliciously cold with ice. Curious as to where this was obtained at that time of year he eventually found that it came from the Guler Ice Cave.

Jack Aerni 'discovered' it again in 1895. Experimentations on the storage of vegetables and in particular potatoes were made in 1928 after the construction of steps leading down into the cave. This met with little success. Although owned by Messrs W. H. Dean of White Salmon and Charles Coate of Husum they were managed by Mr. Christian Guler. He showed a reporter from 'The Enterprise' how firm the potatoes were after storage. In 1939 an article in 'The Sportsman's Guide' refuted the fact that vegetables were stored there.

Like other lava tubes in Oregon and Washington the 'caves' in this area of the Gifford Pinchot National Forest are formed from a particular type of lava, Pahoehoe. The source for the lava in this area was a vent, now partially filled with water and called Lake Wakipi in Indian Heaven Wilderness. Guler Ice Cave was formed less than 20,000 years ago, much younger than the basalt of the Columbia Gorge which ranges from 1 to 15 million years old.

My next flirtation with lava tubes was during a visit to the North West Caving Association Regional meeting in

Trout Lake from Friday 22nd May 2009 until Sunday the 24th. However, I was getting married on the Saturday afternoon. Arriving on my own by lunch time on the Friday I was fortunate to meet up with, initially, Claude Koch a respected caver who had discovered many tubes in the area. For the very few early arrivals a trip to the Pillars of Fire cave was the choice and we were duly taken by Claude. The cave is found three miles away from Trout Lake, a few yards behind the ironmongers shop.

A low wall had been built around the entrance to stop mud flowing down the entrance shaft. A tricky climb led down and into a large passage. I was wondering why everyone, apart from me had really stout knee pads. I was to find out quite quickly although it did not stop me enjoying the sights within. A flat out crawl was met soon after we had entered. This was, thankfully, sandy floored, much different to a crawl deeper inside that even the thick 'knee-padded' people found sharp. That crawl led nowhere in particular. However, the piece de resistance was a huge stalagmite type formation that had been formed from dripping lava. One of the largest that anyone had ever seen on any of their previous exploits. I was pleased. Some thin tree roots hung eerily, unmoving in the gloom deeper inside. This was a good experience and I bought thick pads and gloves for future trips! The evening slide show about lava tubes by Brent McGregor was a delight. His pictures of lava tubes were very professional.

The next day had to be a quick foray as I had to be back in Portland by 2.30 at the latest to get ready for my wedding. Two trips were on offer and even though I had wanted to do the harder of the two trips, Resurrection Cave, I had to be content with the easy option of a morning trip. This was to Cheese Cave. Found deep in the forest it had a huge new wooden cover over the top. As time was pressing I set off on my own. Using a stout fixed rope I descended the steep slope into a huge passage. I wandered very easily up this looking at the walls for flow marks and 'splash concentrics', solid circular ringed ripples on the floor. At the far end the remains of the old cheese racks lay on the floor but a prodigious metal 'fire escape' ladder took me to the roof and the underside of a building displaying much plumbing underneath, thankfully not discharging into the cave. Beautiful lava drips hung from the ceiling. Back out I had a fast drive back to Portland. Although I was back in good time for a scrub and change out of caving clothes into better ones I was delayed by Sandie's brother Rod who plied me a shot, OK then two large shots of whisky. This made me 10 minutes late for my wedding! We went to Hawaii for our honeymoon and were based on Maui. A pretty island we did many walks not only in the lush forests but also around the Haleakala volcano. We did much snorkeling and even visited some minor lava tubes including a trip into the far reaches of Hana lava tube.

Sandie had enjoyed the experience of Guler Ice Cave, so I persuaded her to visit Ape Cave on the side of Mount St. Helens a month or so later. This is a very publicised and easy to find cave as it is well signed. Open to all, Ape Cave is the longest lava tube in conterminous America at 2.5 miles. Amazingly this cave was totally unaffected by the 23rd May 1980 catastrophic eruption of Mount St. Helens when the mountain lost 400 metres of its height. Although a popular venue, we experienced the cave all to ourselves. Well, we did arrive at 07.00 as we had other plans for the day.

Entry into the cave was easy. Firstly by cemented steps and then down a very solid metal ladder-way. We entered a huge passage 13 metres below the surface that was at least 11 metres high. At the bottom of the stairway there was a choice of two ways. One was down flow and the other up. We chose the shorter down slope section of three quarters of a mile first. This was mainly easy, spacious walking leading to a blockage at the end. Some half a mile down the passage the tube shrinks both in width and height. At this point there is a remarkable 'Meatball' suspended between the walls. This round lava ball 3 metres above the floor was wedged while the lava was still flowing through the tube and is a comparative rarity.

We saw many lava tube features including contraction cracks of all sizes, splash concentrics, flow marks, lavacicles and 'gutters'. Gutters are formed when the lava flow does not occupy the whole width of the passage. Glaze on the passage walls and ceilings were formed by the burning of superheated volcanic gases.

We returned to the base of the ladder to explore the one and three quarters of a mile up flow direction. After one hundred metres we entered the largest chamber in the system. From here on the caving became more difficult. Many boulder falls littered the floor and several short but awkward climbs slowed progress. An hour later we climbed out through a small hole to daylight up a solid metal ladder, very impressed with what we had negotiated and seen. A pleasant walk through the wood then took us back to the car park.

A few days later Sandie and I returned to Bend and the lava tube systems there to check a few details for this book and to update some information as well as taking some pictures. We had a very early start from Portland stopping for breakfast at the Huckleberry Inn below Mount Hood at Government Camp. I chose, at Sandie's recommendation, to have a short stack of Huckleberry Pancakes. A full stack is three pancakes whilst a short stack is two. They were the best pancakes I had ever tasted but I don't think I could have eaten three on this occasion but on a later visit I did, washed down by never ending coffee! We usually stopped there on our travels in that direction.

Whether it was the full feeling or heat we somehow found it more difficult to locate the tubes we had explored almost twenty years previously. The wooden ladder allowing the exit from Pictograph Cave was gone so we had to make a there and back journey clambering over the awkward huge boulders. Arnold Ice Cave did not exist as the wooden ladder was totally submerged in ice and we could only penetrate a metre or so. We did manage however, to explore another cave that we had not visited before. Called Boyd Cave it is located close to the road. The passages below were accessed via a wooden ladder. We did this six hunded metres long cave because we could no longer access Skeleton Cave, as it was gated and access denied. Another cave we visited but could not gain access to was Wind Cave. Again this was fortified with a huge and impregnable metal girder fence. A tiny door in this over the top fortification needed a key.

I became a paid up member of the Oregon Grotto (Club), which is affiliated to the National Speleological Society, in the hope of doing some trips with other people. I had complained bitterly about not being able to find caves and wanting to explore more tubes. Roger Silver was a long standing member of the club. Although a great guy he was quite secretive about giving information out as to the whereabouts of the caves. However, he then offered to take me to the 1¼ miles long Ole's Cave. After a one and a quarter hours drive and clutching Roger's G.P.S. we set off walking into the extremely thick forest. Roger thought it was less than a mile to the entrance. The road was quickly left behind and the only sounds we heard were the cracking of dead branches as we stepped on them. I don't know whether Roger was having me on or not but it did take longer than I had expected to locate the cave. Perhaps he didn't want me to find it again.

Ole's Cave was discovered in 1895 by Ole Peterson who owned a farm near the Lewis River below the cave. He gave guided tours and was Washington State's first 'commercial' cave.

As with all the tubes I had so far encountered access was through the roof. This impressive spot was adorned with beautiful ferns. A short down slope section was explored before the main upslope passage. We entered this section via quite a tight, though thankfully very short crawl. A large passage continued until Roger stopped me and asked what I saw ahead three metres up the wall. I looked and eventually could make out a rock feature looking exactly like the bust of George Washington. There were many features of volcano-speleology. Further on we passed a possible way out upwards via a very difficult climb. Shortly after this we arrived at the end. Here I decided to climb out. This was fun and not too hard but Roger decided to return the way we had come.

We met back at the entrance and set off for the return walk to the car again implicitly trusting Roger's G.P.S. Well, we stumbled, fell and staggered through almost impenetrable forest on a bee line to it. After what seemed ages we were nowhere near the road let alone the car, so zigzagging on many bearings we eventually found it. If that is what G.P.S. navigation is all about give me map and compass every time or even a blow by blow account on how to reach a cave. That is not the American way though. In some ways I agree with that ethos as it helps to conserve the caves and only cavers go to them.

Later that year I was still trying to meet people for underground trips. I had no success even with grotto members and it was not until Martin and Liz Grain, friends from England, came to visit that I went underground again. They were delighted to be shown Ape Cave. It was not until May 2010 that I went underground again having purchased the latest copy of 'Curious Gorge'. I was having a great deal of enjoyment climbing mountains being especially pleased with climbing Mount St. Helens and South Sister near Bend. Only 100 people are allowed to climb Mt. St Helens each day. This number is strictly controlled by a permit system. I also visited many amazing waterfalls but I really wanted to visit more lava tubes. Scott Cook's latest updated and expanded 'Curious Gorge' guide included another cave, Falls Creek Cave, which I was very pleased to see.

The drive there was pretty straightforward as Scott was very precise with his directions to reach the parking area in the middle of the Gifford Pinchot Forest. The rough track was not too rough for the car whilst the walk to the cave took only five minutes firstly around the rim of a blocked depression to reach a point where it was possible to climb down into the next collapsed part of the system. A short passage took Sandie and me into a third collapse and the main entrance. It is possible to abseil in to this third hole through a hole on the left from a conveniently sited tree. The passages are huge from the word go. The cave is very extensive but no-one hardly ever goes to the end as the going becomes incredibly tough going.

Walking down the main passage for fifteen mutes or so took us to a turning up into an impressive passage on the left three metres up the wall. This wonderful passage is an oxbow and returns to the main passage. Across this is another side tunnel that has to be climbed up into. Fortunately I had a rope for which to safeguard Sandie on the 5 metres climb. This again loops round to join the main passage. The climb down was a little harder than the entry one so I belayed Sandie as she climbed down. We decided that we did not want to spend more time here so retreated and visited some spectacular nearby waterfalls.

On a later visit here I was working for a company called 'Rare Earth'. The bunch of clients was to be taken to Falls Creek Cave and abseiled in via the hole above the third entrance. I rigged it as I would have done in the UK. That is to say a releasable abseil rope so that any one stuck by catching their clothing or perhaps their hair in the abseil device could be lowered to the floor quickly. I had also rigged a safety rope. When Jarrod, the owner of the company arrived he could not believe what he saw. Without any discussion why he stripped the lot down and replaced the abseil rope as a fixed rope that could not be released in the event of anyone getting stuck and the safety rope was dispensed with! It certainly appears to me that much improvement is needed in American instructed circles. The only safety was having a person at the bottom of the abseil rope pulling hard down if anyone lost control! Needless to say I did not want to work for them again, even though I was getting paid and tipped!

A week later I went on a meet organized by the Oregon Grotto. Although there were not too many I met them at Trout Lake Ranger Station. One of the mainstays of the group Kim Lauper was the coordinator. He has an encyclopedic knowledge of all the St Helens area caves. I became friends with a guy called Josh Hydeman. He was as keen as mustard and wanted to do much more caving. Eventually we managed many trips together. Josh worked in a coffee shop in Portland called Heart. Each time after we had finished caving we would have coffee. He supplied the coffee and cafettiere and I supplied the stove. This was a lovely way to round off a good trip. Relaxing in the forest with sunlight filtering through the trees gave a wonderful feeling of well being.

The venue for this exploration was Deadhorse Cave. I had heard brief stories about this one especially about a tight squeeze just beyond the entrance which was reached after a short walk. On the way up we looked at the lower entrance. The main entrance was an inconspicuous hole on the left of the track. I now had a boiler suit and more importantly the obligatory thick kneepads. Entry was easy and after only a very short distance the Inner Chamber was entered. From here the way on looked rather snug. I was not filled with confidence when people smaller than me had difficulty. When it was my turn there was no way I was going to fit let alone turn around at the bend.

I decided that as I had nothing to prove I would enter by the lower entrance and find my way to meet them. Shortly after getting in I met a rather fine stream-way, unusual I thought for a lava tube. I followed this up to a junction and where I heard voices. Going upstream a little further there were some small but attractive cataracts. When I met the group they seemed surprised to see me. We explored a little more before exiting to a warm and balmy late afternoon.

More adventures followed. One time I was visiting an outdoor company in Bend so on the way there I stopped off close to the 'city' of Sisters and had a solo trip into the fine Skylight Cave. The following day was wet. I had arranged to meet Kim at Cougar, about an hours' drive from Portland, in Washington State. After picking Josh up from Heart and after the obligatory coffee we drove to Cougar. We were to explore caves on the south side of Mt. St. Helens and went around Scroll Cave, Joe's Cave and Kim's Cave. This last one was a fine if short cave having extremely rough crawls on aa. The formations too were quite spectacular. We also did Becky's Cave and a new find by Josh was very tight that became Josh's Cave. Finally we did Dogwood Cave where I saw my first lava roses.

Lake Cave near Ape Cave was visited with Josh. I found this an excellent trip and the cave was correctly named. There was a lake at the bottom on the first occasion but on subsequent visits it was absent! Entering at an upper level we explored a passage on the right just beyond the entrance porch that was very beautiful. Wonderful ochre coloured rock lining one wall being especially so. Again all the passages were large. At the end of the upper level a fixed metal ladder down gave access to the main body of the cave.

However, my next cave was part of a joint meet with the Oregon Grotto and the Seattle Grotto. I met everyone at Trout Lake and we were to be camping at the cave in the forest. We were to explore Dynamite Cave and it turned out be a very impressive one. Not only is it long but was very tiring. However, there were compensations as the lava formations were stunning, bridges, flows, upheavals, lavacicles, roof pendants and not forgetting the bees and mosquitos infesting the entrance! Once inside the going was immediately rough over a myriad of boulders to reach a six metres overhung pitch down to the continuation of the passage. At the bottom of the pitch a passage doubled back underneath to reach an area known as the 'Sand Castles'. Unfortunately much damage had been to these.

Continuing down the cave we reached a point where we down climbed a three metres high flow of lava. It looked as though it was a waterfall captured on film and stuck there except that this was solidified lava. From the bottom of the climb down we entered a low, wide chamber. The way on was down a thirteen metres high magnificent lava flow that gradually steepened until it was vertical. An impressive sight when viewed from the bottom. Unfortunately the trip ended at the base of the pitch but I wanted to come back to finish the exploration at some stage. I was amazed at how long it took the group to rig the pitch. It took the best part of an hour when on a later occasion I managed to rig it in less than 2 minutes! Re-belay is a word that does not seem to exist. Just chuck a rope down and if there is a rub point put a rope protector on.

In August after Sandie and I had climbed the 3,157 metres high South Sister near Bend we went to a meet organised by the Oregon High Desert Grotto (O.H.D.G.). I had met Brent McGregor and his partner Kara Michaelson at the Trout Lake meet in 2009 and it was good to see them again. They are very genuine and kind people. Matt Skeels was the main coordinator for the O.H.D.G. and had arranged this trip. Our first foray was to Little Belknap Crater Cave. Sandie and I had climbed Little Belknap a few days previously so knew roughly where we were going apart from the fact we had not spotted any caves that particular day. It is an extraordinary walk across a moonscape of desolation being just one massive boulder field with a rugged path through. It was a hot day and I was glad to be going underground.

The cave starts with a ten metres abseil to reach an easy walking passage. Although an exit can be made from the end of this, for very thin people only, it was fun to S.R.T. out. Sandie not being proficient in this technique was willing to be hauled out using a 2:1 hauling system. This greatly interested the rest of the team as they had not seen anything like it before. The rope for the descent was belayed around a huge skylight. Close by was Little Belknap Crater No 2, a short through trip. Other caves followed after we had driven a short distance over the McKenzie Pass. Ectomorph Ice Cave entered by a tight squeeze and Incline Cave. Sandie and I had to visit Ectomorph Cave the following day as she thought she had left her expensive sunglasses there. Alas not, but it did give me a chance to take some pictures!

At the end of the month another foray by members of the Oregon Grotto had Sandie and I in Christmas Canyon with Kim, Josh, Tom Peterson and his son Mike. It was a most memorable day as we explored some very beautiful caves, especially Pillars of Hercules with its fine lava pillars and many areas with lava roses. The other memorable cave that day was Perseverance, a very aptly named cave as it involved much rough crawling. Two others were explored, Cougar Cave and the previously visited Dogwood Cave. Another meet with club and I managed to do New Cave another good and long one, though quite easy

Sandie was really enjoying all this underground stuff so we decided to go to Lava Beds in Northern California as there are some fine lava tubes there. This area was much revered and talked about by the grotto members. Camping there was a dream in the very spacious campsite. Organised sites like this are so well prepared with tables and barbecue pits as well as being relatively cheap. Toilet facilities were good and exceptionally clean. It really was a case of what we didn't do whilst there as we really made the most of our time there. There are some twenty five marked cave entrances described in a little booklet. The best ones we visited were Hercules Leg Cave, Labyrinth Cave and the superb Catacombs Cave, the best trip of all. In all we did eighteen caves in the three days we were there. However, within the National Monument there are a total of 746 caves!

On the way back we decided to pay another visit to Arnold Ice Cave, a year on after the last visit, as I had heard that it was now devoid of ice! The rumour was correct.

There was no ice whatsoever to be seen anywhere. Unfortunately I did not have any abseiling gear or ascending gear and was unable to access the passage below, although I did have a rope. The in-situ ladder that had previously been captured by the ice had disintegrated and was lying crumpled at the foot of the short drop.

I felt now that Sandie was ready for the big one, Dynamite Cave. Going with Josh we made good time and I lowered Sandie down the six metres high pitch before once again visiting the 'Sand Castles'. Josh and I descended the thrirteen metres high flow and down the 'Blind Pit' where there were some amazing lavacicles. Unfortunately we were not able to do the extremely dodgy looking traverse at the head of the thirteen metres pitch into the short continuation of the cave. On the way back prior to going for a meal we explored Poachers Cave a segmented tube.

Before returning to Britain two more trips stand out as really great fun. The first was to Little Red River Cave. This is the highest segment of the Ape Cave complex that also includes Lake Cave. There was also a vertical element to it. Firstly we had to get a key for the gate. Calling in at the U.S. Forest Service office we did not have to give any information regarding whether we were cavers or not. In essence we could have been cave vandals. I felt the United States Forest Service (U.S.F.S). should have much tighter controls as who they give keys out to as it appears that just about anybody could get one.

Fortunately Josh had been to the cave before and knew the way. We did not get too wet on the short walk as rain fell persistently out of a very grey sky. Once in the cave we quickly met the pitch that was easily rigged. Not only was the cave very pretty but also had a 'red' river flowing down the lower half. Finally our last trip was to Dry Creek Cave. We had firstly explored New Cave again before finding this. The walk was a staggering two yards from the forest track and consisted mainly of hands and knees crawling, but it was a lovely trip with many fine lava features. Unfortunately that was my last lava tube exploration. They had been fun to do and unusual. Josh had been very supportive and I just loved the way we always had coffee. Not only before we left Portland but after the trip. On a final note the longest and deepest lava tube in the world is Kazumura with 40.7 miles of passages and is 1,101.5 metres (3,614 feet) deep. It is located on Hawaii near Kileau.

Unfortunatley Sandie became ill and unable to work and I could not get a job either. As such I came back to the UK towards the end of 2011 with Sandie following a few days later. After a month she realised she could not settle here and needed expensive medication. It would have cost a fortune and would not have been provided by the NHS. All her family lived in Portland so she took the decision to return to the US. As my residency had expired I had to remain here as I was able to work. A painful split!

Chapter 14

Return to north Wales, the slate and mineral mines of Snowdonia

Returning to North Wales shortly after coming back from America my interest in the slate mines of Snowdonia was reinvented. Having renewed my C.I.C. I regained my trainers and assessor status for the Local Cave and Mine Leader award. As such I was able to explore the slate mines of Snowdonia. It was much more friendly on an increasingly aging body! I have always been in awe of the caverns hewn out by incredible hard and dangerous work. These hardy miners worked in such primitive conditions with an absolute minimum amount of safety equipment. At best when working on a vertical face a rope wrapped around the body sufficed. As such horrific accidents occurred and much loss of life. Nowadays, of course, with modern protection exploring mines is a relatively safe experience.

Working for some of the outdoor centres in Snowdonia still enabled me to instil the spirit of adventure in people within these man made caverns. None more so than Gaewern Mine. This is a part of the Braich Goch system at Corris where the lowest part of the mine can be enjoyed by tourists on a 'magical' trip through King Arthur's Labyrinth. Gaewern is a different story.

The walk up the hill from the road is ahort although steep and when I first went there there were some old tin sheds where a local lad, Jeremy, did some amazing art work in slate. Unfortunately many of these were destroyed by vandals and his workshop burned. That said some of his work remains with a particular piece looking much like a vulture. It leers down at you as the mine access path is ascended.

The entrance is totally hidden from sight until a corner is rounded and the huge opening is seen in all its glory. Here harnesses are donned and fitted with cow's tails, a short piece of rope having two loops with karabiners attached. Cow's tails are used for protection on wire traverses as a progression is made along narrow ledges above some quite significant drops. Both tails are connected to the wire and alternately taken off to pass a re-belayed part of the wire, always being attached to it by one tail. At one point in the trip there are some very fine, perfectly white formations on the roof just above one of the wire traverses, quite remarkable. The once wet exit has been cleared of debris and is now dry.

Before any mine can be undertaken as an adventure trip on a commercial basis it has to be inspected by a Mine Inspector who will detail a specific route to be taken. This is marked out on a survey. He also has the prerogative to condemn any route being used if circumstances dictate as well as advising people not to use any mine.

Another great trip is Rhiwbach Mine above Cwm Penmachno, not far from Betws-y-coed. To reach this it involves a longish walk up through levelled mine workings to enter a forest. At the far side of this is the entrance. Gated, it needs a key to pass. The long wet tunnel leads to a chamber with a large lake, where a trip around it, in an inflatable boat, is possible. Further along the tunnel is the best part. Well, for me anyway. A stream cascades down an internal incline. At times the water is quite lively! A shuffle out and away from the top of this leads to a climb up a waterfall, great fun. Although looking fearsome it is actually quite easy to ascend. The final crowning touch is the climb out of a ventilation shaft. Fixed with a rope the shaft is ascended to the surface. The climb is unusual in that artificial holds have been bolted onto the wall to make it an easier climb. Protection is by using cow's tails that are clipped on to a frequently fixed rope. Now much higher up the hillside the walk back can be unpleasant in bad weather. There are many variations of trips here set up by a local entrepreneur, the owner of a company called Go Below.

At one time there was a miner's community here living over 400 metres up the hillside. There were living quarters, a shop and a community room used both as a school and chapel. It was a very bleak place to live indeed. The ruins remain and are a stark legacy of the hardship endured by the people who existed there. Today it is just as bleak as it was in those days.

Other trips include Wrysgan, an easy upward way through big chambers to emerge several floors higher; Cwmorthin and the aptly dubbed 'The Last Great Adventure'. This last is a through trip from Croesor Mine through to Rhosydd Mine. Starting off benignly enough there are tyroleans, abseils, boating across lakes, climbs and all with the threat of the roof crashing down. Nowadays the trip is much safer thanks to the in-situ ropes. At one time swinging, rotting bridges had to be crossed with little if any security. I think the scariest trip for me, however, was into Ratgoed with Pete Rigby and Mark Waite. Ratgoed is part of the Corris slate vein. Mark has set up a company called 'Corris Mine Explorers' and regularly takes people around the real Braich Goch on whole or half day trips. This is above King Arthur's Labyrinth. Back to Ratgoed and although it is only a short trip there appeared to be hanging death all around. Rockfalls seemed to have happened an hour or two before. Sharp slate abounded and moving around was fraught with the threat of gaining a severe laceration. Slate really can be extremely sharp with razor like edges. No wonder the miners years ago lost limbs. The one pitch was, however, secure. Small consolation as the rest was somewhat worrying to say the least. Cwmorthin Mine situated above Tanygrisiau close to Blaenau Ffestiniog has a variety of trips and the one that goes down and ends up below Llyn Cwmorthin was a really good one. It is a very complex mine on many levels but is a place I, regretfully, only visited once.

Minllyn Mine above Dinas Mawddwy is a small mine but has a very dramatic entrance. At the start a stream flowing through a fine arched tunnel is passed through to the floor of a deep pit and the entrance proper. The rest is easy enough but with some deep water in places. The trouble with this mine is that it is quite a long, steep climb to reach but is a very good introduction to mining. A wall plaque inside reads 'better to light a candle than complain of the dark'. I wonder who placed that there?

It was very pleasing to venture into these mines as a guide, trainer and of course an assessor. I think people often take on board the hardships the miners endured to create these voids rather than nature creating hers. That said I feel that not enough attention to safety is given. Quite often I have seen groups going into these mines in shorts and with little in the way of protective clothing, whilst in caving, nowadays, people are properly clothed to cope with the environment. I think that as mines are man made they are as a fairground attraction people believe nothing can go wrong. People have become blasé about them and treat the experience as an instant adventure fix. Like anything man made humans are not infallible. As slate is very fissile it is almost impossible to ensure that rocks do not fall. Slate is a layered rock and can fracture without warning. Caves are formed by a slow and secure process and nature usually keeps the integrity of the rock. Very occasionally in thinly bedded rock roof falls have occurred in caves and these areas are known so people keep away but many rock falls occur in mines hence the continual assessment by a Mine Inspector.

Apart from the slate mines there are some great trips to be had in the mineral mines of Snowdonia. My favourite is Pandora Mine where lead and zinc were once mined. It is found above the A5 near to Betws-y-coed by following the turning off that road by the Ugly House. In Welsh this is Tŷ Hyll. Close to the parking area the mine starts off as a wet wander along a passage to where the character of the mine develops vertically. Part way down a chamber is entered where there are some extremely pretty formations. The descent of the shafts to arrive here can be quite damp at times but the main watery bit is the descent out of the pretty chamber. The start of this is a traverse across a wall to where a hang gives a partially dry initial descent to join the point where water falls on to your head. Another good trip is Bwlch y Plwm. As its name suggests this is a lead mine and again is a vertical ecperience although drier than Pandora.

The good thing though about mines for me is I can still enjoy being underground without having to bend and stoop. A new knee in 2015 stopped me from crawling around so no more Pippikin Pots!

Epilogue – Twilight Years

Caving has given me countless wonderful experiences in life which have been undertaken with many great people. A new knee as mentioned in the last chapter and limbs that have started to ache ensures that there are many days when my body feels as supple as an iron bar. Whilst still having a great interest in the world below ground level, it is now impossible to do the trips I once did.

Many of the sights I have seen have been some of the most beautiful in the world. Going on expedition to Papua New Guinea was, perhaps, the greatest experience of all. The enormity of it and living in a rain forest as well as being a part of a rain forest community for almost two months was very special indeed.

So what now? Instructed caving has become a happy memory. I suppose the answer is to undertake trips that I feel able to do, ones that do not involve tight crawls, athletic manoeuvres or perhaps even, big pitches. I have to admit that I especially enjoyed being on rope and the technical side of rigging pitches whether they were straightforward, intricate, big or small. My days of caving two or three days a week has become a thing of the past as

I spend more time climbing and walking above ground. That said one memorable evening was spent with Pete Denver. Pete and I climbed a lot together in the 80's and 90's and sporadically since having first met in the Cairngorms in 1975. Pete had always had an interest in caving but preferred to be on the outside in the vertical world.

We left Buxton this particular evening for the short drive to Owl Hole, a re-discovered cave in Dowel Dale armed with a long extension ladder. Parking the car just off the narrow road close to the cave we lugged the ladder into the depression and propped it up against the wall below the enticing opening above. I climbed up and secured the ladder at the top before opening the gate. I was totally amazed with the formations I saw inside. All glittery and sparkling obviously not very frequented at that stage. After going a short distance a left turn took us into the fine 'Crystal Pallas' via a short ladder descent. We continued further to the very pretty 'Gour Chamber'. Returning to the junction we went upslope along 'High Passage', taking great care not to damage any of the fine formations, to reach 'Hoggmorton Aven'. Although the caving was easy great care had to be taken to avoid damage to the formations. It is interesting to note that the depression was at one time full to the brim with rusting metal, bits of cars, old fridges, washing machines and all manner of other rubbish. Talk about landfill. Fortunately the hole was emptied of all this by the co-operation between the Derbyshire Caving Association and the County Council to return the hole to its former glory in the early 1990's. It is the second largest open pot entrance in Derbyshire!

True, original adventure is difficult to find nowadays. Cavers that have the drive and perseverance can experience places that only a few people can get to. The number of caves already found and explored on the planet is estimated to be around 10% of the total. So, with 90% of caves still to find, let alone explore, the cavers of this world have much excitement in store for them.

It was a privilege to be involved with original explorations and to reach places where only half a dozen of us or so out of 6.5 billion people have ever stood. In some of these places more men have walked on the moon! Being able to recall those experiences by reading my diaries, by looking at my photographs, reliving those times, brings all my feelings of excitement flooding back. I often wish that I was twenty years younger to be able to feel the excitement of being in a deep cave, to be on rope all day descending beautiful symmetrical shafts; noisy rivers twinkling in my light; still, limpid, ripple less lakes; exploring huge galleries and to see marvelous formations. Watching caving expedition D.V.D's is no substitute for the thrill of feeling the rope stretch as I prepared for the big prussik, the clink of karabiner gates on my cow's tails snapping shut over re-belays and the shouts of 'rope free' after each pitch.

There are trips I would have enjoyed undertaking. Who knows though, perhaps one day I may just get to enjoy them. Two stand out as exceptional and ones I would certainly like to explore, given the chance. One is the Systema Badalona in the Spanish Pyrenees and the other is perhaps the most beautiful and decorated cave in the world, Lechuguilla in New Mexico.

In a deep cave, rescue is at best slow, if indeed possible at all. Great care, concentration and diligence are required all the time to avoid accidents whilst exploring these wild and very remote places, often more so than being at the Poles or on a high mountain, I have been lucky in having some really great friends. They have, without exception, been very careful and, perhaps, even safer than I. Without doubt caving altered the way I lived my life, even more so than climbing, but I have no regrets, just happy memories.

As age progresses different types of holidays have presented themselves. Not least cruising! Yes, you read it right, cruising. I suppose like going on coach trips I always thought that it would never be for me, ever. Having met Gaynor she was more into an easier life. She was a horse rider, especially enjoying eventing, but nowdays into golf to which I have no interest at all. But a couple of cruises later with her saw me in the Caribbean and a couple of easy caves in the warmth of Aruba were fun. Called Qudiriki and Fontein they were followed up by Hato Cave on Curacao. Harrison's Cave on Barbados also gave a memeorable show cave experience. The good thing about cruising is arriving in a different place or country each day. Many different and varied trips can be arranged on board, snorkeling, sight seeing, culture even walking and cycling. How pleased I was when I saw, that often, visits could be made to caves! Not full on trips but gentle ones with only a small number of people able to book on to these. Whilst in Belize a tyre inner tube trip down Branch River Cave was fun. A trip to Canada allowed me to experience a cave near Kingston, Ontario called Tyendinaga, another show cave. Whilst cruising in the Mediterranean a visit to Postojna Cave was made 25 years after my last visit. It was just as pretty as I had remembered it but infinitely busier whilst Predjama was the same as it was all those years ago. Perhaps its big sister was taking all the trade?

Finally, on a long trip to Crete in February 2018 with Gaynor I visited the cave of Dikteon Andron. Gaynor sensibly stayed behind in the car park overlooking the fine Lasithi Plateau in the village of Psyhro above which the cave was situated, and read a book. The cave was pretty unremarkable but steeped in myth and was by far and away the most dangerous show cave I have ever visited! It was here that Rhea, according to mythology, hid the baby Zeus away from his offspring guzzling father, Chronos. The cave was excavated in 1900 by David Hogarth a British archaeologist where he found traces of cult worship.

The walk was a very steep one of around 25 minutes up a rough stony path to where it levelled and opened out to give a fine vista over the Lasithi Plateau. There was no trace of a cave until a pay booth appeared and the occupants wanted money. Having paid half price, well it was out of season, the cave was just around the corner well out of sight of prying eyes beyond a secure fence. There is an 84 metres descent down the extremely steep entrance slope. As depth was gained so did the darkness. Lighting was virtually non-existing with only two lights giving a faint glow. That combined with the total lack of any steps having their edges painted white. This made for a harrowing descent. I guess that by paying half price they only had half the lights lit! Nevertheless once the bottom of the steps had been reached there were some fine formations. The ascent back up the steps was tiring. At one time a run up them would have been the norm but that day it was a slow ponderous ascent. Arriving back in the car park, having having found a newly paved path, lunch in the nearby restaurant was a traditional affair complete with Greek (Cretan) music.

At school I had no interest in learning although I did obtain three G.C.E's. English was one of my worst subjects. However, fast forward to 2007 I found myself writing walking guide books although I had written and had published a rock climbing guide and a couple of caving guides. One of these called 'Vercors Caves' was published in 1993. The next one, 'Selected Cave Guide to Britain and Ireland', was one that I edited with help from Don Rust.

This was published in 1997 and nicknamed 'Top of the Pots'! For both these books I self published a supplement in 2005. Having started to correct some north and mid Wales walking guides I was invited to write my own by David Perrott of Kittiwake books. I have now written 30 books in the past 11 years for several publishers not least by Myrddin ap Dafydd of Gwasg Carreg Gwalch book publishers of all things Welsh.

Writing three books a year nowadays it keeps my body active and the grey cells alert. I go out when I want to do the walks for these guides and not because I have to. As an instructor it is expected that you go out regardless of the weather. Preparing these books it is easy to take rests when doing the walks. Walk a few yards rest and write the notes or even take a picture. I try and put between 20 and 25 walks into each book. It is a leasurely way to enjoy the mountains although I still go out for fun. In February 2019 after recording all my mountain, climbing and caving days in diaries since 1961 I completed the 214 Wainwrights of the Lake District.

That brings me right up to date but here's hoping I can visit more 'Starless Rivers' in the not too distant future, even though they might be show caves. The mind is very willing but the body ...

Glossary

Abseil: To descend a rope using a friction device. In caving the use of a Petzl Stop is the usual item of equipment for this, although there are many other devices. The Stop has a handle that locks when you let go of it. For instance if you get hit on the head by a falling stone and are rendered unconscious, it stops you from plummeting to the floor.

Affluent: French word for inlet.

Aven: An upward tapering shaft that is often blind at the top, but sometimes with a passage leading off.

B.C.A.: The British Caving Association, the National Governing Body for cavers. Previously known as the N.C.A., the National Caving Association.

Bed: A layer of limestone.

Bedding Plane: This is the horizontal void that varies in height from a few centimetres to several metres, between one layer of rock and another. They are usually low and wide.

Belay: The attachment of a rope to a secure point (or points) at the head of a pitch.

Breccia: Sharp, angular rock on shaft walls that is often loose.

Carbide or Calcium Carbide: When water is dripped on to this rock it gives off an Acetylene gas. Carbide is placed in the bottom part of a generator with water in the top part. Control of the dripping water regulates the flow of gas which is lit to give a good all round glow of light. It was especially good for expedition caving but is now superseded by L.E.D. lighting. This is cleaner and much more user friendly.

Choke: Often referred to as a boulder choke. A passage that is full of boulders or with a mixture of mud and rock blocking the way ahead. It has been dug out to allow people through. They can be dangerous and suddenly collapse if not supported. The boulder choke descent of Notts 2 is a fine example of determination and engineering skills to secure the 40 metres descent to join solid rock close to the main passage.

C.I.C.: The top award for cave instructors is the Cave Instructor Certificate. This allows instructors to operate in any cave system in the country.

Clint: The up-stand or block of rock separated from another by a gryke on a limestone pavement.

Column: A column is formed when a stalagmite and stalactite join together.

Cows' tails: These are short lengths of dynamic rope attached to the central maillon on a sit harness. A short one is used for descent and a large one used on ascent of a rope.

C.R.O.: The Cave Rescue Organisation. Founded in 1959 this is the Yorkshire based rescue team.

Cumec: Volume of water flow measured as cubic metres of water a second.

D.C.R.O.: Derbyshire Cave Rescue Organisation. This concerns itself with cave rescues in the Peak District and areas close by.

Difficile: One of the French descriptive terms for grading climbs. Gradest start at Facile and continue through Peu Difficile, Assez Difficile, Difficile, Tres Difficile to Extremement Difficile with the addition of plus or minus to further quantify the difficulty.

Doline: See shake-hole.

Glaciere: A cave that traps cold air and forms ice.

Golok: Another name for a machete.

G.R.: Grand Randonee. A main walking path in France, which are all numbered as in GR 10 in Corsica, a well known and frequented long walk.

Gritstone: A sedimentary rock that is very rough and forms 'edges' or cliffs up to 30 metres high and is a perfect climbing rock. Mainly found in the Peak District and he Yorkshire Dales. It is found above the limestone and is a younger rock some 250 million years old.

Grotte: French for cave.

Gouffre: French for abyss or chasm or pit.

Gour or Rimstone Pool: These are pools of water held back by a rim of calcite. They can be tiny or as in the Grotte de Chevaline large enough so that they have to swum and their rim abseiled down into the next one.

Gryke: The fissure or gap between blocks of limestone on a limestone pavement.

Gua: The Indonesian word for cave.

Gupha: The Nepalese word for cave.

Gutter: A gutter is formed in a lava tube when the lava flow does not cover the whole floor. When the lava becomes solidified a narrow trench forms on one or both sides of the tube.

Helictite: Formations that grow out horizontally from the cave wall and formed partially by hydrostatic pressure. Usually irregular in shape and can vary in length from a few millimetres to half a metre or so.

Jama: Slovenian word for cave.

Inkasion hill: Rock-fall or collapse which is consolidated with sediments.

Jammers: These are used for ascending rope, prussiking. One is linked to your chest harness and is called a 'chest jammer or Croll'. It is attached directly to the central maillon on your sit harness. Another is linked into the central maillon with a safety cord and has a foot loop coming from the bottom end of the jammer. This is called a hand jammer.

Lapiaz: Limestone pavement. A fine example in Britain can be found at the top of Malham Cove near Settle, Yorkshire. The vertical gaps in the pavement are called grykes and the up-stand of rock, clints.

Lava tube: A tunnel formed when the surface of a lava flow, pahoehoe lava, a smooth type of basalt, cools and solidifies to form a roof while the molten lava continues to flow through and drains away.

Lavacicle: Formations resembling round-tipped stalactites and icicles which are found in lava tubes. They are formed when lava splashes on the roof of a lava tube, cools and solidifies while it is dripping downwards.

Limestone: A sedimentary rock laid down in a warm, tropical, shallow sea some 275 – 390 million years ago. It is composed of billions of sea creatures encased in carbonate mud.

Maillon: This is properly called a maillon rapide. A steel or aluminium semi circular or delta shaped maillon is used to link the two ends of the harness to make a secure fixing around your waist. It can be loaded in a multidirectional direction. All the equipment needed for S.R.T. is connected to this.

Master Cave: This is the point where all the water from several systems collects and flows through a cave to resurge to the outside. A good example of this is the Kingsdale Master Cave in Yorkshire. Here water from many pots high above collect and flow into a long sump to emerge in daylight at Keld Head after an underground journey of almost 2,500 metres.

N.C.A.: National Caving Association, the old name of the British Caving Assciation.

Neve: Hard compacted snow more akin to ice and ideal for climbing.

Pahoehoe: A type of lava in which lava tubes form. It has a ropey appearance.

Pendulum: A swinging movement part way down, or at the end of a rope to gain a feature on the opposite side of the shaft.

Phreatic: Or phreatic tube. This is a passage usually formed under the water table and is elliptical in shape. It is enlarged by a process of solution or corrosion.

Pitch: A vertical drop of varying depth inside a cave for which rope is required for descent.

Pontonierre: This is a thin rubber membrane with feet that goes over a fleece under-suit to keep dry in water that is below chest deep. In essence a 'rubber baby grow'.

Prussik: Two spring loaded jammers that attach you to the rope. These are called the chest and foot jammers. From the lower end of the foot jammer a piece of rope is attached to form a foot loop with a short safety connection returning to your harness. Both feet are placed in the foot loop. The hand jammer is pushed up the rope and as you stand up in the foot loop the chest jammer automatically rises up the rope. It is then possible to sit down and move your hand jammer up the rope. This method of prussiking is called the 'frog system' because you emulate a frog moving or the 'sit, stand' method. A tandem prussik is where two people ascend the rope at the same time!

Re-belay(s): The placing of an additional belay(s) for a rope to avoid a rub point on a pitch.

Resurgence: The point where the stream exits the cave after its underground journey.

Rift: A narrow but high passage between walls formed along a weakness in the rock.

Rigging: The term used for fixing ropes to anchors above a pitch head where the rope is placed in such a way that it hangs clear, away from any rock projections to avoid abrasion. Re-belays or deviations also help in keeping the rope in space!

Ropey lava: Pahoehoe lava. In the cooling process the lava flow takes on a corrugated surface resembling coils of rope.

Runner(s): Short for running belay(s). These are placed at intervals so that if the climber falls he only falls twice the distance above his last runner. For example if the climber was twenty metres above the ground he would only fall 6 metres and not all the way to the floor if a running belay has been placed 3 metres below him.

S.P.A.: Single Pitch Award., the lowest category of rock climbing assessment. The others are M.I.A., Mountain Instructor Award, for summer climbing and M.I.C., Mountain Instructor Certificate. This allows people with this award to operate in the mountains in winter conditions. The highest qualification is the British Mountain Guide allowing these people to operate in any mountain area in the world as this is a universal qualification. There is also now an indoor climbing wall qualification. There are also several walking awards from simple low level walking, winter walking and European Walking Leader.

Scialet: This is a local French word used for a cave and used in the Savoie and Isere regions.

Serac: A huge and often unstable block of ice that has catastrophic results when it falls.

Shake-hole: Doline is the correct geological term. This is where the ground has collapsed into a void below leaving a funnel shaped depression. Often cave entrances are found at the bottom of these.

Sink: This is the point at which the surface stream disappears underground.

Spit: A short metal threaded sleeve drilled into the rock to which hangers can be screwed. Hangers have a hole for either a maillon or karabiner to be clipped enabling the rope to be attached. Having drilled the hole for the sleeve a metal wedge is placed into the base of the sleeve which is then hammered home into the drilled hole.

S.R.T.: Single Rope Techniques. The method used for descending and ascending secured ropes in caves.

Stalagmite: This is a deposit of calcium carbonate on the floor formed by water droplets splashing on to the floor of the cave from the roof of the passage. They are usually larger than stalactites.

Straw: Or straw stalactite. These are hollow tubes of calcium carbonate (calcite) hanging from the ceiling, just like drinking straws. They can be short or long. When the inside of the straw becomes blocked, water flows down the outside rather than the inside depositing calcite carbonate (calcite) on the outside. It becomes thicker and more pointed and becomes known as a stalactite.

Sump: A passage completely filled with water with no airspace normally only accessible to cave divers. Short, known, sumped passages can be free dived.

Swallet: A term used to describe where water sinks and is a common term used in Mendip. Sometimes this is called a Slocker.

Tandem Prussik: 2 cavers climbing the rope at the same time. Often used on big pitches.

Tyrolean: A rope placed across a river or void so that cavers can pull themselves across from one side to another suspended beneath the rope.

U.L.S.A.: University of Leeds Speleological Society.

Uvala: A term to describe when two or more dolines coalesce.

Other titles by Des Marshall from Gwasg Carreg Gwalch:

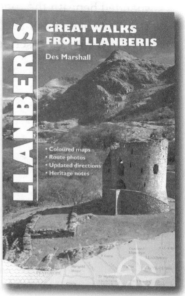

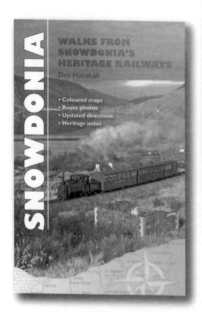